With warm memories
and affection

Ever —

Don

NOTES FROM A BATTERED GRAND

ALSO BY DON ASHER:

The Piano Sport

Don't the Moon Look Lonesome

The Electric Cotillion

The Eminent Yachtsman and the Whorehouse Piano Player

Blood Summer

Honeycomb

Raise Up off Me: A Portrait of Hampton Hawes

Angel on My Shoulder (Stories)

DON ASHER

NOTES FROM A BATTERED GRAND

A MEMOIR

Harcourt Brace Jovanovich, Publishers

NEW YORK SAN DIEGO LONDON

HBJ

Portions of this book previously appeared in different form in the following publications: *Harper's Magazine*, *The Paris Review*, *Zyzzyva*, *The San Francisco Chronicle*, *The San Francisco Examiner*, *Jazzletter*, *The Electric Cotillion* (1970), and *Honeycomb* (1979).

Drawing on fifty years of high times and hard knocks, I may have lost or transposed a few details of name and place. On-the-spot improvisation was sometimes required, but I've tried to stick as close to the melody as possible.

Library of Congress Cataloging-in-Publication Data
Asher, Don
Notes from a battered grand: a memoir/Don Asher.
p. cm.
ISBN 0-15-167281-4
1. Asher, Don. 2. Pianists—United States—Biography. I. Title.
ML417.A825A3 1992
786.2'092—dc20 91-34598

Designed by Trina Stahl

Printed in the United States of America

First edition
A B C D E

For Lois

PROLOGUE

During the thirties and forties in Worcester, Massachusetts—that dear, drab, redbrick pile that gave you Robert Benchley, S. N. Behrman, Bob Cousy, Abbie Hoffman, and the songwriter-recluse Einar Swan (who died at thirty-six, leaving a poignant legacy: "When Your Lover Has Gone")—the most prestigious job in town for a piano player was the Pollywog Lounge of the Bancroft Hotel. That maroon-upholstered room off the lobby of Worcester's sole major hotel was pitch dark but for the faint green luminescence shed by a number of murky glass tanks filled with tadpoles, minnows, and luxuriant flora. Here politicians, professional athletes, columnists, and gamblers convened; businessmen rendezvoused with their secretaries, the upper crust mingled with the underworld, wagers were laid and intrigues undertaken. It was the city's polestar, tips were sometimes extravagant, and pianists vied with, undercut, and bad-mouthed one another for a chance at the Pollywog Lounge's piano stool. For the last three years of my residence in Worcester, it was occupied by a pink-haired lady of indeterminate age named Vivian. She brought in her own organ, which she played alternately with the piano, swiveling around like a technician at a console; occasionally she worked both keyboards simultaneously, one hand on each, necessitating an ungainly stretch (thirty years later news photos showed Rose Mary Woods similarly contorted while operating the Oval Office tape-recording system). Vivian wore gowns of a metallic hue that contributed an eerie sheen to the pale glow from the fish tanks, and played long, incongruous medleys of such diverse tunes as "Indian Love Call," "Donkey Serenade," and "Tico Tico." I never attained this musical pinnacle; in effect I circumvented it, embarking on a more ambitious course that would admit me to the preeminent cabarets and ballrooms of Boston and San Francisco society, entering via the back door of assorted waterfront dives, back-street saloons, and what were known then as turnpike toilets.

How do the seeds of a career emerge from the vagrant impulses and mindless days of childhood, coalesce and gather force? A chemist friend has suggested: as neatly as the precipitate in a beaker, once the proper ingredients are found and combined. But more often, I think, via happenstance or coercion than any such ordered synthesis.

In 1935 my widowed mother started my thirteen-year-old brother, Herbie, on piano lessons. It was automatic among Jewish families of the time: the firstborn got music lessons irrespective of finances or aptitude. (Herbie was named after my mother's cinema heartthrob, Herbert Marshall. She assumed he would be called Bart for short, as was Herbert Marshall by his intimates; but through the age of twelve my brother was called Fatso, and after that Hub or Herbie; not until he was nearing the threshold of middle age did the variations condense in the comparatively dignified Herb.) The lessons, administered by Mrs. Wheeler next door, cost a dollar an hour. This was a considerable sacrifice for my mother. (Her husband had died a few years earlier, leaving precious little. A brilliant, urbane, troubled man with at best a tenuous interest in family and livelihood, he had spent the last years of his life gadding about New York, Boston, and Philadelphia with his sidekick and protégé, the playwright S. N. Behrman, who had hit it big with his first play in 1927.) The west-side Jewish community gathered round the young widow and her two sons, and set her up with a candy business that she conducted from her home—selling tins of Mary Ann Chocolates and Robin Hood Sweets to the wives of businessmen who had weathered the market crash. Many of her customers were the same women who had helped arrange the business for her. They would arrive for their weekly purchases at our house on Edgewood Street bearing gifts of used coats and dresses and occasional pairs of woolen trousers or bleached-out shirts for my brother and me. Their gracious concern spilled over material borders. On a still summer night my mother phoned one of these benefactors in whispered alarm, relaying her fears of a strange man prowling the neighborhood. The woman's attorney husband immediately got on the phone and prevailed on the police department to dispatch an officer to check on the vulnerable widow and sons. Our rock pile of a street, after untold years of inflicting sprained ankles and pocked car fenders, had been paved that morning. Within a half hour of my mother's anxious call, a cop came plodding down the street on horseback, kicking huge chunks out of the soft tar. While his horse relieved itself on our front walk, the officer poked his riding crop into the hedges and bushes of a few backyards, found nothing, and retreated the way he had come, creating a parallel phalanx of gaping potholes. The next morning it rained heavily, and I joined the neighborhood kids filling the largest hollows with minnows and salamanders from the swamp behind Edgewood Street. The hoof-shaped craters would wait three years for a repair crew and were my earliest intimation that we are overseen and governed by the unmindful and the incompetent.

But my brother and Mrs. Wheeler. The bell rang early for Herbie; he didn't have a musical bone in his body and had scarcely bothered going through the practice motions. (Today, incidentally, he is worth a large bundle and could comfortably buy and sell the aggregate of surviving purchasers of Mary Ann Chocolates and Robin Hood Sweets.) He was let off the hook in less than four months. Mrs. Wheeler, though she had few students and a sick husband and, God knows, could have used the dollar, concurred in my mother's decision with an alacrity that would have been an embarrassment had Herbie been capable of that emotion. Now it became the kid brother's turn. I was nine. Mrs. Wheeler sat beside me in a straight-backed chair in her vine-infested parlor, tapping her ruler in time with the metronome. When she wasn't teaching she was gardening, and sometimes absentmindedly began the lesson still wearing her blue-necked white cotton gloves—the same kind our mothers made us wear when we got poison ivy. She was a small, spare lady with rough, open-pored skin, accentuated by steel-rimmed spectacles and coarse dull-gray hair drawn to a tight bun on the nape of her neck; I thought of her as the Lady with the Iron Head. I don't remember being enthralled by the Czerny exercises, the simplified Bach and Mozart. But I was more of a scholar than Herbie—no, more of a drudge—and acutely sensitive to finances. On the rare occasions—a birthday, the first day of Hanukkah—when my mother took us out to the Lido Café for lunch (Venetian murals and a strolling fiddler in a theater usher's uniform), if Herbie ordered something other than the lowest-priced items on the menu I would cry in a fury, "But that costs seventy-five cents!" and kick him in the shins under the table. I don't know where this miserly trait came from. I don't remember ever going hungry, missing a meal; there were always full bottles of milk in the icebox, bowls of hard candy and fruit on the dining-room sideboard—my mother must have managed her resources exceedingly well. But even today, in my sixties and fairly well-off, I have enormous difficulty picking up a luncheon check or popping for a drink, satisfying myself with the tacit, unjustifiable rationale: I was a Depression kid.

The point is, I could not bear to see that weekly dollar handed to Mrs. Wheeler in vain. So I buckled down, three to four hours a day, year after year. And an astonishing thing happened: One day (not all of a sudden, though it seemed that way) the drudgery was past, I had traversed the endless desert of scales and arpeggios in parallel and contrary motion, double thirds, exercises from Czerny's School of Velocity, and the parade of the hammering octaves, put it all behind me and reached the blessed oasis where I was making music. I had assimilated the modest culture and intelligence Mrs. Wheeler had to offer and was sent across town—at a dollar a *half* hour—to Martha Cantor, Worcester's foremost classical piano teacher and sister of theatrical producer Arthur Cantor. One of her students was my classmate Barbara Coppersmith, now Barbara Carroll and playing opposite Bobby Short in New York's posh Carlyle Hotel. (I drop these names not for vanity's sake, but to point up Worcester's considerable cultural connections; it was a factory town, but not a tank town.) My hands were moving with ease and fluidity now; I could play Bach fugues, Haydn sonatas, and Chopin nocturnes with a competence several cuts above high-school-assembly level. But I still wasn't all that thrilled. Something was missing that I could almost touch. It's an unworthy, callow, and demeaning thing to say—but simple and true—that the music did not make me smile or tap my feet or snap my fingers. Elevating, pure, enchanting, for all time, yes, but it just lay there; I couldn't rid my mind of the idea that I was playing long-dead composers or that the notes were fixed indelibly on the pages, not to be tampered with . . . And something else was in the air and on the airwaves, something livelier, more flexible, exuberant, slapping a grin on my face and luring me down vibrant alleys. Benny Goodman, Earl Hines, Jimmie Lunceford, Artie Shaw, Count Basie, Woody Herman, the King Cole Trio. Name bands and combos were stomping through town, appearing at the Plymouth Theater and Mechanics Hall and Danny Duggan's lakeside Dance Deck, the names shining like garnets on the grimy marquees. On a Sunday afternoon at the Plymouth you could see a movie, a stage show backed by Charlie Barnet or one of the Dorseys, and the Fats Waller Sextet (filling the intermission!) for fifty cents. Forty miles down the road at Boston's Hi-Hat, the blind genius Art Tatum was making solo appearances that would leave aspiring pianists incredulous, exhilarated, and ultimately depressed, knowing that what they were hearing could not be done. "It's cartwheels and magic," a dumbfounded older player said to me. "He puts us all in the deep shade." We could only sit at an immense distance from his roaring blaze and try to warm ourselves.

It was this music that entered my bloodstream permanently, setting up little eddies and currents and explosions before imparting a pulse as natural as breathing, as constant as heartbeat.

PART ONE

REDBRICK TOWN

1

To my last breath I will marvel at the number of—I hesitate to call them clubs—taverns, joints, converted stores, renovated barns, gutbuckets, subterranean holes-in-the-wall (saloons was the kindest word our parents used, garbage dumps and cathouses the most disparaging) that prevailed in and around Worcester during the two decades spanning World War II. And the immigrant proprietors who allowed us—rank novices, the rawest of young kids—to bang, toot, and honk for their degenerate clientele sold us beer and hard liquor without requesting identification, though many of us had not even the fuzz of a first shave on our cheeks (was it possible the cops on all those beats were bought?), and paid us to boot—a dollar-fifty to two dollars a night, roughly half of union scale.

To our dismayed parents these dilapidated havens where my musician classmates and I served our teenage apprenticeship in spartan horn-piano-drums trios were virtual sewers in terms of fragrance and the class of inhabitants, catacombs of depravity peopled by lowlifes: besotted men with hacking coughs and gray pallor, and brazen women with blotched skins and reputations who wore slinky dresses and drank like deckhands. Our parents' visions may have been slightly feverish, but no less heated were our own imaginations, which effortlessly transformed these reeking, smoke-filled dens into storybook honky-tonks, replicas of the fabled river-town saloons, gangster-run speakeasies (offering bootleg gin and whores in silk dresses along with the music) and funky-butt brothel parlors that were the mythical cradles of jazz; we were drawn to them as leeches to a bruise, babes to the breast.

The names were Valhalla, Logan's Tavern, Babe's Silver Dollar, Somerset Café, Sundome, Blue Marlin, Jan's Waterfront Café (several miles from water, stranded high on the Pleasant Street Hill like the ark on Mount Ararat), and the improbable Good Ship Madam Zucchini, another landlocked dive in whose basement—forbidden to younger musicians—stag shows were held, naked women cavorting to a zillion choruses of "Hold That Tiger" (as we called it) and prostrating themselves on the floor to indulge in an unutterable drama (rumors reached our tender ears of cigarettes snapped from patron mouths and smoked from *other than oral cavities*). The nautical motifs of the lakeside places—Yard Arm, Windjammer, Jolly Roger, Rod and Reel Club—were numbingly similar: bars in the shape of half dories, hurricane lamps, seashell and starfish ashtrays, bogus portholes, signal flags, buoys and fish netting strung across ceiling beams, a ship's wheel over the bar mirror. A veritable flotilla of simulated vessels imparting a sense of perpetual voyage and salty adventure. During the spring and summer, cigarette butts bobbed thick as hake in the oil-streaked water around the pilings, and the tiny distant coals of canoers' cigarettes sparkled across the black lake like fallen stars. In the winter, as a kid skating around the wooded islands, I remember the distant yellow chain of club lights strung along the shore, and the crude distorted sounds—faint clatter of snare, goose honk of sax, like an ancient scratchy record on a wobbly turntable—leaking through the indistinguishable windows, spilling toward us over the silver glare of ice. Common to almost all the clubs, landlocked or lakefront, were the fat jars of pickled pigs' feet, eggs, and sausages spaced along massive oaken bars, justifying one third of the ubiquitous "Dine & Dance—Lager" signs scrawled in blue and red neon loops across bug-spattered plate glass.

We called ourselves the Classical High Gang and dreamed of becoming Benny Goodmans, Jimmy McPartlands, and Gene Krupas, our illustrious forebears in the celebrated Austin High Gang out of Chicago. Our parents yearned for a Henry Ford, Felix Frankfurter, Enrico Fermi, or Hank Greenberg—even (bending a little) a George Gershwin or José Iturbi.

My path was eased by the early death of my chemist father. A battery of uncles exhorted me to abandon the crazy course I had chosen and follow in the sensible footsteps of my brother, who, following in those of my father, had matriculated at The Tech (as Worcester Polytechnic Institute was called by ambitious Massachusetts parents of humble circumstance seeking scientific eminence for sons lacking the credentials for MIT). "It's an unnatural life you're pursuing," the uncles said, "an upside-down world." "You're turning day into night." "Think of your poor mother." I was resolute; in those days the sons of middle-class Jewish parents did not often become nightclub musicians, and my tenacity perhaps had less to do with strength of character than the state of being fatherless. Marcia, my mother, had no capacity for dissuasion; she was (and is) a gentle, tolerant, and proper woman. (In her later years she mildly boasted that neither cigarette smoke nor whiskey had ever passed her lips. S. N. Behrman, who had been a short-lived beau before her marriage, had sent me, on the occasion of my bar mitzvah, a fifty-dollar bill with this accompanying admonition: "Spend it on anything you like except liquor, as your mother never liked drunkards.")

A musician I looked up to, "Duke" Goldman, lived across the street. He was two years older and was working weekend nights at a brawling basement grotto called the Bucket of Blood (didn't every northeastern mill town in the forties have one?). When he packed up his drums every Friday and Saturday evening and lugged them out to the trumpet player's car, he told his parents he was playing for a school prom or church social or a house party on Salisbury Street (Worcester's Beacon Hill). He carried mothballs in the pockets of his blue gabardine suit, and in his bass-drum case a bottle of Airwick to set alongside his drums at the Bucket of Blood in a feckless attempt to neutralize the reek of booze, smoke, and sweat that impregnated his clothes; he had begun drinking ale and red wine, and chewed Sen-Sen the way the rest of us chewed Juicy Fruit. After school every day he practiced his drums to Count Basie and Jimmie Lunceford records. His mother became increasingly disturbed by the direction Duke's life was taking—his grades were terrible, he evinced no interest in college or a normal profession, the bags of an anxious businessman sagged under his eyes—and was knocked reeling by the daily practice sessions. She said to my mother, "Marcia, it's like getting hit in the head with a coal shovel over and over." Though no scholar, Duke too had a gift for imagery, which he applied to musical dynamics. *Forte* (loud) was Primo Carnera jumping rope on the uncarpeted floor over your head, and *fortissimo* (very loud) was a pair of drunks at three in the morning staggering down a brick alleyway lined with metal trash cans. He lent me his records and suggested I drop by the club some weekend night. "If you can stand the smell you got it licked," he said, subverting a popular erotic injunction of the day. "There's a piano player in the joint across the street you won't believe, sounds almost like Tatum. Colored guy."

On a sweltering Saturday night in June I caught a bus to Duke's place of business. It was a part of town I'd never been to: brick tenements like squat bullies among the seedy storefront cafés and one-story frame houses, the gray stoops burdened with silent, sullen-looking people in chemises and undershirts. The streets smelled different, a musty, acrid odor like rotting fruit cores left in butt-choked ashtrays. A neighborhood alien rather than scary, for at fourteen all pilgrimages are possible and you believe wholeheartedly in your own inviolability. I saw the gory neon sign Bucket of Blood across the street, but it would take me the better part of the evening to reach it. I was passing an even more unassuming establishment—"Dominic's Café" painted on insect-caked glass backed by ratty-looking bamboo blinds—the door open to the humid night. And what poured out that door was as wide and surging as a swollen river. A skinny white drummer and the colored piano player Duke had spoken of: a big heavy-shouldered fellow in a blue shirt and brown pants. His eyes seemed remote, inwardly focused as he played, and his smooth, plump, sweating face glistened with ardor and tension.

But the sound . . . it was jubilant, cocky, it leaped and shouted. I can't say how long I stood in the doorway more inside than out, oblivious to the shadowy, questioning faces, washed by echoes of all the music I had ever heard or read about—the Harlem house-rent parties (where legend had it the players could devour a pig's foot or swig from a bottle of beer while the left hand alone pumped both melody and rhythm), the strut of southland cakewalks and brass band parades, and endless, linked choruses of pile-driving boogie-woogie that went lickety-split like a night train slamming across prairie tracks. Heads were snapping and fingers popping on the little patch of dance floor, the piano player's galloping stride springing off walls and bodies and needing no support, drums merely aboard for the ride like a kid hanging piggyback on the massive blue-shirted shoulders, a weightless toy train hitched to a life-size diesel. The little room seemed ready to explode, hardly able to contain the cadences pouring out the doorway and into the street, engulfing me in waves of vibration that set my scalp tingling and tripped a wild, grainy current down my backbone. When the set was over I edged my way through the jostling crowd, homing in on the blue shirt and sweating dark face, as single-minded and needful as a hungry pup sniffing a backyard barbecue.

IT MUST HAVE been near to midnight when I finally crossed the street to the Bucket of Blood. Down a long flight of warped wooden stairs to a fetid basement cavern with smoky lanterns hung on the water-stained concrete walls. The place had the look and smell—my imagination told me—of the caves of hell. A half dozen couples were jitterbugging to "Them There Eyes," the tinny trumpet-sax-accordion-drums sound rattling around the high, unforgiving walls. It was like stumbling on a bad makeshift barbershop quartet after hearing a hundred-voice professional choir sing Handel. At the end of the set Duke introduced me to the older musicians, bought a Coke for me and an ale for himself.

"You should have come earlier, we only have one more short set. You can ride home with us, except we usually stop to catch the guy across the street; he goes to twelve-thirty."

"I already have."

"What'd you think?"

I opened my mouth to answer and ended up fluttering my fingers.

"Didn't I tell you? Guess how old he is."

"Twenty-five, thirty?"

"He's a senior at Commerce High. His name's Jackie Byard."

"I know. I'm going to be studying with him."

2

Worcester's colored district, like that of most New England industrial towns at the time, was small and discreet; it centered around Clayton and Carroll streets, a half dozen blocks east of the Plymouth Theater. If you lived a circumscribed life on the west side of town and did not frequent shoe-shine parlors or car washes or ride the New York, New Haven & Hartford line, you could advance well into adolescence before seeing your first Negro. I saw mine at the age of nine on a downtown shopping trip, hands strung between my aunt and mother. When he had passed beyond earshot my aunt said over my head to my mother with an unnerving, whispered urgency at odds with the mild sunny day, "Black as the ace of spades." Five years later I would find myself on the threshold of a black world, my first step on a frustrating lifelong odyssey to pick the brains, embezzle the rhythms, master the soulful secrets of the race—destined to become a "nigger lover," as the phrase would soon gain currency in political and artistic circles, to the anxiety of my mother, who was too genteel a lady to express her concerns for my physical safety and cultural welfare in any but the most roundabout locutions. *They're very fine people, dear, don't misunderstand me, but they have had a different background and upbringing . . .*

Every Friday afternoon I went straight from high school to Jackie Byard's house on Carroll Street. I arrived at 1:30, and when I left the shadows were lengthening. I paid him seventy-five cents; it was a long time ago. If I stayed on toward supper time I guiltily gave him a dollar, which was my entire weekly allowance, and for that he was grateful. If members of his family needed the parlor that afternoon, we'd go down the street to the Saxtrum Club (a blend of saxophone and trumpet), a converted store that was a place to hang out and jam for central Massachusetts musicians and road bands coming through, both black and white. Roy Eldridge dropped by, and Anita O'Day, Gene Krupa, Cozy Cole, Frank Sinatra. Jackie, at eighteen, was the club's resident luminary and official host. On nights when there were no sessions at the Saxtrum, he'd lock the door early from the inside. Neighbors said the practicing on the ancient upright went on all night—scales and exercises, parallel and contrary motion, hour after hour, random excursions and improvisations mingling with snatches of Chopin and Bach. If he knew there was someone listening outside the door—and before midnight there was often a knot of us, like kids huddled around a bakery shop drawn by the rumor that free samples might be given out—he'd slide into some whomping way-back whorehouse piano, a big, pumping, joyous sound, and in our imaginations it was like being present at a spectacular parade, hearing a whole history of the music from the New Orleans cribs and levees on up the river.

MY DAYS AT Martha Cantor's North Main Street studio were numbered. I did not tell her I was simultaneously studying elsewhere. But she had detected something coarse and alien infiltrating the texture of my playing, and she was puzzled. "Your legato lines are losing definition and clarity, Donald, and I can't seem to put my finger on the difficulty."

Concurrently Barbara Carroll (née Coppersmith) was getting herself seduced, drawn down the same sordid, enchanting alleys. She had made her pilgrimage to Dominic's Café, which was becoming a mecca for southern New England piano players. (Hearing Jackie in that environment was like encountering Horowitz on a drink-stained spinet in a back-road motel cocktail lounge.) I would see her near the front of the line at the Plymouth Theater on Sunday afternoons and in the tiny cubicles at Carl Seder's Music Mart listening to King Cole and Teddy Wilson records, head bent, eyes closed. Then suddenly she had deserted Martha Cantor and was playing three and four nights a week in the east-side Worcester dives and turnpike roadhouses strung halfway to Boston like dingy boxcars on a coal-littered siding. Within a few weeks I followed suit, divulging to Martha the Dominic's–Byard–Saxtrum connection. She was devastated. Two of her prize pupils jumping ship in the space of a month to vanish, perhaps forever, beneath the waves of vulgarity. She phoned my mother to express her dismay, sorrow, and sympathy, and my distraught tearful mom all but said Kaddish over my watery grave.

DUKE GOLDMAN COULD keep the cat in the bag only so long. One Saturday night his father, whose suspicions had been aroused by the lingering camphoric reek of Duke's blue suit, followed the trumpet player's car at a discreet distance to the Bucket of Blood. He descended the dank stairs and stood appalled on the threshold of that odorous cave; watched, in benumbed silence, his sixteen-year-old son flip a coin with the bartender and win himself a sudsy schooner of ale; heard in disbelief his high-pitched yelp of delight as the Bucket's forty-year-old henna-haired waitress slipped him an affable goose on his way back to the bandstand, causing half the ale to slosh to the floor. That friendly goose signaled finis to Duke's career; he didn't even get a chance to unpack that night. Soon afterward his drums were sold, and the jaunty sobriquet would vanish with them, like a dapper dresser bereft of his buttonhole flower and gloves. "Duke" would revert to Irwin, and at eighteen he would take up a lifelong position with his father's Chrysler-Plymouth agency.

The hit tunes during my sophomore year at Classical were "The White Cliffs of Dover," "Johnny Doughboy," and "I Left My Heart at the Stage Door Canteen." The saloon proprietors, at the first signs of trouble between drink-sodden servicemen, signaled us to break off whatever we were playing and launch the "Star-Spangled Banner" while they called the MPs. The anthem, blatted by a quavering trumpet or saxophone player (natural vibrato), had as much impact on the combatants as an oil slick on a tidal wave. Cowering behind the upright piano, we watched one-on-one encounters erupt into full-pitched battles as ashtrays, beer bottles, and bodies ricocheted off walls or crashed through neon-strung plate glass.

When I got home at around two in the morning the lamp was always lit, my mother waiting up for her youngest and most vulnerable son, her graying head framed dolefully in the yellow window like an old Flemish painting; she looked like she had been there beyond time, immobile and sorrowful, keeping vigil. And her reproachful greeting as I let myself into the front hall—trailing, like the character Joe with the surname of jumbled consonants in "Li'l Abner," a dense nimbus of smoke and fume—never changed: "Dear God, you smell like a brewery," though I was a good year away from that baptism.

At the end of the year a new family from out of state moved next door into the flat above Mrs. Wheeler. A bespectacled couple with a twelve-year-old son, Eric, a spacey, reclusive kid who practiced his violin five to six hours a day. From what little I knew about the violin, he sounded gifted; his tone had no edges and it sang. (It drove my brother Herbie fruit. "What's with the cat fight next door?" he'd say, grimacing and jamming his fingers in his ears.) Late one winter night shortly after Eric had moved in, I came home from work and saw him from my upstairs bedroom window standing out in the Wheeler backyard in his bathrobe, pajamas, and unclasped overshoes. It had snowed earlier in the evening, and a deep muffled quiet lay over the houses and streets. He was standing motionless, head cocked at a funny angle, gazing up through barren branches at the clear glittering sky. I thought, Maybe he's communing with God, but he was such a loopy kid I felt sure he could handle two conversations at once. I raised my window and called down, "What're you doing, Eric?"

"Listening to the earth turning," he said, and added after a moment, "It's always the same key."

"What key?" I asked, going along.

"Five flats, same as Chopin's 'Raindrop' Prelude."

"Ah . . ."

"But you have to listen carefully. It's probably pitched different at the poles."

Eight years later I would not be in the least surprised to read of his solo guest appearance with the Cleveland Orchestra under George Szell.

3

Having no father to answer to, I didn't feel the need to resort to subterfuge, as Duke had done. I told my mother straightaway that I was playing in a club that was a few cuts below the Copacabana, but I was learning my craft and picking up my credits (turning over half my weekend paycheck of four dollars helped the cause) and would soon graduate to the classier places—even, pray God and Neptune, the Pollywog Lounge of the Bancroft Hotel. My candor backfired. An inveterate worrier, wringing her hands over my two-in-the-morning homecomings, my pallor, and my general hyperkinesia (a volatility and shortness of attention span that in someone fifteen years older might have been taken for coffee nerves)—graying steadily via vicarious depravity, she wheedled the name of the club out of Herbie, called up her sister Lila and Lila's husband, Allie (one of the brigade of uncles who had cautioned me against turning day into night), and solicited them to drop in discreetly and check the joint out.

The Blue Marlin was my habitat the winter Eric was conducting cat fights next door: a knockdown, rat-hole dive featuring a crackling neon fish in the window and a unique balcony bandstand, access to which required agility and involved a fair degree of risk. Ascend the board ladder, ten feet straight up, push open the trapdoor while holding onto the top rung with your free hand and hoist yourself, carefully, because of the low-hanging network of overhead pipes. Attaining solid ground—and of necessity stooping—lower the trapdoor. The railing-enclosed platform held an upright piano, a drum set, and two folding chairs. (To say that the quarters were cramped is to say that Bessie Smith could carry a tune.) Though hot air and smoke rose readily to our roof perch, the prevailing and overpowering odor—one part spilled beer, one part stale urine (the adjectives interchangeable)—was less pronounced there, and the arrangement had the advantage of commanding an unexcelled view of both the dance floor and the occupants of the booths, predominantly servicemen from the nearby camps and local girls, whose activities were a source of endless and sweaty fascination to us.

We called ourselves the Tunesmiths: a flagrant misnomer. All the local fledgling combos had similar names—the Melody Makers, Noteables, Harmonicats. Our repertoire consisted of seven tunes, each of which we repeated several times in the course of a night, but with variations in tempo and rhythm. If a rumba were requested, "Tangerine" became a rumba; in like fashion, "When You Wish Upon a Star" served as a waltz and "Tea for Two" as a beguine or samba. When a song or its rendition displeased the servicemen, a barrage of liquid-propelled missiles—half-filled beer bottles—would zoom unerringly toward our cloistered aerie. At first rocket's red glare we'd push the heavy-duty upright over the trapdoor in case the troops chose to advance behind their artillery, while our trumpet player Dennis blew a wavering, futile chorus of "Star-Spangled Banner" (or "Anchors Aweigh" or "The Caissons Go Rolling Along"). There were nights of real fear when you would swear someone had turned on the sound track from the last reel of *Gunga Din*, the scene where the water boy bugler succumbs on the ramparts. With the piano blocking pursuit from below, we could remain inviolate in our parapet until friendly forces came to our aid or, if need be, until Reardon the cop wandered in at ten to one to see that all glasses were off the tables. But for the most part the battles were intramural and confined to the floor. The Tunesmiths were tolerated in the same way that the rank odor and raw bar whiskey were tolerated (the price was right). In any case, by the latter part of the evening a good proportion of the clientele would be in a condition such as to render one tune indistinguishable from another. As for the proprietor, Heinie (his name was Harry something, an unpronounceable German guttural; he and his shopkeeper compatriots were all called Heinie just as the corner grocery run by Mr. Andropoulous was called The Greek's, no denigration intended), he understood that the quality of the music had little bearing on his business. He had had his belly full of older, professional musicians who asked for raises and sometimes got drunk and made trouble with the soldiers' girls. The freckled kid on drums laid down a heavy, plodding, but danceable beat, the pint-size piano player was innocuous, and the good-looking boy on trumpet lent the group a veneer of class in the casual yet confident way he propped his feet on the bandstand railing and aimed his gleaming silver horn at the rafters. (Dennis was this good-looking: When he walked the corridors of Classical High in his gray flannels and blue-lettered white sweater—varsity basketball—a lot of girls' eyes rolled in their heads, their bodies turned awkward like puppet-show Judys, and they giggled behind cupped hands; they all but melted into the walls. But they resented his unavailability for parties and proms; he was always hanging out or working in cheap saloons, off-limits to them. Another thing:

Despite his striking appearance and bearing he could rarely resist a prank or occasion for horseplay, even at the expense of self-ridicule. Playing the "Star-Spangled Banner" at the start of assemblies, he would sometimes deliberately "clam" the high notes or blow a succession of sour, blatting tones—a sound, one of the office stenographers said, that "would bring a herd of sick cows home"—his eyes fixed soberly on the school principal. Such antics put off some of the more desirable girls, who could not understand how someone so artistically gifted and physically endowed could willfully fritter away his talents and self-destruct his image; but of course they were the very traits that attracted his wide circle of male friends.) So Heinie was generally content and resigned to the economic fact that he was getting what he paid for: the most inexpensive ensemble in town.

The war's most immediate and dramatic consequence for the Tunesmiths were the blackout drills instituted by the county civil defense administrator. At the first sound of the air-raid siren—biweekly occurrences at varying hours of night but falling most often on weekends—Heinie would dutifully throw the main switch behind the bar, plunging the café into total darkness. The drills lasted for about fifteen minutes, and as soon as they commenced Dennis and Warren scampered down the ladder to reconnoiter for unattached girls, their descent in that impenetrable gloom a marvel of sureness and agility: nocturnal creatures adapting to their environment. Not yet into that bag—a late bloomer—I maintained solo watch from our sturdy crow's nest, my imagination inflamed.

It was an eerie quarter hour. An immense black sea opened below me, pricked by the glowing coals of cigarettes. Disembodied voices drifted on the deep, a girl's voice squealed in delight, amazement, or outrage; illegally flaring matches sent grotesque shadows chasing around the walls . . . And invariably one voice would detach itself, a delicate plangent entreaty floating up to me like a human bell-sound from Debussy's engulfed cathedral.

"Donny, come on down . . ."

I knew its source—a walking coatrack with a firecracker skin—and didn't answer, which wasn't hard: I was invisible.

"Come on, just for a minute . . ."

Staunch silence from the crow's nest, and a steady trickle of sweat down the ribs as I weighed consequences.

"You comin' . . . ?"

"For Christ's sake, come on down!" a serviceman's voice bellowed.

Footsteps on the ladder, more sensed than heard, then a soft knocking on the underside of the platform.

Without rising I slid the piano stool over the trap door.

Klonk klonk klonk.

"Lemme up, just for a minute. Don't be scared . . ."

Not a chance. I knew an ambulatory collection of spirochetes when I saw one (the rowdy little scrappers in baseball caps from the hygiene texts notwithstanding). But there was a wild ache in my groin and my heart was kicking holes in my chest.

AS THE TEMPO of the war picked up, shipping-out orders arrived with greater frequency. The café's clientele turned over, and the weekend revels gathered momentum, fueled by raw nerves and trigger tempers.

Corporal Moriaty was the agent of events the Friday night Lila and Allie decided to pay their clandestine visit; their timing could not have been worse. Trouble had been brewing all evening. With European orders in the pocket of his jacket, the stocky corporal had been sitting alone in a corner booth for almost two hours getting steadily, sullenly drunk. From time to time he would lurch onto the floor and attempt to cut in on a soldier or sailor. These forays were consistently rebuffed, but the corporal, in an unimpressible state, persisted, and at one point a shrill-voiced sinewy lady with flaming hair, known in the neighborhood as Shanghai Bess, wheeled angrily on him and shouted a stream of obscenities.

By ten o'clock the corporal was in a brutish mood, turned in on himself and mumbling unintelligibly in the corner booth. A quarter hour later he pushed himself up and perversely headed once again for Shanghai Bess. An exchange took place and without warning Corporal Moriaty drove his fist into the chest of Bess's partner. This sailor's breath let go in a whoosh and he dropped to the floor, mouth shaping a soundless O, thrashing helplessly like a fish in a skiff. Bess loosed a piercing scream and went at Corporal Moriaty with her nails, and that's when Lila and Allie chose to make their entrance. I saw them suddenly appear in the archway separating the front-room bar from the dance floor, saw Lila's wide fixed gaze, her nose wrinkling like a pet rabbit's. Now Allie was known to take a few drinks in out-of-the-way pubs, so presumably he wasn't too fazed by the look and smell of the place; still and all, a boy in blue was writhing on the floor and a raging redhead was going at a drunken soldier with her talons extended. As I fatefully waited for Allie and Lila to locate the bandstand, the air-raid siren began its rising octave wail, so close on the heels of Shanghai Bess's scream that it was uncannily like an extension of it. In the bar Heinie dutifully plunged his establishment to black. Another shattering scream, a different pitch from Bess's, ripped the dark, followed by a jarring thud that shook the room like a temblor. Dennis broke off "Harbor Lights" and kicked into "The Caissons Go Rolling Along." "*For Chrissake, lights!*" someone roared. Abruptly they came on, Heinie's hand nervous on the switch. Bedlam below. A tangle of soldiers and sailors on the floor, two prone and unmoving, girls cowering in booths, and Corporal Moriaty and the sailor he'd dropped with his first punch slugging each other with abandon, their bodies periodically flying apart, ricocheting off posts and booth supports. Lila and Allie stood frozen under the archway, positions unchanged, like performers who have missed their cues in a blackout skit. Signaled by Dennis's ineffectual braying horn, their doleful gazes now rose to the rafters, and our three pairs of eyes locked in mute, familial recognition. I saw a beer bottle sail inches past Allie's head; another, lobbed like a grenade, smashed against the bandstand railing, spattering the Tunesmiths with tepid brew. Alongside me Warren, a wild exhilarated grin lighting his face, was babbling into an imaginary mike, ". . . And now from high atop the roof garden of the venerable Copley Plaza Hotel overlooking downtown Boston we bring you—"

"SHUT OFF THEM GODDAM LIGHTS!" I recognized Police Officer Reardon's voice booming in from the bar.

Heinie was standing a little behind and to the side of Allie, looking on the debacle with the sorrowful, torpid expression of someone who has seen formidable horrors firsthand, entire buildings obliterated, maimed children screaming in the streets, and when Officer Reardon bellowed his order and barged through, he knocked Heinie, Allie, and Lila apart like bowling pins. The portly cop came to a dead stop, eyes bugging at the carnage, and, seconds later, unbelievably—Heinie adhering strictly to orders—the saloon once again dissolved to black. Officer Reardon's whistle pierced the dark at ear-splitting pitch, again and again, echoed now by a fainter whistle in the street outside.

There was a splintering crash, followed by a barely human yowl—the sound a cat makes when its tail is trampled—then a feeble drawn-out moan.

"TURN THEM GODDAM LIGHTS ON!"

Like a slide in a projector, the renewed flood of light brought a fresh spectacle—a contingent of white-helmeted, splendidly cordoned MPs wading into the melee with flashing puttees and raised batons. Lila and Allie had vanished from sight.

I found them ten minutes later huddled in a doorway, the sad café emptied out and a good-sized throng gathered in the street watching bruised, disheveled sailors and soldiers being herded into two blue-and-white paddy wagons. Allie's arm was tight around Lila, who was shivering like a struck tuning fork. As I approached she turned her grieving tear-blurred face on me.

"Your poor dear mother . . ." Allie briefly massaged his eyeballs between thumb and finger and released Lila to light a cigar. "Donald, if you're serious about pursuing this avocation, I don't think it's too early for you to consider the purchase of a substantial chunk of life insurance."

A few feet away Warren was taking in the action, gulping a beer he had brought out with him; in his excitement, he gagged, brew spewing onto his shirt and down his pants. Allie, who knew Warren's father, ruefully regarded him—retching, dabbing at his clothes with a handkerchief—then turned to me and asked where the proprietor was. I pointed out Heinie standing forlornly on the curb in his shirt-sleeves and brown corduroy vest, hands in pockets. Rolling the cigar importantly around his mouth, Allie approached him; I followed anxiously, meaning to intercept anything he might say that would compromise the Tunesmiths. Allie tapped Heinie on the shoulder and pointed to Warren. "I know that boy's family, he's barely sixteen. You shouldn't be serving him."

"I vuss given idendivigation," Heinie said with a faint pained smile; he knew an Alcoholic Beverages Control agent when he saw one. "I nevehr sell undil I see broper idendivigation."

"All the club owners serve us, Uncle Allie, it's accepted." A few yards down the curb I caught the predatory eye of the coatrack with the firecracker skin.

"The only identification you might have seen from that kid," Allie said, "was a rattle and a teething ring."

"Go home everybody, bedtime, go home . . . ," Officer Reardon was calling in gruff singsong, steering into the crowd like a sturdy blue tug through roiled waters. The paddy wagons pulled away in tandem, and a few minutes later the neon-lighted fish on the plate glass fitfully flickered out. The Blue Marlin, as far as Friday night was concerned, was dead as a mackerel.

4

The reigning king of the society band business in Worcester County was Kurt "Pepto" Bismel. He had originally billed himself as Pepto Bismel and His Buccaneers—black eye-patch accessories complementing blue mohair jackets and white flannels, and a brigantine flying the skull and crossbones painted on the outsize bass drum. As Pepto's work mushroomed and the class of his clientele improved, he replaced the raffish logo with the more discreet Kurt Bismel and His Melodeers. The band, made up mostly of older full-time professionals in their thirties and forties, now alternated dark-blue suits and tuxedos, and the bass drum, rigged with internal light bulbs, featured a technicolored representation of sunset over Waikiki. Kurt's greeting cards to his Jewish customers (influential beyond their numbers) read, A Happy High Holiday to You and Yours and (at Hanukkah), May Your Winter Festival Wax Warm. On weekend nights he booked a variety of combos into the area's hotels, country clubs, lodges, and catering halls, and from May through September appeared nightly with his main group at Danny Duggan's Dance Deck Under the Stars, the band's battery-operated bow ties (a carryover from the old rakish days) flashing KISS ME on the vocalist's mushy-romantic lines. As kids we had gathered on the lake's grassy bank beneath the bunting-festooned railing, listening free to the sweet smooth music, some of us dreaming of one day occupying a chair in the ornate bandshell, playing "Nice Work If You Can Get It" for starry-eyed lovers by the light of the silvery moon.

The call from a secretary in Bismel's office took me by surprise: Dawn Room of the Aurora Hotel, Saturday, eight to midnight, four pieces, dance. I couldn't imagine how he might have heard of me—he wasn't in the habit of scouting talent in the dives—or, accepting that he had, why he would have hired me. I played neither in his league nor in his style. (Society bandleaders since the days of the tea dance have preferred their pianists to play in the "butterfly" mode, a rippling execution of florid arpeggios and limber treble octaves brought to full flower by "Poet of the Piano" Carmen Cavallaro.) I correctly guessed that his pool of available musicians was depleted on this busy Saturday night and he was having to venture far afield, dipping into the bottom of whatever barrels he could find. Still, though a shade anxious about my ability to handle the job, I was flattered and eager. The Blue Marlin gig had folded. Heinie, following a fifteen-day suspension ordered by the ABC (with the concurrence of the Civil Defense Office) had decided to go with older musicians who carried broper idendivigation, and the Tunesmiths had temporarily disbanded.

"What will I need in the way of repertoire?" I asked the secretary, prepared to dash out and buy a bushel of sheet music at Carl Seder's Music Mart and practice till my fingers bled from the nails.

"It doesn't really matter."

Doesn't matter? "I think I ought to tell you, I don't belong to the union . . ."

"Don't worry about it, we'll get a dispensation. Blue suit, white shirt, dark tie. Valerie Bismel will be leading," she said brusquely, and the line went dead.

During the week I puzzled over the note of disinterest, almost of disdain, in the secretary's voice. On Saturday night I caught a bus to the Aurora Hotel on South Main Street, arriving at 7:45. In the downstairs Dawn Room I recognized Arnie, a dissipated-looking saxophonist who worked the Bucket of Blood and other joints; I had sat in with him a couple of times during the previous spring. Though only in his early twenties, he had about him the sour look of a hornman who has spent a drunken decade in the third-rate reed section of a territory band out of Grand Island, Nebraska. He was on his knees setting up the drums for a bony sparse-haired man with pitted skin who sat aloofly on his drum stool with a curious uplifted gaze. I figured Arnie had lost a bet of some kind to put him in such a servile position. Mounting the narrow stage, I noticed that his sole horn propped on its metal stand was a massive baritone sax, which seemed a strange choice of instrument for a quartet. Valerie Bismel was nowhere in sight. Arnie greeted me in a glum, distant manner—leading me to believe he wasn't all that thrilled to be playing with me again—and introduced me to the drummer, Roland. I held out my hand; his stayed at his side. "What does Valerie play?" I asked, retreating from the shock of Roland's stony gaze: he was blind.

Arnie pointed wordlessly to a tambourine lying on top of the upright piano. I had heard that on low-priority jobs Bismel occasionally used his wife, who qualified as a union member by virtue of a disputable competence with maracas, claves, and other hand-held percussion instruments. But as leader? Fronting a blind drummer, a novice piano player, and a hard-boozing practitioner of that croaking frog of reed instruments, the baritone sax? Something wasn't quite kosher here.

The first couples were beginning to file into the room. They looked to be about age twenty, and all were startlingly alike in appearance: the boys in dark suits and wearing uniformly somber, absent expressions as if temporarily baffled by the surroundings (*Have we come to the wrong place? Is this the right night?*), the girls in long, pastel gowns with corsages pinned to the shoulders, sweet-faced, many smiling, but with a similar air of distance and puzzlement. The silence, as they entered in twos and milled aimlessly about, a few gesturing with their hands, was the silence of a deserted concourse; they might have all been blind dates, the conversational barriers not yet fallen.

"What are we playing for, a college dance?" I said.

"You might say that," Arnie answered with his crabbed, one-sided smile.

"They're sure a quiet bunch."

"You would be too."

I cocked my head. "How d'you mean?"

Roland said, "Don't you know it's a deaf-and-dumb dance?"

I glanced from the flat barren glare of Roland's raised face to the eerily silent promenading couples.

"Hartville Academy," Arnie said, "we played it last year. It's all percussion."

"You're saying I don't get to play?"

"You can play or not play, it doesn't matter." He tapped the drumsticks on Roland's hands, which turned palm upward to receive them. "They only hear vibrations, maybe some resonance from the bottom of the baritone's range."

"I start loud and get louder," Roland said on a note of subdued glee.

"You're gonna wish you brought these," Arnie said with his twisted smile, displaying a pair of rubber earplugs.

I glanced back over the mute congregation, the light, dazed smiles and careful movements, my skin tingling as if someone had drawn an icicle across the back of my neck.

Valerie emerged from a side door, smoking a cigarette and sipping coffee from a paper cup. A thin-lipped small-breasted blonde of about forty in a shiny, black, sleeveless gown, her fleshless arms ringed by an assortment of loose-fitting bracelets that made me think of abacuses. She nodded curtly to me, dropped the cigarette sizzling into the paper cup, set it atop the piano, and picked up the tambourine.

"All right, Roland," she said, and the slightly built, balding drummer, good to his word, laid down a measured thudding barrage in the high-ceilinged room, to which the silent scholars began to move in a slow carousel. Valerie called out a tune I didn't know. "Play what you want, suit yourself," she said in a bored tone and began to shake the tambourine in vague synchronization with the drums, her bracelets setting up a faint, cacophonous obbligato.

"Do the blues in B-flat, man," Arnie called, screwing in his earplugs.

Chording behind the sax, straining to hear the honking bass notes poking through the thicket of vibration, I studied the features of the dancers circling stiffly in two-step as if in cadence to some ghostly marching band, a sweet gay melancholy on their turned-aside faces.

Boom rum *boom* rum . . . Roland's merciless drums thudded off the mute figures and barren walls with a muffled roar like chunks of plaster hurled in a mausoleum. Valerie shook her tambourine tirelessly, grimly—its tinny jangle swallowed in the percussive din—and glanced repeatedly at her watch. (Her pixie-style platinum hair put me in mind of the pale fringe on an old floor lamp that once adorned our parlor on Edgewood Street.) As heat from the massed bodies rose in the shuddering room, the planes of her narrow face grew unpleasantly taut and shiny, as shiny as the mirrored ball that spun its shafts of thin light through the dust motes, spangling the scuffed floor, threading a shivery web over dark suit, pale gown.

Boom rum *boom* rum . . .

At intermission the students gravitated to a soft-drink counter set up at the rear of the hall or sat passively in bentwood chairs along the walls. Arnie waited until Valerie departed for the ladies' room, then slipped a pint bottle from his frayed gabardine topcoat, swigged copiously and came up grimacing. "Taste?" he wheezed, holding out the bottle. The orange-and-tan label said Old Tom Glenn. I had yet to take my first drink; I was going to be one of those rare musicians who steered totally clear of booze and dope, remaining everlastingly alert, keen-sensed, on top of my craft. (I had seen what could happen: Bix cold in his grave at twenty-eight, Fats Waller cut down in a Pullman berth at thirty-nine.) I thought now, There won't be many other nights like this, what the hell. I wiped the neck of the pint on my sleeve, unaware of the inherent discourtesy of the gesture, and took a slug. It went down like diesel oil.

"Taste, Roland?" Arnie said, retrieving the bottle.

"A triple with paregoric chaser," Roland said dryly, reaching out a cadaverous hand.

With the start of the second set an apparently rehearsed pattern commenced: at approximately two-minute intervals males proceeded to cut in on one another in close sequence so that no one was left uncoupled, the sweet-faced lasses accepting their new partners with composure and locked smiles . . . rum *boom* rum *boom, qrrrrasssshhh* . . . Roland was losing concentration; the rhythm, previously spooled out as evenly as a thick-slatted picket fence, had loosened, clattering like billiard balls down a flight of stone stairs. Bass drum, snare, cymbals, tambourine racketed and shivered, soles grated the floor in sandpaper shuffle, the revolving ball, sifting the dust, laid down its checkered counterpane. Between choruses Arnie longingly eyed his folded topcoat. After two more intermissions he would be grinning foolishly, playing odd deliberate squeaks, blatts, and honks on his monstrous horn, examining with morbid glee the impervious countenances passing before him for signs of reaction.

When at midnight Valerie said perfunctorily into the mike, "Good night from Kurt Bismel and His Melodeers and thank you all for coming," many of the couples continued traversing the floor for minutes after the last drumbeat, like an echo from a forgotten battlefield, had faded.

Arnie sank to his knees and began dismantling the bass-drum pedal. I asked if anyone was driving in my direction. Valerie, buckling her coat, a lighted Pall Mall in her mouth, shook her head. "I'd like to accommodate you, son," Arnie said from the floor with his mirthless corner smile, "but I promised Roland here I'd walk his seeing-eye dog."

Two blocks from the hotel I caught the last bus home. My head, laid back against cracked leather, rang like an anvil, and I thought of Duke's fortissimo metaphor, the three-in-the-morning drunks reeling down the brick alley lined with trash cans. Outside, the June night was velvety. I watched the bus's ghostly reflection in the moon-bleached department-store windows, a drunk teetering in a darkened doorway. I had partaken of a second slug of Arnie's diesel oil; my old lady would be right as rain with her front-hall reproach tonight.

But cool and crisp in my coat pocket was my first nonsaloon union-scale paycheck, a princely $3.50. I caressed it now with pride of achievement, and a foreboding of departure. I was on my way, the road crooking its finger—a rocky journey that would see me eventually across the stupefying heartland to the white hills and chandeliered parlors of San Francisco.

The bus stopped at Harrington Corner and a group of prom couples boarded, the boys dressed in dark blazers and white flannels, their dates in soft-colored gowns with affixed corsages and sheer wraps around their bare shoulders. Except for a certain liquid ease of movement, a liveliness of gaze, they looked little different from the Hartville Academy girls. One came down the aisle ahead of the others, slim and creamy-skinned and honey-haired, her dress a flouncy pale blue taffeta. The anvil ceased in my head and my face felt blunt and awkward; I prayed there would be somebody a fraction as beautiful on the road for me. She smiled shyly, embarrassed by the high glare of lights, the raw scrutiny of nighttime workers like myself. Just before the driver started up—the sudden lurch that would have the students grabbing wildly for straps—there was a hush as she passed my seat (the faintest scent of lilac lifting off her dress), the quietness broken in that fleeting moment by the rich, delicate, almost tuneful rustle of blue taffeta . . . And I thought Duke, with his keen sense of dynamics, would appreciate how precise and subtle a description of pianissimo that was.

5

A momentous month unfolded. I gained something and lost something, each of priceless value: a membership card in the American Federation of Musicians, Local 143, and my virginity—to one-third of Shanghai Bess.

The latter event came about on a frigid March night. Dennis and Warren and I were having a brew at Dominic's Café, listening to Jackie Byard—wondering why fans weren't piling up in the street, breaking down the door—and discussing future plans for the Tunesmiths, when Bess spotted us from the bar and sauntered over to our table. "Haven't seen you kiddos since the torpedo hit

Heinie's." We had heard that many of the Blue Marlin girls had found new quarters; when a saloon shuttered for any length of time, the regulars would disperse, make contacts elsewhere, and seldom return. Bess seemed subdued and a little drunk; I could still see those lethal extended claws, hear the bloodcurdling scream blending into the air-raid siren. She sat down and asked us to buy her a bourbon and soda. "I've run out of loot. Buy me two bourbons, I'll take on any two of you."

The Tunesmiths considered Bess and then each other.

"How do we decide which two?" Warren said.

Bess shrugged. "I dunno, throw fingers."

"Instead of two bourbons for two," Dennis said, "what about three for three."

Bess slapped her palm smartly on the table. "Done and done."

We left in Warren's father's Pontiac. "We can't go to my place," Bess said, "my girlfriend's entertaining."

"We could use my living-room couch," Warren said, "but I have a feeling my folks wouldn't dig it."

Dennis tapped Warren on the shoulder and said crisply, "Green Hill Park, James."

We found a secluded, darkened roadway; on either side patches of crusted snow gleamed like mica. It was about fifteen degrees outside. Warren shut off the engine. I was in back alone, Bess between Warren and Dennis. "I ain't stepping foot outa this car," she said and slithered over the seat, dropping like a bundle of sharp bones into my lap; her red hair brushing my face had the smell of a mouse in a boarded-up attic. "For Chrissake keep the motor running," she said to Warren. "Who's first—you?" She swiveled around on my lap, bones grinding.

"I guess. I'm already here." My voice sounded calm and collected, but my hasty heart was bouncing like a Mexican bean.

Warren started the motor. "Hold it," Dennis said, opening the front door. "Come outside a minute."

"I told you I ain't leaving this frigging car!"

"The piano player," Dennis said patiently.

I met him outside. Our breaths mingled and plumed amid the silvery trees.

"Take this," he said, squeezing a flat, rubbery coil into my hand.

Legions of spirochetes in tiny baseball caps were breaching the walls of my imagination. "Which way does it unroll?"

"You'll find out."

I opened the door and climbed back in. "Will you turn up the frigging heat," Bess snapped in her shrill, mynah voice.

Warren pumped gas and I began rapidly stripping off everything, throwing coat, shirt, pants, underwear, socks over the front seat.

"What the fuck, are you nuts? It's minus zero out," Bess said.

You sleep with a girl you take everything off, was the way I heard it.

Warren and Dennis, their heads and shoulders festooned with my clothes, were breaking up in front.

Bess hiked her skirt beneath me, tore off something with a sound like a kitten playing in a pile of leaves. The rubber unrolled on the second try.

The inch-long red nails that had raked Corporal Moriaty weeks earlier dug into the goose-stippled flesh below my ribs like honed ice tongs.

"You're tickling me," I gasped. I felt a brief burning sensation.

"What's happening," Bess said, her hands flattening out on my frigid buttocks.

"I guess it's over," I said.

"I've had 'em young before but this puts the cherry on the fruitcake. NEXT!" she hollered like a drunken stevedore, heaving herself up and me off.

Half-dressed, sitting numbly beside Dennis in front, I heard the hard breathing behind me as if from a long distance. There was nothing to look at, the windows were completely fogged up. The idling motor rocked the car very gently. Dennis had found a half pint of Four Roses in the glove compartment and was taking nervous, short slugs as if steeling himself for what lay ahead. I marveled a little at this. He could have had his pick of unsullied Classical High girlhood, and here he was sharing an over-the-hill saloon trollop of dubious hygiene (a *shikker* and *bummerkeh*, Uncle Allie would have said) with a pair of callow sidekicks, one uninitiated. Maybe the camaraderie was important to him, or the Classical girls weren't putting out. Or, despite his golden-boy image and middle-class upbringing, he was uncomfortable with the wholesome and conventional, drawn the opposite way for no more complicated reason than that the music and the inseparable seamy life of the clubs were vital to him. Most of us—and few had his choices—would soon leave behind this passing fascination with the lurid. Dennis wouldn't because he didn't live that long . . . But all this conjecture came later. Mainly I was sitting there in a stupor, glad I had gone first and wasn't fretting like Dennis, and wondering why I didn't feel any different, only stickier. And when Dennis finally clambered over the seat, passing Warren like two overgrown kids on playground bars going in opposing directions, he would last no longer than I, and Bess's petulant voice, edged with disgust, would rise behind me, "Pop one more cherry on the fruitcake."

It would be Dennis's last civilian fling. He passed his preinduction physical the following week, and in no time at all, it seemed, was on his way overseas. Such a handsome, stylish kid with his wavy blond hair and slim build and careless smile, looking so grand in his gray flannels and herringbone jacket, white bucks riding the bandstand railing, ankles crossed, the very model of casual poise and grace as he passionately angled his silver horn into the smoky upper reaches in simulation of his idol, Beiderbecke, investing our ragtag trio and squalid bucket of a bandstand with a touch of panache. (I used to fancy Beiderbecke's ghost up there with him, a kindred and benign spirit, ever tolerant of the fluffed notes and fledgling technique, flattered by the ardor of Dennis's imitation.) I confess I was deeply envious of him, of his looks and the ease and confidence with which he moved and wore his clothes, the unself-conscious flair about him, his swooning coterie of girls—his non-Jewishness, if I looked far enough within myself. At the time I thought he was the embodiment of everything I wanted in life, and within twenty-four months of our sordid gangbang at Green Hill Park he would die like a beaten dog in the rain and mud of northern France.

COE WITTIG LED the quartet at the notorious Good Ship Madam Zucchini. His uncle, Dink Foley, ran the joint. A roly-poly, unsmiling man addicted to checked suits and silk bow ties, Dink was reputed to have links with both law enforcement officials and the Mob, which allowed him to conduct certain clandestine operations in his basement room—stag shows and films, after-hours drinking, card games—with impunity. He would have preferred to have been called by his given name, Raymond, or better, Mr. Foley, but "Dink" was acquired, Coe told me, during his early school years when he wore a beanie, or dink, to conceal a scalp disease, and Dink it remained.

Coe was only seventeen, though he seemed much older, and attended the Sheffield School for the Blind. (You might think two blind drummers in a city the size of Worcester—actually there were three—somewhat unusual, but consider this: An older, sophisticated cousin of mine from Chicago paid her first visit to the city that spring. As I was showing her through the downtown area she remarked, "This street looks like it's been hit by a syphilis epidemic." "What are you talking about," I said. "Look, for God's sake—people with crutches, canes. That couple coming off the curb, not a day over forty—they're *stumbling*. Unless everyone's drunk at two in the afternoon it's a city of the halt and the lame," she said. She might have said, "the halt and the blind"; either way, I think she exaggerated a little.) I had known Coe at Classical before the accident that cost him his sight and had jammed with him a few times. A small, slight boy with a raw look about the mouth. The school corridors had been awash with rumors of wild and lecherous activity in the Good Ship's basement, and kids were always bugging Coe for a gig or nonprofessional entrée to the downstairs sector of his uncle's joint. But Coe couldn't help them, for even he was denied access, at least while he still had his sight. After the accident Dink threw all the work he could to his nephew—the four nights a week in the dine-and-dance room upstairs as well as the stag shows below decks—assigning a bartender to chauffeur him and help set up the drums when Coe's older brother wasn't available. (His divorced mother, Dink's sister, worked days at the Klavin-Schaft Knitting Mills and was usually too beat nights to help out.) "The kid makes up for lack of visual comprehension with a helluva beat," Dink told people. For the basement work he could be easily cued by the piano player when the girls wanted changes of tempo or rhythm. And as the boy was devoid of sight, he, Dink, could hardly be accused of corrupting him, could he?

The week of Dennis's induction I ran into Coe and his brother at Easton's, a downtown confectionery. There was a stag affair the following afternoon, Saturday, he told me, for a foreman at the Klavin-Schaft Mills celebrating his coming marriage. The regular pianist had the flu and would rather save himself for the evening if a satisfactory replacement could be found for the afternoon show. Coe had been making calls all day; a raft of weddings were scheduled for Saturday and the older professional players were all booked.

"Do you want to take it? It's just piano and drums. You could use the money, I guess." Coe knew I was fatherless.

"I'll do it," I said, trying not to appear too eager, remembering all the juicy rumors I'd heard.

"You're union now, aren't you?"

"Not yet. I've been thinking maybe it's time—"

"Well, you aren't going to be able to join before tomorrow. It's one-thirty in the basement. Ring the buzzer high up to the right of the door. There'll be a guy at a peephole. Tell him you're with the band. I'll tell my uncle it's a busy weekend and I couldn't get an older guy."

"Dink ain't gonna like it," the brother said.

"What do I wear?" I said before Coe could change his mind.

"Anything with a tie. Do you know 'Hold That Tiger'?"

"I will by tomorrow."

I ENTERED BY the street door carrying my two cushions (for building a high perch in case a rotating stool wasn't available—a Humpty-Dumpty posture Martha Cantor was unable to dissuade me from, which I trace to early explorations standing at the benchless player piano in the back of Carl Seder's Music Mart) and was directed by a busboy through a narrow verminous-looking kitchen and down a flight of concrete stairs. Pressing the buzzer alongside the latched door, I reflected that so far a good part of my professional career had been spent like a bat or rodent in rafters and cellars. An oblong panel slid back and two eyes round and intense as a weasel's snapped into place.

"What?" a mouthless voice said.

"I'm with the band."

The eyes glared and glittered, then the panel slid shut.

A half minute passed. The door opened and Dink Foley stood squatly before me. He was shorter than I, which was short, and his ice blue eyes rose unblinkingly to mine. In his blue-and-red-checked suit and floppy polka-dot bow he looked like a fireplug decorated by school kids.

"You're the musician?" The voice, coarse but not loud, rumbled like coal down a slow chute.

"Coe said to be here at one-thirty to play the show."

He was regarding me with an almost sorrowful air. "I was expecting someone of more advanced years. Just hold it right here a minute." I watched him toddle across the floor, his short, splayfooted steps somehow reinforcing the fireplug image, to where an aproned bartender was helping Coe set up his drums alongside the piano. Dink put his head close to his seated nephew's and spoke animatedly for a few moments, pudgy hands poking out of starched white cuffs, gesticulating; Coe obviously hadn't got around to telling him about me. Standing just inside the room I could feel the billow of moist, heated air as if a furnace door had been opened. Metal hurricane lamps gleamed through a gray-blue haze of smoke like old streetlights in a fog. Beneath the low cinderblock ceiling some two dozen men in suits and sport coats were sitting at two long tables forming an L. Busboys in soiled white jackets were clearing the remains of a roast beef, baked potato and ice cream lunch. The men were smoking cigars and drinking coffee, highballs, and brandy. Their faces were sweaty and their ties pulled askew; many had shed their coats.

The uncle was beckoning me. I crossed the linoleum floor under the mill hands' amused scrutiny.

"Must be the broads' agent," someone called out, and someone else: "Guess the cushions go under the asses," setting off a charge of raucous laughter.

They had the right idea but the wrong buttocks. Dink said to me in his coal-chute voice, "It's too late to do anything about this, the show will start in a few minutes. My nephew has informed you of the routine?"

"I'm all set," I said.

"I don't want to see you drinking anything stronger than iced tea."

"He's Jewish, Dink," Coe said, "they don't drink till they're middle-aged and then only sweet wine."

"Five minutes," Dink said and waddled off.

Coe tested his snare with rolling sticks. " 'St. Louis Blues' twice through, low-down," he reminded me. " 'You Do Something to Me,' one chorus, then 'Hold That Tiger' way up. I've played these dames before. They'll stay on 'Tiger' for fifteen, twenty minutes, so keep repeating. When they're ready to go out they'll cue you and you cue me."

There was a stool for the piano, an old bulky upright with the front off. I dropped the cushions in Coe's drum case, spun the stool up and played a few chords. What came out sounded like an organ-grinder's nightmare. "Jesus, Coe, it's way out of tune."

"Nobody said we were playing the Waldorf Astoria," Coe said, rattling his sticks.

"I begin to see why there're no horns on this gig."

"Believe me, it won't matter. This is no debutante ball."

The wall lights dimmed, and the men suddenly quieted as two women in brightly colored kimonos appeared in an entranceway hung with beaded strings at the far end of the bar. One was white, the other coffee-skinned. "*Hooooo*-ee!" a voice hollered. "Get 'em on out!" Shrill whistles pierced the gloom. The colored girl's hair was tinted reddish orange and hugged her head like a cap of spring coils; the other's dazzling yellow hair rose in a massive beehive, her beefy face thick with rouge and powder.

Dink rapped his knuckles on the microphone, and Coe played a long roll on the snare.

"We have arrived at the coup de grace of the occasion. What more perfect condiment to spice your after-dinner drinks than these contrasting ladies of countless stage and screen performance"—Dink extended a pudgy arm toward the curtained entrance—"Bridget and Dinah, and I need not inform you which is Dinah!" Loud guffaws erupted from the tables.

" 'St. Louis,' two, three, four, *go*—" Coe called, launching a medium-tempo beat on tom-tom. Bridget moved out first to the minor-key strain, simultaneously chomping gum and blowing air up into her face, gold spike heels cracking the linoleum like canister shot. A spotlight bloomed off to the right, grazing my eyes and pinning Bridget to the smoke swirl. Kicked by Coe's heavy-footed bass drum, she sidled in angular, lumbering movements, hips and belly thrusting, drawing sweat from her upper lip with a finger, the spangled multi-layered kimono flaring in the blazing cone of light, revealing great swaths of powdered flesh. Suddenly she was glaring at me, mouthing two syllables: *slow-er*.

"Slow it down, Coe," I yelled.

"Hold it back, hold it back," Dink's voice rumbled somewhere behind me.

I entered the major-key chorus, Coe easing the tempo back, shifting from jungle tom-tom to snare and high-hat, as the clatter of heels intensified—Dinah moving out in a second spotlight's blaze with a frisky, mannered prance like a painted carousel pony come to life. Strange, agitated cries were breaking from the tables, rude, high-pitched, birdlike sounds mingling with hoarse rebel yells. The girls were working opposite sides of the room, utilizing a variety of movements, shimmy, sashay, shoulder-shake, strut, sheer outer garments gliding gracefully to the floor as the twin light-circles chased erotically after them, grazing, pinning, overrunning . . . Bridget's glum, busy-jawed beef-heart puss in stark contrast to sleek Dinah's fixed, impersonal smile (eyes slightly downcast) as she drifted down the tables of sweaty, ogling, grin-cracked faces, periodically breaking into her jaunty, dainty, painted-pony prance, a maneuver the bulkier Bridget wisely eschewed.

Coe was back on tom-tom cueing my entrance to "You Do Something to Me." Bridget had positioned herself at the intersection of the tables and, rooted to the spot, proceeded to bump furiously, pelvis synchronized to Coe's jungle-thunder as Dinah flitted tantalizingly around her, her few remaining silks billowing like some gaudy-winged lascivious butterfly, doin' that voodoo.

Trying to follow Dinah on her sinuous course, I was flubbing notes, though it hardly mattered, what with the booming drums and the mill hands' yelping outcries. For a fleeting moment her glance caught mine, and even through that yellow-lit murk she must have detected my yearning; the faintest of acknowledging smiles rippled across her gleaming face.

"Ready for 'Tiger,' way up—," Coe hollered, beating a preamble tattoo on his cowbell. And Dinah suddenly cried, "Oh ring dem bells!" in high piercing put-on southland falsetto. The abandoned cry pricked me with a thousand needles of desire.

Coe's rat-tatting snare and thudding bass drum efficiently booted the ladies into the up-tempo rag; they had kicked off their spikes and were angling toward the center of the floor, the last spangled garments cascading and blossoming about their bare feet. The formality of striptease was dispensed with: both ladies were abruptly, glaringly naked. A near-frenzied roar exploded from the tables. Bridget shimmied cumbrously about the floor, all jiggling breast, buttock, and belly. And Dinah, God almighty, Dinah was . . . nothing finah in all of Carolinah. Of more pressing concern, "Tiger," committed to memory less than twenty-four hours earlier, was giving me grievous trouble. A godawful tune to play solo, it makes you *flail*, and the blistering tempo was forcing my eyes to the keys, away from a spectacle I would have crawled Worcester's seven hills on my knees for . . . With dollops of sweat dropping from my chin, bedeviled by the jangling notes and chewed-up hammers jumping in my face like jackrabbits, I battled toward the turnaround of choruses, a two-bar breather allowing time for one more quick, depraved glance, a jellylike flash of— Incredibly, she was staring at me, Dixie eyes blazin' through the smoky haze . . . My descending glance never got past her mouth, which was articulating two distinct syllables: *Fast-er*. Faster? I was stumbling as it was, grappling with the tune like a picknicker with a damn bear.

"Pick it up, Coe!" I yelled.

"Follow the drum, follow the drum—" Dink's raspy voice scratching at me.

Raising that tempo was like tightening the flea collar on a choking cat; I felt my hands cramping, the beat slipping away.

"Forget the melody," Coe hollered, "just chord!"

Sound advice. My corner sight, scorched by flaring arcs of light, hooked onto Dinah working methodically down the tables with her detached, downcast smile, ignoring the shouted smut and lechery (*Lookit the ass, y'could break a duck's egg on it . . . Bite them nipples, betcha they'd bite right back*), sweat stippling her sleek, dusky face and torso like oil on waterglass. A companionate sweat filming our faces, blooming on our shirts, Coe and I drove desperately into a third churning chorus.

Some kind of eye signal had passed between the ladies: they now commenced a coordinated sequence of high-energy contortions, a writhing, thrusting, and grinding to Coe's intuitive rolls and rimshots, using the basement's spartan appointments—bar corners, pillars, tray stands—as (the phrase a year or two away from my vocabulary) male surrogates, climaxing in a roughly choreographed event at opposite ends of the juxtaposed tables—snatching lighted cigarettes from uncomplaining mill hand mouths and dropping like stricken ballerinas to the grimy linoleum, where they proceeded from supine positions to indulge in an abandoned and lavish drama that pasted a crooked, uncontrollable grin on my flushed face. Enough to say that the rumor that had reached our ears at Classical—of cigarettes puffed by dancing girls utilizing unorthodox apparatus—was now verified. The emotions of the Klavin-Schaft workers had been raised to a rabid pitch. A small, redheaded man in shirtsleeves, tie wrenched askew and eyes pinwheeling with desire, broke from his table and assumed missionary position over the recumbent Dinah. I was suddenly tasting bile; all semblance of song and beat had snaked out from under my fingers, leaving a meandering, unrhythmic flow. Dink and a bartender moved in on the gross coupling and with a minimum of fuss pulled the crazed fellow to his feet and escorted him back to his chair.

Relieved of her unsolicited suitor, Dinah raised up on one elbow, eyes fixed on me like hot, melting candles, mouth shaping a perfect O—abruptly swallowed behind snapping teeth: *Out*—reinforcing the message by drawing a supple finger across her glistening throat.

"Goin' home, Coe!" I called hoarsely, and with a surge of adrenaline, port in sight, retrieved the thrashing lines of melody and rhythm and pulled myself safely through the last eight bars.

The ladies got to their feet and padded unsmilingly to the beaded exit, all vestiges of grace and debauchery left behind with their discarded raiment as the room blew in a yowling, table-banging ovation.

Dink Foley was tucking a bill into my coat pocket and at the same time lifting me firmly by the elbow. "That's all she wrote, my friend. You didn't work here today—you played for Miss Sullivan's dancing school or the taffy-pulling at St. Andrew's, comprenez-vous?"

The lights were up, busboys retrieving garments (and a pair of still-smoldering cigarettes) from the floor, as Dink ushered me to the door. Behind us the shouting mill hands clamored for more, glasses pounding the table.

"I'll just say good-bye to Coe."

"I'll do it for you."

I came up into the bright April afternoon blinking and sweat-streaked, lurid visions of Dinah—that astonishing nakedness like a luminous, bawdy statue of a dusky Madonna come upon in the gloom and dust of a coal cellar—hanging on the rim of my mind's eye. The bill Dink had given me was a five—a fin for forty minutes' work and a spectacular freebie peep show. I was as sure as I'd ever be that I had chosen the right profession. It wasn't until I reached the trolley stop that I remembered my cushions. Back across the Good Ship's dance floor, through the rat's-nest kitchen, down the concrete stairs. The same pair of weasel eyes greeted me.

"I was with the band. Forgot my cushions."

"Forgot *what?*"

"Cushions. To sit on. They're in the drummer's case."

"Stay where you are." The eyes vanished; the panel remained open. What my sight encompassed in that narrow oblong took the heart out of me and the bloom off the dusky Madonna. A cleared table. Dinah, prim and businesslike in horn-rimmed glasses, seated alongside Bridget; both marking lists with pencils, making change from cigar boxes. A dozen men queued before them in adjacent lines. But for the yellowish gleam of wall lamps through the pall of smoke and the fact that the ladies' attire was limited to gold-flecked spike heels, they might have been selling tickets to a church raffle.

A WEEK LATER this communiqué arrived from Local 143 of the American Federation of Musicians:

Dear Mr. Donald (or Don) Asher:

It has come to this office's attention that an unreported

dinner-show on the premises of the Good Ship Madam Zucchini on the afternoon of April 12 was worked by member-leader Coe Wittig in conjunction with a nonmember pianist (to wit: yourself). Though this board sympathizes with physically handicapped member Wittig, it cannot condone such infractions, which serve to undermine the prestige of the Local and result in lost revenue from work dues and pension payments.

It is of course your privilege to remain outside the membership roll of Local 143, A.F. of M. The exercise of such a privilege denies you working access to union-affiliated establishments throughout Worcester and environs, which currently constitute some 93% of all premises either employing musicians or available for live music. In addition you are prohibited by this Local's constitution and bylaws from associating in any musical capacity, whether it be formal work, rehearsal or "jamming," with duly enrolled members.

If you desire to make application please report to the union offices at 10 Franklin St. on Friday, April 30, at 4:30 p.m.

Very truly yours,
Francis ("Bunny") McNaughton
President-Treasurer
Local 143, A.F. of M.

There was no proficiency test at the time; the local simply went for body counts. I took the oath in the fly-spattered second-story union offices with a South High guitarist named Mousey Doyle, fourteen. Mousey was a giggler from way back and set me off. We giggled straight through the oath of obeisance to the local's constitution and bylaws. When the giggling fit persisted through the concluding pledge of allegiance to the flag, the white-headed, tobacco-chawing president-treasurer turned his back on Mousey and me and hacked noisily into the cuspidor by his desk, an indisputable personal comment on the bearing and manliness of the new members.

6

If there is a distinguishing feature that sets the musician apart from the family of union-connected professions, it is that our pension funds are of no great concern to us. Unless we succumb to the scourges of the trade, booze, drugs, and road accidents (which decimated the ranks during the decade of big-band one-nighters), our life expectancy is bright and the span of our performing careers will match it. Some years ago I watched Rubinstein, close to ninety, half-blind and stiff-haunched, bend laboriously to retrieve dozens of long-stemmed roses flung at his feet by a packed hall of shouting worshipers. Count

Basie was rolled to the grand piano in a wheelchair during the last months of his life. His regal compatriot, Duke Ellington, was asked a year before his death at seventy-five if he had given any thought to retiring after a half century on the road. The illustrious pianist-composer was nonplussed by the question. "Retire to what?" he replied. "I'm a musician."

We mostly die in harness. There is a reason beyond a constant and compelling process of exploration and discovery (what Eugene Ormandy described as the perennial search "to find what is good and what is missing"). We are doing something we love. A lot of child remains unadulterated in us after other careerists have journeyed irrevocably into adolescence and beyond. It has to do with our toys—our instruments—that we have been tooting, sucking, breathing into, strumming, plucking, caressing since childhood; they have now been mastered and are used to make both music and a livelihood. But they are still our toys. To drag fancy a tottering step further—in many respects we continue to live like children, celebrating our good fortune at having escaped the family furniture store, insurance agency, junk business. Our work (play) hours are short—three to four (comparable to the kindergarten half session)—our free days like a perpetual summer. If demon-free, we eat and sleep well (staying up as late as we want, as the child would like to do) and instinctively avoid stress. If you watch a musician, especially one who is improvising, playing well, on top of his talent, the ideas flowing and the circuitry from mind to hands functioning with ease and precision—if you look carefully, behind the often trancelike concentration you'll see in his expression something carefree, blissful, abandoned; it is akin to the look on kids' faces climbing playground bars, building a snow fort, playing king-of-the-mountain. Could there be a neural affinity between kids having fun and grown-ups making music—the urge to block out everything extraneous and jump for joy?

AN EXHILARATING YEAR and a half was about to commence. Remarkably so considering that it was a sexually barren period, which I could rationalize by a single-mindedness of artistic purpose and psychic scars left by the less-than-rhapsodic initiation at the hands of Shanghai Bess, strident queen witch of Worcester's netherworld. (For weeks following the encounter I had examined myself countless agonizing times for the first incontrovertible signs of *Spirochaeta pallida.*) More realistically, I simply had not yet discovered the knack of seduction, though it wasn't for lack of trying.

Jackie Byard had split for Boston and more challenging vistas—we had all known his talent was too large for Worcester; the only surprise was that he had stayed so long—leaving me to my own devices. But the legacy had been passed on; his imprint was on me, at least a shallow facsimile of it. My repertoire had expanded to the point where I could get through an entire night without repeating tunes, and I was beginning, in a small white way, to swing. (There were rare days when my fingers seemed to perform their dance without conscious effort, when intricate harmonies and swarms of notes rose off the ivory board like jinns from an old bottle and I was, for the allotted time, the operator of a magic music box.) The piano had become my toy, addictive, unpredictable, infinitely complex.

TINY'S CAROUSEL ON Route 9 between Worcester and Boston was one of the class of clubs known as turnpike toilets, but in the upper reaches of that category and a professional step forward for me. The stage turntable, I'd been told, used to revolve, but the circuitry broke down one night in 1937, and ever since it had sat there like a dead donut ten inches off the floor. A sign over the bar said, "Our waitresses are ladies of unimpeachable moral character," and the band, a quartet, featured a Negro on tenor sax, a friend of Jackie Byard's who played rings around everyone in town. I later learned that I acquired the job (following an undistinguished audition) and held onto it by grace of

Tiny's having come up before another of my uncles, a fairly well known Worcester County judge, on an extortion charge. My uncle had given him a small fine and probation, and Tiny was the soul of deference and congeniality throughout my tenure at his club. "A fine, upstanding man, your uncle the judge," he'd say at the slightest provocation. Tiny hired only strippers six feet tall and over. Glamazons, he called them. I believe the coinage originated with Billy Rose at his Diamond Horseshoe. Tiny's six-footers had names like Belle Adonna, Beryl Bang! (exclamation point hers), Eve Cherry, and Ginger Rhale. They rarely brought in music, simply asking for "some slow blues" or "any jump tune, medium tempo, 'bout like this"—snapping a thumb and middle finger in a brisk ellipse—or " 'Satin Doll,' medium-slow, couple choruses, stop time on the bridge; when I'm down to the bra and G-string double time and out."

Tiny, according to my uncle the judge, was a man "of humble origins and acquired manners." Burly and barrel-shaped, with a comical rocking motion to his walk, he intoned in a soft husky voice such expressions of civility as "Happy to be making your acquaintance," on being introduced to a new customer, and "Try the veal parmigiana, it'll enliven the palate." His introductions of the acts were equally florid: "Now for your postprandial pleasure, the pulchritudinous Ginger Rhale . . ." The second night of Ginger's engagement Tiny changed her billing to "Silverella." A lissome ebon-skinned beauty ("I grew up on a boulevard of broken lights," I had overheard her tell a guy at the bar), she emerged from behind a red-velvet curtain in glittering silver headdress and swirling layers of diaphanous mauve and scarlet, tracing a sinuous course between the tables under a pale-blue spot to a Fats Waller medley of "Ain't Misbehavin' " and "Keepin' Out of Mischief Now." Gutbucket tenor and boiling drums propelled the medley through a progression of crescendos, spurring Silverella to impassioned maneuvers—now strutting like a thoroughbred mare, now swinging her head to the floor, legs taut as a stork's, and straightening abruptly with a rapid-fire shimmy of shoulders and switching of hips—all the while loosening strategically placed strings, allowing raiment to spin tempestuously from her body in incarnadine streamers. Thundering tom-toms, mingling with the crowd's raucous exhortations, built to a frenzied pitch, rolling into the climax—the blue spot winking out on a vision that stormed the blood: Silverella, throat arched and arms akimbo, revealed in all her extravagant glory but for a phosphorescent coat of silver paint, collarbone to toes (and this fifteen years before *Goldfinger!*), shining diabolically in the black light. A hollering foot-stomping ovation followed her regal exit through the swirling red curtain. She colored my dreams, Silverella, the most erotic fantasies I've ever known, and she departed before I could muster the courage to speak a word to her.

Beryl Bang! was equally statuesque but more accessible. She had recently graduated Pembroke, was funny and imaginative, and told me she had perfected her supple, feline strut by conjuring a metamorphic image of herself as a Persian cat strolling along the top of a fence on a moonlit night. Her legs went on forever ("Do they go all the way up?" asked a leering businessman as she sauntered past his table; "All the way to heaven, dearie," came her over-the-shoulder retort), and her raven hair fell like a lace shawl about her shoulders. Toward the tail end of her engagement I plucked raw courage out of the smoke blue air:

"How about a bite of supper after the last show, Miss Bang!?"

She wore three-inch spikes; I was five-feet-six and her green gaze, which seemed to descend on me from the eaves, was not unkindly. "Honey, look at me and look at you and tell me what we're gonna do together."

Strippers, I was learning, appropriate for their art the best, bluest, gutsiest tunes of the day, and that year and a half at Tiny's was probably the happiest time I've ever known. Home at two in the morning and up at seven for school; trying to nap in the late afternoons but too keyed up in anticipation of nightfall, the lights, the funky vibrant club and long-legged glamazons, and the music that sent the blood leaping and bucking in my veins.

A fresh, rhythmic pulse (the Negro players called it "snap" or "dip") was beginning to infiltrate my playing, a resonance from the year with Jackie Byard and from listening to the Carousel tenor man, who could alternately melt and scorch and took thrilling, perilous excursions on "Mood Indigo" and "Stella by Starlight" and "Green Dolphin Street." His name was Junius—we called him Junie—a strange, visionary, exotic man, part black and part Choctaw Indian, goateed, with skin the hue and sheen of mulberry. When I asked him how he got such a pronounced dip in his playing or, more specifically, what he did on the bridge of such and such a tune, he responded with mystical pronouncements: "You got to ride the car to the end of the line," and "If you didn't bring your cleats, stay off the field," and "Always take your best shot and go to the wall with it." In a more constructive vein, he suggested I listen to some old piano-roll rags and wrote out a list for me. "It's where everything comes out of. Get that promenade feeling down and it'll open an alley up the middle of your style wide enough for a moose to swing in. Inside the same eight bars there's sass, there's ecstasy, there's heartbreak. And listen to the Iowa boy, Beiderbecke, the cornet on 'I'm Coming Virginia.' Same thing." I listened. Bix's horn, rising from a morass of tubas, banjos, and trap drums, rang like a carillon in the mountains, lonely, sorrowful, and piercing. And those old rags that made my skin prickle and sent quick shivers down my spine—what was there in them, even the jaunty ones, that left such a residue of sadness and ache?

7

My dear, widowed mom was right to worry; at seventeen I was becoming skin and bones, consumed by the fiery demanding music and feverish nights of unrequited lust (*those strutting skyscraping glamazons!*). An anxious euphoric light shone at the back of my eyes, and I was beginning to drink a fair amount. Beer and ale mostly, a little gin, an inchoate, foolhardy addiction to Southern Comfort. I wouldn't be surprised to read a survey one day indicating that a lot of musicians drink because they're having a good time and are intent on sustaining the level of exhilaration—or having a miserable time and seeking release. We drink because we're happy, excited, inspired; also because we're dejected, nervous, fearful, anxious, unsure, self-conscious, uninspired. In short, for mostly the same reasons everybody else does. (We're luckier; we don't have to get up mornings.) But the singular coercive element in our case is the availability, the enticing proximity of the bar. Like the peanut-butter and cookie jars in the kitchens of our childhood, it is always close by and often open (free). Less consciously, we strive to emulate our heroes, the accomplished pioneering veterans whom we respect and, in a few instances, revere. It's easy to become a voluptuary in this business. A future friend, the superb jazz pianist Hampton Hawes, would tell me that many musicians of his era got strung out on dope paying homage to the music's archpriest and prime innovator, Charlie Parker, reasoning that "if they went out and got fucked up like him they might get closer to the source of his fire." Hawes's answer to my inquiry about his own addiction to booze and heroin before he was twenty was at once incisive and poetic: "You're standing on the curb, young and unsure of yourself, and see seventeen cats swing by in seventeen green Buicks. Now these cats are all grooving—confident, sophisticated, independent, not hurting, unafraid. Wouldn't you start to wonder, What's with the green Buick?"

AS IT MUST to all nightclubs, the IRS came to Tiny's Carousel—dispassionate agents armed with padlocks—and I gravitated back to Worcester, a solo spot at Vincent's in the Shrewsbury Street Italian section. This was a shiny and opulent cabaret, incongruously situated among the neighborhood groceries, laundries, and pizzerias, and frequented by members of the thriving Worcester–Boston–Providence axis of La Cosa Nostra. I never learned who Vincent was. The manager, Guido, owned two cocker spaniels, and every night at closing time he'd set out twin yellow bowls of food on either side of the leather-padded door beneath the zebra-striped awning. Inside were a black-marble fireplace and lots of mirrors on the crimson walls; from different angles they glittered and flashed with light thrown from the banquettes' silver and glassware. The bar was separate, a small horseshoe affair called The Paddock with black glass-top tables and framed photographs of racetracks and horses. In an alcove between the supper room, where I worked, and the bar was a combination coat-check stand and cigarette counter operated by a pretty, faded woman attired in mesh stockings, satin corselet, and pillbox hat. This was Guido's sister, and I would soon become overly familiar with a phrase that she invariably appended to her offhand remarks: "It's fairly common knowledge, but for the love of God don't quote me."

At that time you could distinguish the Mob-patronized clubs (Vincent's was one of the smaller and more sedate of these establishments, which often featured elaborate floor shows and eight- to twelve-piece bands) by the preponderance of good-looking young women who appeared to be unattached—it took an immoderately courageous or naive outsider to find out—and middle-aged men in conservative suits. The younger men dressed more elegantly but still along reserved lines: dark suits of shiny material and monogrammed white shirts and light-colored silk ties, the sole note of ostentation residing in the cuff links and tiepins that gleamed opulently in the restrained bar lights. The mobsters enjoyed contemporary music and the kindred arts—singing, dancing, comedy. They liked to conduct their business and relax in sleek and animated surroundings and could grow misty-eyed listening to a pretty girl sing a sentimental tune.

I backed singer Amy Avallone and played solo segments around her. She was a full-bodied, sloe-eyed woman with olive skin and a marauding walk. ("Honey, I only walk down wide corridors 'cause I bruise kinda easy," I heard her say to an aging mafioso.) She came in that first night wearing a luxurious fur coat, a monogrammed leather folder under one arm, and a blue silk gown over the other; she dropped the folder on the piano. "Let's run over my charts before the place fills up."

I glanced through the arrangements; they were elaborate and overwritten, dense with notes. My reading skills were modest at the time, and the notation looked—in musician's argot—as decipherable as flyshit on a screen door.

"I know most of the tunes, why don't we just fake them."

"I paid good loot for these charts. You can read, can't you?"

"Let's save ourselves trouble. Just write out the order with keys and number of choruses."

She leaned her elbows disconsolately on the piano and for a moment seemed to be studying her reflection in the polished wood; then she muttered something under her breath that sounded like a resigned "What a pity." When I got to know her better I realized the phrase had been "Crap city."

She opened each of her three nightly sets with "Once in Love with Amy" and closed with some sprightly, maudlin jumper like "Aren't You Glad You're You?" The mafiosi ate it up. Part of my job was to boost her to a sitting position à la Helen Morgan on the baby grand in one of her strapless sheaths (she wore a different one for every set and a week would elapse before I noticed a repeat). A rich and heady perfume came off her throat and shoulders like mist off a still pond, and I'd retreat from these exquisite exertions reeling.

Between her sets I played ballads and show tunes of the day, trying to impress with a lot of gloss and technical display—cross-handed embellishments, full-keyboard runs and rhythmic variations on old war-horses like "Alexander's Ragtime Band"—what musicians call flagwavers. I thought it wouldn't hurt to get on the right side of these guys. (Guido's sister had told me he'd tried a pair of strolling fiddlers when the place first opened, "but the clientele wasn't all that crazy about the horsehair shafts poking into their lobster Newburg. They lasted three nights and no one's heard of them since. It's fairly common knowledge, but for the love of God don't quote me.") What sometimes drifted across my mind as I served up my flagwavers to the blankly pretty women and blunt-featured men was an account I'd read in *National Geographic* of primitive Indian tribesmen in the remote upper reaches of the Amazon displaying "extraordinary emotional responses" to a recording of the Beethoven violin concerto.

Guido took me aside one night. Unlike his conservatively dressed clientele, he wore a brown shirt and yellow tie with his pinstripe suit. Complaints had come his way: People were having trouble recognizing the melody, and a highly esteemed party at a reserved table had remarked that the piano player couldn't seem to keep a steady beat, sadly mistaking my embroideries for rhythmic instability.

"I like you, you're a nice boy," Guido said. "Amy wishes you'd use her music, but she's happier than she was with the last guy. Now, you want to make an old businessman happy? My friends are simple goodtime Charlies, they don't like a lot of adornment. Knock off the fancy flourishes, cut down the DiMaggios [arpeggios]. Leave us hear the melody, *capisc?*" And he drove a short, playful right to my midriff and slapped my cheek in a friendly but brisk manner.

Later that night an old and battered mafioso approached the piano while I was playing a medley from *Oklahoma!* His face was deeply seamed, and coarse tufts of gray hair sprouted from the backs of his thick hands. They lowered onto mine, at first merely covering them, then gently pressing them into the dead keys as if he were reluctantly squashing a pair of harmless but repulsive insects; "The Surrey with the Fringe on Top" went flatter than a doormat.

"Play 'Ciao, Ciao, Bambina.' It's for my wife." His voice was a hoarse whisper. "Play it every ten minutes until I tell you to stop." He raised off my hands, which involuntarily retained their crushed-bug position, and dropped a five-dollar bill on the piano; it fluttered like an autumn leaf, brushing the keyboard, coming to rest in my lap. To my considerable relief I knew the tune, thanks to a lot of weekend wedding receptions over the past two years at the Italian-American Social Club (where the smell of chicken parmigiana and veal scaloppine got permanently bred into my bones), and found myself smiling in recollection, thinking "Eat Eat Babe Ruth," which had been the Puerto Rican bass player's designation for "Ciao, Ciao, Bambina." (As mnemonic aids he had devised his own translations of the Italian titles; thus "Chiove" became "Anchovy" and "Non Dimenticar" "Please Don't Dent My New Car.")

Guido wandered in from the bar, grimacing painfully and banging the heel of his palm against his ear like a long-distance swimmer emerging from a heavy surf. "What's with the same song, you're sounding like a broken record." I told him of the unusual request and pointed out the party who had made it, in a corner banquette. Guido took a look and said, "Keep playing it."

At the beginning of my third week a special consignment of tinted long-stemmed wine glasses arrived for the supper room's service bar. I began to notice that on the nights when the density of the crowd was just right a certain note in the treble, struck singly, would set the top row of glasses chiming. No one else paid this tiny miracle any heed. It always sent my mind flying back to my sixth-grade geography class—an account of a nineteenth-century earthquake in Madrid that rang church bells in Boston.

Now that I was reactivating my Italian repertoire and playing unadorned melody, a steady stream of drinks began arriving at the piano. I was drinking beer and ale at the time, as I said, but had not yet made inroads on the heavy stuff. I tried to cut off the flow; if a drink were pressed on me or arrived unsolicited I let it stand on the piano until it went flat. Guido noticed this aberration and spoke to me during a break.

"It's not a friendly attitude."

I told him if I accepted every drink offered me I'd be finished by thirty. (A piano-bar player I knew in Provincetown handled this problem by announcing at the start of the evening, "As I'm allergic to both booze and flowers, thunderous applause and the clatter of silver dollars will do nicely. Thanks a million.")

Guido gave a sad little smile and laid a parental hand on my shoulder. "Always accept the drink. The bartender will send up colored water. Order an old-fashioned, we'll load it with fruit, you'll have yourself a nutritious snack, *capisc?*"—followed by the right to the midsection and the friendly slap across the face.

I soon began to retch at the sight of maraschino cherries and orange slices. A stranger dropped into the club late one night, an out-of-town boy by the looks of him—charcoal suit, checked shirt, white scarf—and seeing three untouched old-fashioneds lined up in front of me, said, "You seem to be overloaded here." He hefted one and took a generous slug; a contemplative expression came over his face. "I see Guido's still pouring the same old swill." The next night I asked the bartender to substitute gin rickeys sans gin and very light on the lime juice. He had never been overly friendly toward me and greeted my request with mute contempt. I think I can safely interpose a blanket judgment here: Bartenders are not enamored of musicians. They begrudge us our short hours—roughly half theirs—and our frequent (union-sanctioned) intermissions. A businessman at Tiny's Carousel once tried to buy the band champagne cocktails. The bartender told him, "Pouring champagne for this crew is like feeding a pig strawberries," and his accompanying smile failed to conceal the underlying rancor.

After a month backing Amy Avallone I helped her on with her coat one Saturday night as she was leaving. It was either mink or a class muskrat and gave off a fragrance like a moon-splashed field of jasmine. I opened the door for her and blurted, "How's about going somewhere for coffee?" She glanced at me in a sidelong, questioning way, smiling and frowning at the same time; a low chuckle rose in her throat. "You tired of living?" I watched her swing voluptuously across the street on spike heels, her breath pluming in the chill morning, and slide into the front seat of a black Chrysler. A man in a dark, shiny suit sat behind the wheel, smoking. At my feet Guido's cocker spaniels were scarfing noisily from the twin yellow bowls. The club door opened, and the elderly mafioso who had flattened my hands on the keyboard a week earlier came out. He breathed deeply of the crisp air, buttoning his overcoat.

"Guido tells me your name is Asher," he said in his soft hoarse voice.

"That's right."

"Your father's the judge?"

"Uncle."

He nodded sagely and gazed down at the busy spaniels; an almost angelic smile crept over the bulbous weathered face as he stooped laboriously to fondle one of the golden heads. "I see you dogs're dining out again tonight," he whispered.

8

The Classical High Gang was breaking up. A few had gone the way of Duke, into the family business, selling cars, shoes, apparel, wholesale liquors. Others, discouraged by the prospect of eking out a living from music in a town where many of the clubs used bands on weekends only and union scale was depressingly low, retreated to the nonperforming corners of the trade—tuning pianos, teaching beginners in studio cubicles on the narrow downtown side streets, selling sheet music, records, and instruments at Carl Seder's Music Mart—or, under the pressures of marriage and anticipated children, revised their expectations, settling for weekend gigs and nonmusical daytime jobs. The rare gifted ones, recruited by the big bands sweeping through the area—Will Bradley, Jimmy Dorsey, Stan Kenton, Charlie Barnet—were fitted for uniforms, packed their bags, and left for the road. Several took off on some chance pursuit or dream or whim and were never heard from again. Of those who were drafted or enlisted, two died and one was maimed. Most of our nonmusician classmates, whose prosaic evenings had been spent in movie houses, in front of drugstores, and on gymnasium floors—who had envied us our dramatic nightclub pallors and lurid evenings in the proximity of raw booze and tainted women and suddenly no longer did—went to college.

BY THE TIME I graduated Classical I owned a Studebaker and a virulent case of hay fever, which kept me out of the army and on very bad nights left me positioned onstage with my back to the audience, a handkerchief knotted about my lower face like a bandit chief's bandanna. I possessed in addition something infinitely more valuable—improved reading credentials, which secured for me the piano chair with the Hal Harganian band at a 500-seat show club on the Worcester–Boston road called the Foxes and Hounds. It had been a dance hall in the twenties. The weather-worn facade displayed a steaming ten-foot roasted chicken and yard-high glass of vino on a table the size of a barn door. This outrageous supper had been repainted many times and shone rubbery and indigestible in the parking-lot floodlights. Inside, under high, gloomy rafters, an acre of white-clothed tables and cane-bottom chairs stretched to a proscenium stage fronted by a three-foot-high parapet papered in stone-wall motif—the whole enclosed by a wraparound mural depicting the world's longest fox hunt. The waiters wore red cotton coats and white riding breeches. (Our uniforms were tan slacks and dark brown jackets of a burlap texture that bore the label Buckskeen Joe and came from Harganian's brother's surplus store in south Worcester.)

This sagging elephant of a place was owned by Morty Gelb, one of those harried, decent, sad-sack proprietors whom everyone, from the most valued customer to the lowliest busboy, calls by his first name. A long, wrinkled face like a road map of busted dreams, and a self-wounding gallows humor. "Don't stare too hard at the tables, fellows," he'd caution the waiters, "my insurance doesn't cover snow blindness." To a headline comic: "The agency said you'd draw like flies to molasses. I forgot, it's winter, there're no flies." To himself, wistfully: "It was a night like this that a thousand speckled trout went belly-up in the Housatonic." (A variation ran: "On such a night flocks of migrating birds collided with the Empire State Building, littering the avenue below with tiny corpses.") When I caught a cold one weekend and kept a box of Kleenex at the end of the keyboard, he sidled past the piano, hands deep in the pockets of his baggy brown slacks. "I don't blame you, I feel like crying too."

During my year's residence business ranged from slow to brutal. No one knew how Morty stayed open. The cuisine was bare-bones Italian and the entertainment basic turnpike-midway revue: Indian-club jugglers and tank-town comics in luminous suits ("I know someone's out there, I can hear breathing"); chanteuses with five-and-ten charts and plastic orchids pinned to the shoulders of ballroom gowns singing "June Is Bustin' Out All Over" and "How Are Things in Glocca Morra?" with semaphore arm signals; Debby and Dick musical comedy teams and Trixie and Cuckoo, the Dancing Terriers. We played stop-time choruses of "How Much Is That Doggie in the Window?" for Trixie and Cuckoo as they cavorted in their turtleneck sweaters, paced by a trim peroxide blonde in rhinestone-studded tights.

I joined the Harganian band in the middle of Trixie and Cuckoo's engagement and asked their mentor, whose name was Sandy, if she'd care to join me for spaghetti and meatballs after the show.

"Baby, the only way you'd get me to eat anything out of that kitchen would be to truss me up and force-feed me like a goose."

"Why would anyone want to force-feed a goose?"

She studied me a moment. "That's how they make pâté de foie gras. Where you from?"

"Down the road. Worcester."

"That figures."

"I guess we travel in different circles."

"I wouldn't bet against it."

It turned out she was sleeping with the comic, Stan, who was just a few years older than I but looked thirty-five to forty, depending on how miserable a night he'd had. A skinful of bones with a ragged look in his eyes, like a man who has witnessed frightful visions at too early an age, Stan worked so hard for laughs he'd often end his act with sweat standing out on his gaunt face like lather on a horse's flanks. The meatball–chicken leg crowd smelled his vulnerability. Cries of "Back to the drawing board, kiddo!" and "Bring on the broads!" pierced the stale air and hung in the rafters. The centerpiece of his act was a great white hunter–fag routine perpetrated in rolled-up pants and Frank Buck helmet. He told me how he'd practiced for weeks perfecting the mincing walk using a method devised by a well-known Broadway character actor; this entailed promenading while squeezing a subway token between the buttocks. Hailing from Rhode Island, without access to tokens, Stan had started with a nickel, graduated to a dime.

Morty took him aside in the bar one night. "Stan, you're a young kid but already your stuff's got barnacles. I know we ain't exactly on Avant Garde Row here but—you need a fresh concept, a new approach. Check out the Boston and New York clubs, see what the frontliners are doing." Then, perhaps suffering a twinge of compassion, he lightly patted Stan's shoulder. "Ah, it's a cockamamy business, what can I tell you . . ." Turning away, Morty gazed forlornly out over the sea of near-empty tables. "Anybody got a hose? We'll spray the joint and see which customer gets wet."

I brushed up against my first future celebrity at the Foxes and Hounds. Orson Bean opened his low-key monologue in the modulated tones of Harvard Yard: "When I was a small boy my father said to me, 'Here, Rover.' He always wanted a dog . . ." In the attendant silence the clatter of forks hitting the plates resounded like clapsticks on a movie set.

Morty said to him midway through his engagement, "Orson, you're a nice kid and you've got some fairly clever material, but you're not gonna reach the masses with lines about Martian house pets. I mean, we ain't exactly on Avant Garde Row here . . ."

He was in the second slot on the bill, sandwiched between one of the semaphore-armed warblers—or, as Morty alluded to her, "Miss Bloodbath of nineteen-fifty" ("Why does my booker keep dumping on me like this? Maybe there's a snafu in the agency, the guy handling the clowns and dog acts got assigned me by mistake")—and the headline act, Phil Philby & Phamily. Attired in matching seersucker suits and polka-dot bows, Pop, Mom, Daughter, and Son perched on stools of descending size and played smiling freckle-faced medleys of golden oldies on assorted banjos and mandolins. The zinger in their act came when Philby père accepted a Sunday funnies section and pair of garden shears thrust at him from the wings, and by a legerdemain of rapid snipping and tearing fashioned a comic-strip tree while the family (backed by the Harganian band) strummed and sang Kilmer's "Trees." Orson was fascinated by this bit and studied it from different vantages in the room. He also got a charge out of the sign posted on the band-room door by our hip Armenian leader:

ACHTUNG! ALL MUSICIANS

FORMAL SHIRTS
(Meaning Studs, Studs!)
SPIT-SHINE SHOES
(no sandals)

FOUR-IN-HAND
(50¢ Fine per Soup Stain)

NO CHIN WHISKERS
(Muttonchops Okay)

NO JUICING ON STAND

Or

BUTTERFLY BOW CLEAN SHORTS

(Clip-ons Cornball But Okay)

SWING!

Hal had perfected a rare stunt on his trumpet, which did nothing to mar his reputation as one of central Massachusetts's foremost showman-leaders. Perhaps the keenest trial the horn-playing leader is subjected to is the attempt by unthinking patrons to converse with him while he is in midchorus. Hal would try to indicate by a quivering of brows and bulging of eyeballs that he was occupied for the moment and incapable of lucid discourse. Patrons do not seem to understand this; they grow impatient and vexed when conversation is not reciprocated. I watched a woman one night request a tune from him while he was playing the lead on "People Will Say We're in Love." After repeating the request several times and getting no satisfaction, she reached up—we're on a three-foot-high stage here—and began tugging the sleeve of the arm holding the horn. "Hal, didn't you hear me? My husband wants you to play 'Button Up Your Overcoat.' " Hal stopped playing; it was the only time I ever saw his composure give way; he looked down at the woman with a tight, controlled smile. "Mrs. Palmer, I am not a freak in a sideshow. I am not capable of playing the trumpet and talking to you out of the corner of my mouth at one and the same time."

Later that night inspiration struck, triggered by the Mrs. Palmer exchange. Hal found that by fixing his embouchure at the far right corner of his mouth, he was able—after weeks of arduous home practice—to speak simultaneously out of the left. The lips on that side would pucker and part like miniature tent flaps and the words would emerge slightly garbled in a kind of subdued W. C. Fields harangue—"Practice a little patience, Mrs. Levy, soon's we finish this selection we'll get to yours pronto"—all the while the trumpet blithely tootling on, its tone somewhat tinny and attenuated due to the reduced supply of breath. The strange thing was I never saw a patron curious about or surprised by this skill; musicians, to a man, were awed. One night the drummer, Warren—my old Blue Marlin *compadre*—hand-printed a sign and surreptitiously taped it to the front of Hal's music stand; it said, Drop a Quarter in the Bell of the Horn and Hear the Freak Speak.

Hal had another endearing routine, which he often perpetrated in conjunction with the freak-speak maneuver. Spotting a pair of regular customers entering the club during the entr'acte dance sets, he'd cut off the band and start playing "Sophisticated Lady" or "The Most Beautiful Girl in the World" with a quavering hearts-and-flowers hand-shake vibrato, simultaneously announcing over the PA system in the W. C. Fields drawl, "Here she comes, folks, Mary Ann Beeson, belle of Ferguson Tool & Supply, in tandem with her beloved Wally. Let's give this special duo a great big hand . . ." And the few other couples on the floor would awkwardly, docilely break apart and applaud, the spare accolade reverberating fitfully in the vast hall. Hal had a colorful way of calling off tunes: " 'Rainbow,' three grapes," meaning "Over the Rainbow" in E-flat. If the band's intonation bothered him he'd rear his head back and holler like a crazed logger, "Timmmmmmm-ber!" His business cards, soliciting weddings, bar mitzvahs, and private parties, read, Give Us a Ring—We Would Like the Engagement.

Not yet fully trusting my sight-reading skills, I spent several afternoons a week at the Foxes and Hounds, going over the acts' arrangements. I could have done this at home, but I was discovering something about nightclubs in the afternoon, a singularity of mood, light, and fragrance that I was irresistibly drawn to. The mood at once elegiac for the acts that got buried and hopeful for the troupers to come, the light resiny, weighted, a ghostly gleam reflecting a thousand midnights, and the peculiar tangy barrel smell of spilled drink and stale smoke that always evokes for me the early-morning street-lamp tunes, "For All We Know," "One For My Baby," "Two Sleepy People," "Put Your Dreams Away (For Another Day)." Visions kindled of closed parks and deserted streets, moonlight splashing on old brick.

Today, forty-five years later, the slightest of promptings—a whiff from the open door of a seedy south-of-Market barroom in San Francisco, a glimpse through the slats of a darkened club in the bright afternoon—can summon full-blown, in all their squalor and glory, Dominic's Café, Blue Marlin, Tiny's Carousel, Good Ship Madam Zucchini, Foxes and Hounds . . .

I would miss that antediluvian barn of a show club and the resourceful Harganian, a man of impulse, whimsy, and manifold talents. My year-long tenure with the band ended dismally a few days after Christmas when a fire broke out in the early morning hours. By dawn the Foxes and Hounds had burned to the ground. The blaze's origin was never established, but the timing was suspicious: an hour or two after closing time and just before New Year's Eve. Union scale for performers and musicians was double on that night, and Morty had contracted an expensive show; then too, December business, usually hyped by Christmas parties, had been below expectations. I couldn't help wondering if a surreptitious visit had been paid by one or more of the boys from Vincent's on Shrewsbury Street.

I heard the news via a phone call the next morning from Warren, who was hard pressed to keep a note of perverse relief, even restrained jubilation, out of his voice; he normally left his drums overnight, but last night had packed up and brought them home in preparation for a wedding gig that afternoon. "Take a drive by, man," he said, "it's spooky."

A light snow had fallen during the night. Now, at eight in the morning, the sky was a bright, metallic blue. All that was left standing was a blackened section of brick chimney; nearby a half dozen twisted piano wires jutted from the whitened ash like grotesque flora on a primordial landscape. A small boy in a hooded snowsuit was scrabbling amid the rubble, picking up and discarding bits of debris, scuffing his boots through the thin snow. A car driven by a woman pulled into the parking lot and stopped about twenty yards away. Morty got out, walked uncertainly toward the chimney, then stopped and stood hunched against the cold, hands plunged deep into the pockets of a bulky plaid overcoat, his bare head sunken a little against his chest. An eerie humming sound distracted me. The boy had grasped one of the piano wires with his mittened hand and released it; it sang briefly, a thin mournful hymn in the brittle morning. I glanced back at Morty. He stood unmoving, engrossed, his breath emerging in tattered puffs. I could imagine him murmuring to himself, "On a morning like this the hair rose simultaneously on a hundred cats' backs in Willimantic, Connecticut."

PART TWO

THE BEAN AND THE COD

9

Junie, the Carousel tenor man, had put me onto something, planted a seed of doubt that was beginning to grow and gnaw. As thrilling as the year and a half playing for the strippers at Tiny's emporium had been, I was left dissatisfied musically—an uneasy awareness that there was a secret I wasn't privy to. Now that I had listened extensively to black musicians, I was convinced there was something basic and vital that came easy to them and hard to us. The difference in the levels of rhythmic charge achieved by whites and blacks felt topographical to me, like the difference between a broad, unrelieved plateau and a spectacular mountain range. The playing of the whites was more even-keeled, linear, lacking the sudden dips and spurts, the coiled-spring tension-and-release and unexpected displacement of meter that sent the beat slamming and teetering down the tracks like a highballing express, generating incredible excitement. Somewhere between the two levels lay the answer to a crucial choice I'd soon have to make: whether to pursue a career in jazz with all its uncertainties, perils, and rivalries, or to steer a less demanding course—over the modulated, civilized terrain of cabaret/country club/hotel with its ordered hours and regular income. Which route? Talent would be the prime determinant. Either way, I knew it was time to move on, put the redbrick town behind me. I would end up trying to go in both directions at once and would get myself stretched out in the process.

BY THE MID-1940s the winds of change were blowing strong from 52nd to 140th Street. The convulsions of black-rebellion music exploding out of the dance halls, theaters, and jazz clubs of Harlem had startled white musicians, turned us around. The music was angry, blazing, ferocious, yet always under a tight edge of control. "It's a rogue boat heading for the New World," a black Boston drummer told me, "and Bird and Diz are the navigators."

The navigators knew something I didn't, something I was in dire need of, and I was young and intrepid and naive enough to make my way north of 110th Street, where the boat was temporarily docked. From there I'd look around, get my bearings, and, if the weather felt promising and the coast looked clear, prepare to stow away for wherever the next stop was.

I'd noticed something else—beyond the racial differences in style and rhythmic propulsion: at integrated jam sessions blacks and whites tended to call different tunes. When I'd suggested "Have You Met Miss Jones?" at an after-hours club, a black had scoffed good-naturedly, "That's one of your white-boy tunes." A similar judgment was passed on Gershwin's "Foggy Day." Blacks leaned toward tunes with relaxed, more fluid structures—"Willow Weep for Me," "Georgia on My Mind"—written as often by white as black composers. " 'Willow's more leisurely and doesn't sweat," a black bass player said, "you got time to climb inside it, feel its bones, poke your way around. Your average Caucasian tune is boxy, four-squared, forces you into corners."

Others I talked to found the whole subject of racial-genetic orientation distasteful, awakening the old we-got-rhythm stereotypes and images of grinning darkies dancing for pennies on southern street corners. "All you got to remember when you're blowing," a black drummer told me, "is one simple thing: Rice Krispies. Snap, crackle, pop." Pianist Hampton Hawes was at once more specific and expansive: "Dancing and singing and lovemaking and making music have no more to do with color than making mud pies or building snowmen. Music's color blind. Absolutely. Ofay players occasionally pull my sleeve, talkin' about their whiteness closing them off from certain secrets of the trade. Listen to me: *There ain't no secrets.* We all came out of the same alley. How you play has to do with who you listened to when you were coming up, who you hung out with and picked up on. Gershwin picked up on the Harlem rent-party players and wrote himself *Porgy and Bess.* There's a new young cat, concert player, André Watts, darker'n me, plays Brahms and Chopin like their breath is inside him."

I was unpersuaded and would make many pilgrimages in the coming years to the ghetto clubs and after-hours joints (where passing remarks dropped on an ofay could be coolly withering and edged with menace: *You from somewhere else and lost your way, Jim, or just slummin'? . . . Hey, lemme ast you somethin'—the buckles on the shoes means you're queer, right?*), tracking the elusive secret, searching out the passion and sensibility of the black man. Hoping for a miracle of transmutation.

Harlem was beginning to put on a hostile face for Caucasian tourists. The years when affluent whites could pass a flavorful evening slumming in the district's clubs and cafés were nearing an end. Making the rounds of the celebrated places I'd read of and been told about —Savoy Ballroom, Small's Paradise, Apollo Theater, Royal Roost, and Minton's Playhouse with its faded awning and dingy wall mirrors, where the musical rebellion had ignited in the early forties—I was an easy target for frisky young Harlem bloods for reasons beyond my whiteness.

"Look how slick this boy looks in his green sky. That chapeau come from Switzerland, right?" (An Alpine hat I'd picked out of a Salvation Army bin—kelly green with a debonair band of feathers. "You oughta spruce up your image," a hatcheck girl had told me. "I mean, you don't have height going for you.")

"I guess. Originally . . ."

"What you call a mountain hat."

"Alpine, yes."

"Now what might a elegant lid like that be worth, would you say in the current market?"

"Stop messin' with the boy, Clarence, he's just around to hear the sounds."

"Well now, if he wants to dwell in our sunshine he got to come out of the shade . . ."

A half-formed sense of vulnerability told me it was time to cut out.

"The hat came out of a trash bin. I doubt you could get four bits for it. See you guys . . ." I waved off amicably and headed across the street—solemn dark faces keeping vigil above me, gazing down from lighted brick-framed windows—to the storefront club from which music crackled and charged through the open door into the mild evening like a tangle of high-tension wires.

What I heard inside was something fierce, uncompromising, and beautiful, an abrasive fiery sound that ran roughshod through all previously decreed rhythmic and harmonic structures. Here were the fabled "cutting sessions" I'd been told about—initiation rites that were in effect pitched battles, mostly black on black, for whites were still chary of joining the fray. Musicians spoke of "taking" one another, were scornful of outsiders, and waited eagerly to ambush anyone who arrived with a burgeoning reputation. *Jump, chump, or I'll burn you up, you don't know nothin'*. After a few nights I began to understand that these sessions served as pressure cookers in which one earned acceptance and esteem. Reputations could be made, reinforced, or savaged in the course of one scorching set, and amateurs and imposters got weeded out in a hurry; in the annealing process the music grew leaner, more sublime.

I asked about the policy of sitting in and was told, Anyone can, but you better be able to fly real good or they'll shoot you down, burn you up. And watching night after night in the close-packed, churning clubs I saw how awesome the firepower was onstage, how efficiently those without strong wings were cut down. These were schooled, confident musicians who had found within themselves a core of calm enabling them to adjust to the roaring tempos and turbulent patterns, a cool and secret site from which to launch their blazing cascades of notes. They had done battle in a thousand sessions, knew their horns inside out and could not be fazed by key or tempo. Nor did they show any mercy, constantly raising the ante, calling unconventional tunes with swift-changing harmonies in strange keys at tempos so fast you either flew or fell. I suffered in vicarious misery with a pianist who sat with his hands in his lap throughout a tune kicked off at a vicious tempo, then quietly rose and retreated with a foolish, downcast smile and a pitiful squaring of shoulders that was like an attempt to pull a tattered threadbare cloak of dignity about himself. That was it, you either measured up or slunk away. It didn't take me but a minute to realize I was nowhere near ready for this league; they were lying in wait for the likes of me. If you don't have the price of admission, stay out of the hall. I began to suspect that the skills required for entry might be forever beyond my reach.

Chastised, I returned to Worcester briefly, remembering what S. N. Behrman, who had his hometown pegged pretty good, had told me years after my father died: "Dan and I shared the passionate conviction that somewhere there must be a better way of life." I packed, said so long to my brother and mother ("I pray to God you know what you're doing, you'll get swallowed up out there . . .") and the remnants of the Classical High Gang, and took off for Boston, where I began studies in piano, theory, and composition with a faculty member of Schillinger House.

Jackie Byard and I were running roughly parallel courses—on strikingly different levels. Having blazed a fiery trail through Boston, turning on a coterie of instrumentalists and aficionados with his galloping full-keyboard command, he now took off on an upward spiral for New York—unawed by the firepower north of 110th Street and formidably equipped to do battle. My plan was to study, work whatever gigs I could find, and continue my search in the black clubs of eastern Massachusetts—a gentler enclave where the music would be less convulsive and searing, I imagined, the hostility more manageable.

At the time, Art Tatum was appearing at the Hi-Hat club on Columbus Avenue. The nearly blind wizard was (and is, though he's been gone thirty-six years) the Father, Son, and Holy Ghost to jazz pianists. I had heard the records, of course, but this was my first opportunity to catch him live.

My first sight of him was in the bar, a floor below the main room. I recognized him from album photos. He was short—five-foot-six or -seven, gauging by my own comparable height—and broad, a dense, low-gravity weight to him. The bartender was pouring bottles of Pabst Blue Ribbon beer into a glass pitcher. When it was nearly brimful he handed it to Tatum, who raised the pitcher to his mouth, tilted his head, opened his gullet. Down the hatch in three or four stupendous swallows. What I had heard was true: he drank like he played, lustily, prodigiously. It was an auspicious introduction.

I followed him upstairs to a semidark, two-thirds-filled room. He eased onto the bench, arms loose at his sides, head cocked as if sniffing something in the air. Only when the rustle and conversational hum subsided did he lift his hands.

Some pianists' hands caress the keyboard; others' prance, skip, sculpt, browbeat, or bluster. Tatum's, as I watched transfixed from a side table that night, alternately tap-danced and marched; the dance puckish, airy, fantastic (sly passagework and raffish embroidery suggested Debussy playing barrelhouse), the march that of an assured boulevardier. He cloaked mundane pop songs in symphonic array and dazzling filigree. Playful interpolations—"Stars and Stripes Forever," "Camptown Races"—studded serious compositions. He closed the first set with Massenet's "Elégie," played it straight, shimmeringly, then turned on the engines, transforming it to a blazing, rag-inflected juggernaut of sound. Someone behind me whispered, "Now I understand *The Charge of the Light Brigade*."

He seemed to be connected to a volcanic fount of energy and invention from which he painted endlessly vivid canvases, the hands chasing each other on breakneck roller-coaster runs. If you closed your eyes it sounded like two supremely gifted players, four hands, nimbly frolicking on the same keyboard, having a hell of a time for themselves.

I returned to the Hi-Hat on three consecutive nights and left each time reeling, bewitched by the intricate harmonies and ravishing tone, the mad-dash, throttle-out excursions—my exhilaration tempered by a nagging dejection. What I had heard hardly seemed possible, absurdly beyond reach.

I knew that celebrated artists from the classical world had been to hear Tatum, either at George Gershwin's Seventy-second Street apartment in New York or at the midtown clubs. Horowitz, Godowski, Rachmaninoff, Gieseking, Paderewski: a select fan club indeed. They listened and were wowed. Horowitz particularly enjoyed the interpolations and endless variations on Gershwin's songs, and Rachmaninoff is said to have remarked to a colleague, "If this man ever decides to play serious music we're all in trouble." (I'd like to think Rachmaninoff was half-kidding about the "serious" music.) These surpassing musicians would not have been intimidated by the bravura technique and velocity; they too could fly. It must have been the spontaneity, the bold improvisations forged at dizzying tempos that floored them.

I later asked a classical pianist-composer and critic for one of the Boston papers if he had listened to Tatum, and if he had an opinion. "There's a demonic, almost diabolical quality to his playing," he said. "The furies must have gathered around his crib at birth, something infernal slipped into his mother's milk."

The overwrought references bewildered me. Why the sinister overtone? Can't a comparable fervor and brilliance evolve from godliness? Wasn't the talent divine?

10

Bearing letters of reference from Pepto Bismel and Hal Harganian, I connected with Rudy Yellin's Society Orchestra. At wedding receptions, when the newlyweds posed with bright grins, their entwined hands gripping the engraved silver knife, we played the year's hit tune, "If I Knew You Were Comin' I'd've Baked a Cake."

On a busy Saturday night Rudy would have a dozen or more combos working in the Boston area's hotels, country clubs, lodges, catering halls, and private homes. From a reservoir or "stable" of musicians he was able to put together units of any size and specification to fit a hostess's needs. This pool consisted mainly of middle-aged professionals, family men moderate in habit and mien, who could both read and fake. (Only in the music business is the word *fake* nonpejorative. People are always asking musicians if they read or play by ear; most do both, but this reply for some reason creates consternation, as if an airline captain were to claim to be both pilot and navigator; a Boston colleague of mine responds to all such queries, "I read pretty good but not without moving my lips.") Rudy's stableboys, as they jocularly or plaintively referred to themselves, gave Rudy first call on all nights in return for a guaranteed annual income. They were steady and dependable (some had daytime jobs), maintained a repertoire of current pop and show tunes, and stuck close to the melody on their choruses. The younger jazz and club-date musicians scorned them as "mickey-mouse" or "ricky-tick" players, but a good many could have acquitted themselves creditably in a Harlem jam session, and they ate regularly. The flexible combos in Rudy's organization were fronted by experienced subleaders who had moved up from the ranks. On a busy night Rudy would make the rounds, putting in brief appearances at each function—if only to wave his baton for a tune or two or play a half chorus on fiddle, apportioning his time according to the importance of the account—so that the party giver would be assured that he or she had hired a genuine Yellin band and not some slick substitute.

THERE IS LESS real music to the society-band business than people think; or, putting it another way, the music itself can be a minor ingredient. The success of an organization like Rudy's depends to a great extent on contacts with banquet and catering managers, club social directors, society leaders, columnists, and other community *machers*; this entails constant wining, dining, or alternate forms of cajolery. Competition is keen, and bandleaders will often vie for engagements by outfitting their musicians in exotic costumes to fit an ethnic or thematic occasion. It's the old sell-the-sizzle-not-the-steak concept. Theme parties are the bane of the professional musician's existence, reducing him, in the space of one night, to the level of the meat-market clerk in phosphorescent green vest and paper bow tie on St. Patrick's Day. With Rudy I found myself working class hotels and country clubs attired in striped blazer, Hawaiian shirt (lei optional), serape, Gay Nineties brocaded vest (with straw boater and sleeve garters), balloon-sleeved Greek tunic, coolie shift and hat (endless choruses of "Slow Boat to China"), bowler derby, yarmulke, and accessories geared to Halloween, Valentine's Day, Thanksgiving, St. Patrick's Day, Christmas, and the Fourth of July. It is the closest the professional musician comes to prostitution other than playing the parlor upright in a reconstructed New Orleans whorehouse.

In the blazer-and-vest line, Rudy tried to keep in stock large, medium, and small sizes, but attrition—cigarette burns, drink and sweat stains, split seams (a large trying to squeeze into a medium)—took its toll, and the mediums were often in short supply. A large blazer could hang on a thin medium-sized guy like a gunnysack on a coatrack; or, in a small blazer—bony wrists protruding from too-short sleeves and a hat perched on his noggin like a knot on a stump—he could look like the sorriest rube this side of the Merrimack. A few successive nights in such ill-fitting garb and you begin to feel like the sideshow freak at the county fair.

Subleaders bear the brunt of a party's success or failure. They are illusion makers. Just as the Shoshone shaman is purported to have the ability to create thunderstorms by poking a certain genus of beetle with a stick, the leader's baton can greatly influence a party's climate. He must perceive and sustain the prevailing mood—pump it up if it's flat and create one if none exists—call tunes and tempos accordingly, determine when requests for a cha-cha, polka, or Viennese waltz can safely be interjected and the judicious time for a Paul Jones, conga line, Mexican Hat Dance, or ladies' choice, all of which he must organize and ride herd on. (In Rudy's era the general rule was, The older the crowd the brighter the tempo. For younger dancers a frequent slow-drag ballad—Rudy called them "pants-busters"—was a requisite. When the ages mixed, as at wedding receptions, we had problems, which would compound in the coming decades with the eruption of rock and disco. Otherwise the exigencies and remedies have remained fairly constant over the eras.) The disruptive request—the "Notre Dame Victory March," say, or "Blue Danube"—by an intractable patron when the affair is rolling along beautifully on tried-and-true Porter–Berlin–Gershwin businessman's bounce (what Rudy called "breadbasket medleys" and so designated on the charts) must be handled with tact and finesse. Despite the patron's yahoo demeanor or an appearance of inebriation, he could be the president of the corporation, she could be the director of advertising or the wife of the chairman of the board. The subleader has several options, all in the area of prevarication and delay: "There are a number of other requests before yours, but we'll try to get to it"; "I'll see what I can do later on," delivered with a conspiratorial smile and wink; "We'll be taking a break shortly"—flash of the wristwatch—"Can it wait till we get back?" Then trust time and booze to numb impulse and blur memory. The ill-timed request should be honored only when the subleader has determined that the requester is a high-priority personage; then he can ask for the party's name and announce, "And now ladies and gentlemen, for your executive vice-president, Mr. Higginbotham, and his charming wife, 'I've Got a Lovely Bunch of Coconuts.' " It always helps to have a bead on the firm's upper-echelon people, a matter the society bandleader's office staff can assist with. For these demands on his patience, tact, and imagination, the subleader is well paid: 10 percent of the band's aggregate union-scale wages above his own sideman's wages.

When we managed to hit on the right tempos and choice of tunes for a party, the actual music—pitch, timbre, proficiency, cohesion—became secondary. People hear an overall beat, a happy or romantic sound. Benny Goodman could be on the stand trading fours with Itzhak Perlman, and if the principals were incognito I'm convinced no one in a party crowd would be aware that anything special was going on. As Rudy's 260-pound bass player pointed out, "When you're scarfing fine cuisine or juicing and romancing a chick—even getting a second wind with your old lady—you aren't going to be paying that much attention to the music." By way of example, he suggested I play eight bars of my next chorus with my knuckles or elbows and see if I could detect any reaction out front. I cordially declined.

One of the subleader's most onerous duties is keeping sidemen in rein during intermissions. Country-club and house-party hosts are generally liberal regarding liquor privileges and will allow musicians access to the bar during breaks; in private homes the booze, of course, is always gratis. Hotel management can be paranoid. I have seen maître d's and catering directors blanch at the sight of a twelve-piece band descending on a service bar like a horde of thirst-crazed elk—or, if the job takes place during dinner hours, infiltrating the kitchen, scrounging for rolls, crackers, discarded fruit cocktails, an untouched cutlet—and quickly move to close off access, shunting the musicians into corridors and back rooms. Count on the ace scroungers in the band to try to ingratiate themselves with hotel waiters, busboys, and chefs, paving the way for future kitchen forays. (Musicians are funny about loot. Beyond the eternal cadging of food and drink, they will wear frayed tuxes and dark suits years past their useful life, saving on everything except their instruments—though I've seen a few saxophones braided with rubber bands that bind decrepit keys like loose cabbage leaves to the body of the horn. At a wedding reception in Brookline the Yellin combo I was working with was invited to partake of the buffet. There was a succulent array of goodies: smoked salmon, glazed hams, caviar, shrimp. The band—everyone except me—charged into line. The drummer, stuffing his mouth as he worked his way down the table, called back, "Man, get yourself some of this caviar, it's fantastic." I told him I'd eaten at home a couple of hours ago and wasn't hungry. He stared at me, incredulous. "You're crazy—this stuff goes for sixty bucks an ounce!") At lodges and catering halls a perverse rule of thumb holds: The lower the class of the affair, the more likely the band will be invited to eat.

Musicians usually bring jugs to hotel jobs, especially the first-class establishments where bar prices are steep; these are carried in topcoat pockets and horn cases. Rudy's longtime first-call trombone player, a white-haired father of five, would bring an elaborate carrying case the size (and aspect) of a portable backgammon set—velvet-lined, with three silvered pint flasks engraved Scotch, Bourbon, and Gin, and a half dozen matching shot glasses; he'd dole out the booze in a back room to his buddies and charge others a nominal price. Bandleaders condone juicing as long as their sidemen don't get sloppy or function below par. They have to; a regimen of austerity would lose men to other organizations. Dope, at least the injected variety, is uncommon among society-band players. A junkie would last in the organization about as long as it took him to play two bars of "I Get a Kick Out of You." Not only in Hollywood movies and Nelson Algren novels do bandleaders say to sidemen, "Let's settle this once and for all, Sidney, roll up your sleeves."

Dance sets at dinner parties are sandwiched between courses, the music coordinated by bandleader and maître d' and orchestrated, if you will, to the serving of the meal. The spectacle of middle-aged diners jumping up from their chairs between courses of an elaborate spread and bouncing recklessly about the floor to bright tempos has bemused musicians since the time string trios were introduced into salons. The practice seems to us as intemperate and unhealthful as a vigorous half dozen laps of the pool in the midst of a backyard barbecue. The sight of tightly corseted women with pink, flushed faces and tuxedoed men with beef-heart complexions and paunches bulging against cummerbunds flinging themselves around on full stomachs alarms us. We keep expecting to see them falter, pull up short and pitch over like tipped cows.

Fine cuisine can provide a more direct menace. The occasion was a small black-tie dinner party in a ninth-floor Back Bay apartment. The candlelight was subdued, the conversation cultured, the drinking discreet. You would not think such a setting conducive to danger. At nine o'clock the roast suckling pig was brought in from the kitchen by the catering staff and placed on a table close by a candelabrum. I was working solo and remember specifically playing "Dancing on the Ceiling" on the good Chickering baby grand, leisurely watching the lambent play of shadows overhead, when the liqueured glaze ignited and with a great whoosh the pig went up in flames. The room was heavily draped and furnished; tongues of flame began licking at the appointments. The vivid colors and racing shadows briefly turned the room into a Rubens painting. Two enterprising guests seized the four corners of the tablecloth, carried it with blazing pig through the French doors onto the balcony, and with a frantic cry—"Heads up below!"—dumped the whole works over the side, nine floors to the street. The host doused the drapes with seltzer water, and I rode the elevator down with several guests to see if any damage had been wreaked below. The pig lay in the gutter pretty much intact, flickering palely on its white shroud, the apple still in its mouth. A knot of curious well-dressed people had gathered round, gazing alternately at the pig and up at the sky. An elderly man walking his dog said to another passerby, "I was told this was a safe neighborhood."

My mother was keeping me posted from "down the road" (as proper Bostonians referred to Worcester): My brother had graduated from Worcester Polytechnic Institute and taken a challenging position with Corning Glass Works; a cousin had been accepted at Columbia Law School and another was engaged to a man who owned a Chevrolet agency.

A few weeks after the night of the roast suckling pig, another Back Bay soiree gave rise to a much different kind of incident, one belying the swank surroundings and triggering a lingering humiliation that still stings my memory and can be rekindled by the mere sight of a serviceman in uniform. It was two in the morning when I left the brick townhouse where I'd worked a trio job. It had been a rare and mellow night. Good music—no funny hats and coats—and gracious people; numerous pale glasses of French wine and a heaping plate of top-drawer hors d'oeuvres under my belt. I waved good night to the bass player and guitarist and began walking with my ubiquitous cushions down a leafy side street to my car. The October morning was crisp and fragrant; it made me think of the illustrations on old sheet music—tilted street lamps against a backdrop of silhouetted city towers, a tuxedoed tap dancer wheeling across a vast yellow moon. A lyric of the endearing good-night tune we had played a few minutes earlier, an all-time favorite of mine, "A Nightingale Sang in Berkeley Square," was running through my mind: "Our homeward step was just as light as the tap-dancing feet of Astaire . . ." when I saw two young soldiers approaching under the arch of shadowy trees. Their dress uniforms were smartly creased and bore corporal's chevrons and Korea service ribbons. I thought they must be on leave, sons of local people, and if they'd been to a party in the neighborhood I hoped it had been as groovy as mine. As they came near I nodded to them, a tacit *Nice night.* The taller of the two weaved to his left as if drunk, though a moment earlier they had both been walking abreast in a leisurely erect manner, the bearing you'd expect of soldiers on leave, at least in this neighborhood. Barely pausing, he raised his arm—I had an instant's fantasy that he was going to salute me in a clownish manner—and slapped me hard and flat across the face. Before I could react they both had passed me by, strolling at their previous unhurried pace. In my back vision there had been no sign of belligerence or malice in the taller soldier's expression; rather a placid, benign kind of vacancy. Hugging the cushions under my arm, I felt stupid and childlike, chastened. There was no thought of fighting back. My hands—I couldn't take the chance; and two of them, both taller, heavier. But more to the point, I'd never been in a fight before, I didn't know how. Never before had I been slapped in that way, in earnest, not by a parent nor by any adult or child. My face was flamed and smarting as I called after them, "Hey, what was that? . . ." the timid words dying in the empty street. Unheeding, they walked on, having discharged their mute contempt for a 4-F, malingerer, goldbrick. My gleaming white shirt, the tuxedo, must have especially rankled. I felt confused and ashamed; already I was half excusing the assault. How could they have known that I was not a Back Bay partygoer of their generation (well enough connected to remain a civilian) but a working stiff wearing the unlikely habit of my trade, with a virulent, exempting case of hay fever to boot?

The next day I began to grow a mustache, hoping to add the necessary years to my appearance to slide me past the time-gate of service to country and forestall a reprise assault on some other civilized, woodsy street. It turned out a sorry little scrap that never took hold. Rudy got a gander of it ten days later and said, "Looks like you kissed a wet kitten. Shave it, son."

DURING MY SIXTEEN months with Rudy's organization I was constantly impressed by the musicians' punctuality. No one ever failed to show for a job and rarely did anyone arrive more than a few minutes late. When you consider dozens of instrumentalists on a given night streaming from diverse points over turnpike, highway, and back road to outlying country clubs often situated on unlighted and poorly marked golf-course roads, to private homes secluded on lakeshore or in wooded countryside—not to mention the logistics of unloading drums, music stands, and cases of orchestrations at the entrance of a downtown hotel on a rainy Saturday night and then scrambling for a parking space—the record appears astounding. I wonder if it can be matched in any other profession. The answer lies in the matter of compelling urgency and indispensability—of an allegiance as ironclad as any Mafia family's code of honor. A drummer not showing for a big-band date or a pianist missing from a quartet spells disaster. The music, assuming it ever gets off the ground, is crippled, the party—a catered affair, say, costing in the thousands or tens of thousands of dollars—debilitated, if not mortally wounded, and the society band's reputation blackened. We *have* to be there, and we rise to the occasion. The band office assists by coordinating rides, supplying maps, and advising an early start in case of car trouble. I have seen musicians arrive blinking and befuddled after traversing a maze of back-country roads, disheveled and grease-stained from coping with car breakdowns, or, having abandoned their wheels, lugging horns and bass fiddles from taxis after parting with a fare equivalent to their night's pay—but always *on time.* You can call in sick, but you'd better have arranged for a satisfactory replacement, and never, never at the last minute when a substitute might be impossible to find. To watch a trumpet player with a raging cold blow for five hours in a drafty hall attired in striped shirt, sleeve garters, and straw boater is to weep.

The closest a Rudy Yellin combo came to catastrophe during my tenure was at a private lodge on a lake some seventy miles from Boston. Rudy himself was on the job, a rare night-long appearance; this was a special account, his presence had been guaranteed, and as it was a slow Tuesday night he was not needed elsewhere. We were five pieces and made the trip in trumpeter Billy Hall's big Buick. Billy would be the only horn on the date and the sole frontline melody instrument except for Rudy. (The less said about Rudy's fiddle playing the better. What has been said behind his back, and in the strictest confidence, is that he gets "a tone like a squeegee on a plate-glass window.") We arrived for the nine-to-one lake job at eight-forty after a bumpy two-hour drive. The drummer unloaded his cases from the trunk, and Billy lifted out his trumpet case; it was strangely, terrifyingly light. He opened it and hurried after Rudy, who was greeting the host on the lodge porch. He plucked piteously at Rudy's sleeve. "Rudy, I don't have my horn." It was dead quiet in the dense woods around the lodge, and the lake, as you looked out from the porch, was pitch dark but for dim, distant pinpoints of light. Rudy gave his faithful employee of twelve years' standing a thoughtful, almost leisurely look, in which there was the chilling trace of a smile. "I knew I could count on you, Billy boy." Billy attempted an explanation but trailed off before finishing, repeatedly clearing his throat. Listening from a few feet away, I thought, So that's what a death rattle sounds like. We started the job with four pieces; the music was as thin and bland as last week's leek soup. At around eleven o'clock one of the lodge members had an inspiration and phoned the local high school principal at his home—one of the dim pinpoints of light that had since blinked out—rousing him from bed. At the member's urging the principal drove to the school, some five miles' distance, and eventually appeared at the lodge with a battered but serviceable trumpet from the school bandroom. Billy played out the last hour of the job. But for the next two months his work calls from Rudy's office fell off markedly before resuming their normal seasonal pattern, and for a week or two following the incident, when you greeted Billy on the street or in the union hall, you were greeting a broken man: his gaze wandered; he spoke haltingly and blinked a lot.

With the help of the more experienced stableboys I soon picked up tricks of the trade: carrying a gooseneck lamp and extension cord on reading jobs (most music-stand lights won't accommodate to pianos) and a pocket chess set or paperback book for killing time during long-winded after-dinner speeches; requesting ice water (heavy on the ice) from bartenders during breaks, drinking off the water and replenishing the glass from my coat-concealed half-pint for a tasty Southern Comfort on the rocks. From a Filipino busboy, of all people, I learned how to bring a piano's flat notes up to pitch by strategically wedging folded cocktail napkins between the strings. You'd be surprised by the number of gutted, out-of-tune relics to be found in major clubs and hotels. The consoles and spinets see heavy duty and are constantly being jammed into elevators and bumped along corridors; even the smaller grands get shifted from room to room. I'd lift a cigarette-scorched piano lid and find a note from the previous pianist: "This box is a dirty dog. D and E above high C stick and a couple bass notes don't work at all. If there's a peculiar smell you can't place I pissed in it closing night." Complaints to management are usually futile. Catering managers and nonjazz club owners don't want to hear about defective instruments. The piano was invariably "tuned just last week," or "Out of eighty-eight notes you got eighty-three in working condition; I wish I could count on that kind of percentage in my end of the business," or "I'm sick of spending money on the goddamn thing, next time bring your own" (which a generation of pianists would be doing in the seventies, trundling electric keyboards and fifty-pound speakers down hotel corridors like latter-day Willie Lomans). Keyboards sprinkled with missing notes can take the heart out of you; consider a gardener trying to work with the center teeth missing from his rake. At an after-hours club in Somerville I watched a black pianist dexterously hopscotching a string of non-playing notes using an aggressive stride technique. He called it his Jack-be-nimble style, developed over the years for dealing with "these rotten tomatoes," and thought of his hands as leaping the candlesticks of dead notes. I expressed my sympathy and admiration for his resourcefulness. "There're times you got to come on like Hannibal and the Alps," he told me. "You can't let the suckers beat you down."

The Brigantine Club in Revere Beach was notorious for its rinky-dink atrocity of a baby grand. Ivories were discolored and chipped or missing altogether; the felts looked like they had been chewed by crazed rodents; the strings were coated with a whitish substance that could only be salt (on balmy nights did invisible sea mists waft through the open windows?), and the casing was studded with drink rings and cigarette burns. Early in the evening of my first Brigantine gig I punctured my thumb on one of the ragged ivories and began spotting the keys like a gored bullfighter dripping on the sand. I signaled the leader-saxophonist, who was playing the lead on "The Night Has a Thousand Eyes"; he wandered over, blowing as he walked; gazed at the keyboard, eyes bulging slightly, and wandered back to center stage, still blowing. (Musicians aren't easily disconcerted; they've undergone too many bizarre experiences, witnessed too much craziness on the stand and out front. I once saw a woman at a drunken Gay Nineties brawl pour a schooner of beer into the bell of the tuba player's horn. He gazed at her mournfully and kept on blowing—it sounded like frogs in a bathtub.) Between tunes a waitress handed me a bar rag, then quickly backed off. "You contagious?" she asked from a respectful distance. Naturally, I requested an explanation. "TB," she said demurely. I said I knew I was thin, but not *that* thin. "Well, this movie I saw . . ." Yes, I knew the one she meant and instantly understood: Cornel Wilde as Frédéric Chopin coughing gobbets of red onto the gleaming ivories. During the break I bandaged my thumb and began wedging cocktail napkins between the salt-encrusted strings. An intelligent-looking bystander asked what I was doing. I explained, and he introduced himself: Dr. So-and-so, a gynecologist from Swampscott. In my inquisitive small-town way I asked him what gynecologists always get asked by frustrated lechers: Don't you get nervous examining all those beautiful chicks? His answer was eloquent and instructive (and possibly rehearsed): "My work is like that of the piano repairman who can only afford a modest instrument in his own home. When he hires out to a rich man to work on a magnificent concert grand, he does the best job he can and does not covet it. He understands it is beyond his reach."

I had occasion to return to the Brigantine two months later. Praying the monstrosity had been replaced, I came fortified with Band-Aids and a liberal stash of Southern Comfort. Black Beauty stood in the window just as I'd left her, massive, bullying, unassailable. Disheartened, I lifted the top and found Scotch-taped to the underside a wry and piquant dissertation by a previous tenant: "This vintage instrument has a storied history. It was fashioned for Czar Alexander I of Russia in the fierce winter of 1857–58 by the craftsman Melinkov of Smolensk. Only small pedigreed animals from the czar's private preserve had access to its innards during the long nocturnal hours, and even after a century's lapse their musty fragrance and distinctive nibblings are still detectable. You'll notice the instrument's unusual sonority. Careful examination of the casing reveals the czar's personal crest, an ingenious design of interlocking circles predating this century's famed Ballantine rings and overlaid with a series of vertical grooves, each, by striking coincidence, the approximate size of an Old Gold."

Bandleaders will sometimes join forces and attempt to shame or coerce managers and proprietors into repairing a derelict. But it is a losing cause: many are beyond salvage and will hold a tuning only so long before reverting to their primordial state. As Rudy's bacchanalian trombonist said to the Brigantine's owner, "Here's what you should do with this aberration: Tune it, clean it thoroughly, refurbish the felts and hammers, polish the casing. Then hire a handyman to chop it up for firewood. And you know what you'd have?" The owner shook his head. "A bad fire."

Paradoxically I encountered the rottenest tomato of them all at a sumptuous lawn party on a Wellesley estate. Chinatown was the evening's motif. Paper lanterns strung in the poplar trees and silvered vessels of barbecued pork, chow mein, et al. warming over burners on red-clothed tables; a pagoda-roofed bar at one end of the wide lawn. We dressed accordingly: coolie hats and loose-fitting pastel cotton garments, supplied by Rudy and intended, I gathered, to simulate the garb of rice-gathering peasants. Indian summer weather had prevailed for the past two weeks—blue-and-gold days and velvet nights—but on this night autumn fell like a clanging gate: a brisk fifty-five degrees and a good wind blowing. A half dozen electric heaters had been propped in the crooks of the tall trees.

We got out of our tux coats, balled them up, laid them in the drum cases, and donned our coolie shifts. (We always wore full tuxes in case the costumes somehow got sidetracked or the host/hostess had a last-minute change of mind—discarding our coats and tucking them away in expedient out-of-sight places; which is why Rudy's sidemen's tuxedos looked scruffier than anyone else's.) The garments came in only one size, fitting the small guys like little girls' dresses and making our bean-pole bass player look like a night heron. I played a trial run on the blond Baldwin spinet and—never mind my ears—didn't believe my eyes. The keys went down and stayed down like the plug had been pulled on a player piano in midtune. With a sinking heart I took off the front and set it on the grass. The hammers I had struck were cocked back against the strings as if glued there, yet the tripping mechanisms and felts all appeared in good condition. I called over trumpeter-leader Tommy Tedesco, who was alternately blowing into his hands and blatting fat notes on his horn, trying to warm it. I pointed mutely to the depressed keys (*look, man, no hands*). Tommy lowered his horn, chewed on a corner of his lip, and went off to find the hostess. Less than a minute later a skinny alert-looking kid of about twelve approached. The guests were beginning to arrive, strolling through the mansion's rear portal onto the illuminated emerald lawn.

"I'm William. Mom says you have a problem."

"Watch." I struck a full chord: ten more hammers shot back and stuck fast like flies on molasses.

"Huh." The kid stuck his head inside and poked around. "What are these metal things?"

"No idea."

"But you're the piano player."

"Right. Not a mechanic." It was almost farcical; in what other profession are you so regularly sabotaged by the tools of your trade? Four hours of egg-foo-yung tunes on this abomination and I'd be a shattered man, licking my lips and clearing my throat like Billy Hall, blinking vacantly into the night shadows.

"I wonder if its being out overnight had something to do with it."

"The piano was out*side* all night?" I looked down at the grass; already the evening dew was dampening my shoes.

"The guys who set up the tables and decorations moved it out yesterday afternoon. But we had a canvas over it."

"That wouldn't have helped. The damp came from underneath and swelled the wood. It's hopeless."

William's face suddenly brightened. "Tell you what. I'll stand here and free 'em for you." By way of illustration he grabbed two handfuls of hammers and pulled them away from the strings. "See, now you're back in starting position."

"You're going to do that after every chord?"

"Well, I'll let you play for a few bars and accumulate a backlog."

We were looking brightly, kind of crazily, at each other. I was beginning to learn about the kids of the affluent: they were different, possessed of a special awareness and guile that had nothing to do with the streets. I'd already met ten-year-olds who were masterful con artists.

"Tell you what you can do for me first. Bring me a stiff Southern Comfort on the rocks."

"We don't stock it."

"Gin then."

"One double Beefeater over comin' up."

We got under way, a motley crew of frigid coolies contriving chop-suey medleys—"China Boy," "Chinatown, My Chinatown," "Slow Boat to China," "Japanese Sandman" (nobody would know)—out of range of the overhead heaters, shoes soaking in the damp grass. I'd play a bar or two, then lay out while William grabbed fistfuls of hammers and pulled them back in my face, announcing cheerfully each time, driving me mad, "There you go, Mr. A., back to starting position." Two or three times an hour he took off to fetch me a fresh gin from the bar, Tommy observing this traffic with growing unease, doubtless pondering his obligatory report to Rudy tomorrow and the possibility of someone else in the band finking if, out of friendship, he glossed over any indecorous exhibition on my part. But I'd worked under Tommy a dozen times and he knew by now that if I were going to get bombed, it would be a quiet, unostentatious, professional job.

"Now you know how Lewis and Clark must've felt," William said, depositing another gin and grasping a clutch of hammers.

With the cold stiffening the horn players' fingers and a piano chord infrequently punched in to no more advantage than a flung cowpie, every tune was starting to sound like "Donkey Serenade." ("On a night like this," I could hear Morty Gelb's ghost whispering in the wings, "swarms of bobolinks gorging on toxic berries plummeted like stones to the velvet lawns below.")

The shivering guests were beginning to desert the flagstone dance area, drifting back into the house, when Rudy put in his promised appearance. He sawed off a few bars, wandered over to the piano, apprised the hammer situation (taking cursory note of the backed-up gin glasses), muttered, "Jesus Christ on a crutch," and departed.

On my sixth gin, watching Tommy tuck his hands under his belt beneath the little-girl dress for warmth, I thought, Another year of Rudy, coolie hats, and assorted monkey suits, of moisture-sodden, rotten-tomato pianos, and I'll be reduced to a shadow of a man, devoid of talent, invention, and testicles. Might as well sew up ducks' rectums in a meat market, or trade off with that waiter carrying a tray of fresh foo yung to the warming table; at least he isn't whoring, he's just putting in his hours, doing his thing (to cop a vacuous expression from a future decade) honestly, with purpose, invulnerable to shifting winds of fashion, ludicrous accoutrement, and the whims of parvenu hostesses and ambitious bandleaders . . .

"There you go, Mr. A., back to starting position."

And just after midnight, as William freed the hammers for perhaps the two hundredth time, I gave it up: sat with my hands in my lap, stuporous, gazing at the slender, shadowy pinnacles of trees tossing in a high, cold wind as the band . . . played . . . on . . .

"What's the matter, Mr. A.?"

"Out of gas, William. Beat. Cold and tired. Don't care anymore."

"That's okay, we all grow old sooner or later."

At one bell (a grandfather clock pealing faintly behind the diamond-pane windows) Tommy and company wrapped it up for the two die-hard couples left on the flagstones with a final chorus of "Slow Boat to China"—the fifth time around for that serviceable ditty—and we shucked our coolie apparel and packed up. William helped the drummer with his cases and waved us off, standing amid the littered sauce-stained tables under the Japanese lanterns: "So long, you guys, see you all later at that big tuning fork in the sky . . ."

11

From Rudy's suckling-pig and chow-mein parties I ventured to another part of Boston—as distant from Back Bay as Hoboken from Great Neck—to continue my search for the talisman that would infuse my playing with the heart and soul of Africa without altering the color of my skin.

For a young white traversing the urban ghettos during the forties and fifties a horn case was often a guarantor of safe passage.

"What you got in there, man?"

"Alto sax. On my way to a session."

"Oh? Where at?"

Possessing no such identifying badge and

looking the way I did (a turnpike barmaid had once remarked behind my back, "The breath my seven-year-old uses to blow out his birthday candles would tip him over"), I improvised: a sheaf of music manuscript paper under my arm, or an empty battered clarinet case I'd found discarded in a union-hall trash can. Often I came directly from a gig in my tux; this could prove an advantage—smoothing the rites of passage—or (more likely) a liability, depending on the character of the district I was passing through. I usually took the precaution of removing my bow tie and wearing a beat-up raincoat over the soup and fish.

One of Rudy's sidemen steered me to Coffee John's, an after-hours place on Massachusetts Avenue. The doors opened around ten, but the real action didn't get under way until after midnight, when musicians began dropping by from work to drink and jam. A dingy narrow corridor of a room lined with scarred wooden booths facing a small, cramped stage.

Guileless, fortified by an instinctive faith in my own inviolability and the holiness of my cause, I sauntered one night into a maelstrom of turbulent sound and close-together black faces, hands holding cups and glasses of coffee laced with rye and gin; a low-pitched jumble of voices beneath the music's pulse, the square patch of dance floor packed with weaving bodies. For the better part of a week I hung out (my white friends blanched when I told them where I'd been until four in the morning), standing alone at the beer-and-wine bar, which shut down by law at one o'clock and was separated from the main room by a shoulder-high partition, listening to the music and watching the dancers, ignored but for an occasional curious or indifferent stare, a half frown etched in a questioning glance. On Sunday night I asked if I could sit in. The music was strong and gutty but within my ken. I knew most of the tunes; the tempos seemed comfortable. I sensed that one or two of the pianists could play rings around me, but the rings were concentric and not all that wide. I felt I wouldn't be embarrassed as I would have been at the incandescent Harlem sessions.

The trumpet player nominally in charge of the session nodded (I learned later that many of the participating musicians were out of work, that a handful of key players were paid a few dollars a night for their midnight to four A.M. stints) and the pianist, Lonnie, slid off the stool and leaned against a booth, hands in pockets, his stony gaze sliding past my shoulder. I fiddled with the stool's height, inadvertently lowering it, then spinning it up a few revolutions, hearing mocking, skeptical voices behind me: "Already I don't like the looks of this," and "What's this peckerwood gonna do, tune it?" and "Come back, Lonnie, all's forgiven."

" 'Blue Skies' okay?" the trumpet player said.

"Sure."

"One flat, you got four bars. 'Bout here," he said, snapping his thumb and middle finger in a lazy circle.

The rhythm falling in behind me was jagged and looser than it had sounded from the floor, looser than I was accustomed to—bass and drums glancing off the beat, churning and slipping around it, rather than hammering it down four-square like spikes in a railbed. Several times I felt the meter sliding out from under my fingers. When this occurred the bass player steadied into a fundamental four-to-the-bar stroll, laying groundwork beneath me; at the same time I experienced the childhood sensation of being effortlessly lifted up on his shoulders (as one of the ubiquitous uncles had once hoisted me on a summer morning so I could see the parade unfolding down Worcester's Main Street). The dancers, I noticed uneasily, were drifting off the floor, some shaking their heads. "It don't get it," I heard someone say. I struggled through two more tunes, hands cramping and sweat dropping off my chin onto the keys until the board was slick as an ice rink. The dancers never returned.

The bass player, whose name was Lucius, a slim graying man with high cheekbones and a burgundy cast to his skin, took me aside after the set. "You want a honest critique?" he said and continued even as I nodded earnestly, mopping my face. "The dancers was off balance, that's why they deserted, they couldn't pat their feet right or make their proper moves. You was playing rhythmic enough, don't misapprehend me, but it was too straight-ahead and ricky-tick, if you catch my drift. We're used to a wider beat, space and margin to move around in. It's like a woman sashaying down a wide alleyway swinging her hips and buns, used to plenty of leeway, you picture it? (Shades of Amy Avallone!) Now that alleyway suddenly *narrows* on her and this fine bitch is getting bruised, *hurting*, so naturally she's going to cut out. What you got to do is listen to me and the iron and skins [drums] more intensely . . ."

I knew what he meant, sort of. Whether I could do anything about it was another matter. The twin legacies I had to overcome were my white upbringing and a current debilitating schedule playing businessman's-bounce show tunes, horas, and Viennese waltzes with a clam-and-chowder society band.

I don't know why they kept letting me sit in; it must have taken guts, or simpleness, on my part to ask. Perhaps they were flattered by my interest in their music and derived satisfaction from the role reversal at a time when there were no black teachers in the public schools; or they may have found amusement in the spectacle of Master Charles getting turned on, trying to dwell in their sunshine—tolerant of me because I was just a skinny, earnest, funny-ass kid and not too obvious a nigger lover.

I BECAME AWARE of a grudging cordiality as I poked my head in each night just after twelve bells. "Here comes the gopher in the watermelon patch" (Nestor, the bartender) and "Where's the sergeant-at-arms? Who let this white trash in?" As I made my way up to the stand a gruff, good-natured raillery followed me. "Better be wearin' your asbestos vest, boy . . . This paddy's gonna get his feathers clipped again . . . What's he gonna play for us tonight, 'Ol' Man Ribber' or 'Short'nin' Bread'?"

There was a beautiful tawny-skinned singer who occasionally sat in. She worked in a show bar on Columbus Avenue and would arrive after one-thirty in a luxurious leather coat, a silver tiara riding a towering knot of blue-black hair, eyes liquid and glittering with the night. Her name was Auraline; a chain smoker with a rich, deep, grainy voice (which was *why* she smoked, she insisted, to retain that timbre), she was always a little stoned, or seemed so to me, saying funny, unconnected things, her luminous, heavy-lidded eyes looking at you and sliding past you at the same time.

"Don't bust your conk, baby," she'd say to me, apropos of nothing, "everything's gonna be everything."

One night after I'd backed her for a set she introduced the musicians, inventing names she didn't know or remember ("On drums, bringin' a little bit of Georgia to Massachusetts Ave., Rufus Funk, Junior"), and when it came my turn—"Let's give this up-and-comin' boy on piano whose name I'll think of in a minute a hand for steppin' across town to do his stuff. He's sweet an' unspoiled and *ser*-ious, so all you hungry-ass chicks out there with big eyes keep your hands off him, hear?" The crowd snickered and guffawed, enjoying the banter.

Off the stand, blowing plumes of smoke over my shoulder, she said, "You starting to get it, baby. You only got one main obstacle to surmount, as I see it, which is that when I grew up tapping my feet and clapping my hands, singing 'Joshua Fit the Battle of Jericho' in my uncle's church, you were singing 'Abide with Me.' But don't pay it too much mind," she advised, her liquid eyes gliding past me, " 'cause one of these days you're gonna score a touchdown and fifty thousand people'll be watching the game."

She had a cousin or half brother, Wesley—both were vague about the relationship—with the same distracted opaline gaze. Wesley washed cars during the day and came to Coffee John's every night, sometimes sitting in on conga drum or beating a woodblock with a drumstick during Latin tunes. He spent a lot of time in the men's room, and when he wasn't there or on the stand he flitted genially up and down the line of booths, stopping to chat and sample a spiked coffee. In regard to me, he gave generously of his counsel.

"What this boy should do is spend some nights at the Arcady Lounge over on Huntington, observe how those ace bitches synchronizes their hips and butts to the drummer's accents—that's where he'll learn to swing."

"Now what would you know about swing, Wesley?" someone chimed in disdainfully. "You couldn't swing a Mickey Mouse watch on a rubber band."

"I'm sayin' the ec-*dysiasts* is where it's at—those righteous ebon girls wriggling their saucy dusters!" Wesley exclaimed, eyes widening and gleaming in opalescent splendor. "Couple nights at the Arcady that beat'll begin to sink in like pilin's in a riverbed. Can't help but happen!"

The next time I saw him he'd forgotten the ecdysiasts; New York City was where I should go to pursue my education. "If the boy's serious in his endeavor"—the discussions seemed always to be directed past or lobbed over me, as if my presence were an obstacle to be circumvented—"he's got to earn his credits. The only place to pick up that final diploma is the University of the Streets of New York."

"The Apple is cool," someone else observed somberly, "but rotten at the co'."

"I've already been," I said. "It's rough."

"It's where you got to go to pick up the pearls," Wesley continued, unheeding.

"You got to slog through some heavy mud to get to them pearls," the other said, dubious.

"There's nothin' new, man," a third interjected. "There's nothin' *new!* You don't have to set foot off your back porch. Just hang out, pick up an' get nervous like the rest of us."

"In that town," Wesley said with a touch of awe in his voice, "without the proper credits you can't even cross Lenox, never mind Park Avenue."

I no longer felt the need to carry manuscript paper or an empty clarinet case with me, and had ceased standing alone at the bar; in the crowded, cozy booths my jug became communal, alternating with the pints and half-pints of my colleagues. On the bruised upright (which was treated lovingly, tuned once a month) I was starting to get it, at least some nights I thought I was (*it* is as hard to define as pornography, but I know it when I hear it), assimilating the displaced, driving rhythms and crackling improvisational patterns, sharpening my ear and expanding my repertoire. My fondest dream was that the Coffee John's regulars would one night rise en masse as I came off the stand, shouting, "The blue-eyed devil plays black!" From Lucius and Everett, a massive older pianist with a wild tangle of snow-flecked hair and a rollicking, bravura stride style fashioned after Fats Waller, I was discovering what "time" meant—the *quality* of the beat, just as timbre is the quality of the tone—and learning to function at very fast and very slow tempos. At slow tempos the beat has to *swell*, Lucius told me, and passed on a concept a West Coast bopper had laid on him: "It's like taking yourself a mouthful of good wine, swishing it around, savoring it before you let it go down; the swallow is that beat finally dropping." On up-tempos Everett showed me how to stay loose and relaxed by visualizing myself riding a train "rocketing along at a good clip, ninety miles an hour or more, but it doesn't trouble you 'cause you're sitting there cool and collected, your body swaying and rocking naturally with the train's pulse, which is the drums and bass. You don't need to be stomping your feet and getting all cramped up and over-excited."

But the supreme lesson I was beginning to absorb—and it's an abstract and elusive one—is that "time" should be as natural as a heartbeat pumping pure, fresh blood into a tune.

THERE WERE OCCASIONAL nights when the clientele turned over or out-of-town musicians dropped by, and the attitude toward me could change as swiftly as the sky on a March day. As soon as I walked in I could feel, like a radio's hum before the sound begins, a tension rise in the room, the friendly or incurious looks of the previous weeks suddenly vigilant and somber. When I sat in, a standard tune would be called in a strange key at a murderous tempo—much faster than the regulars would ever kick it off. I couldn't help but remember what had befallen musicians with suspect credentials at the ferocious Harlem sessions, where the take-charge players had showed no mercy, ambushing newcomers and forcing them to retire in disgrace. Once I floundered badly through a headlong "Perdido"—the conclusion greeted out front by embarrassed silence, broken by an angry voice I recognized as Auraline's. "Raise up off the boy, biggie, you don't need to show all those feathers." The intent was plain: Master Charles lured into the deep end of the pool before being blown out of the water.

If you didn't bring your cleats, stay off the field.

Auraline slipped an arm around my shoulder as I came off the stand, sweat-soaked and confused. "Don't pay those uppity dudes any mind, baby. They'll be pickin' trash out of the gutter while you're riding the elephant down the main street, just wait 'n' see. Everything's gonna be everything."

It was a sobering reminder that despite the previous air of congeniality and counsel, the barrier was still there and always would be—made up of divergent experiences, humor, temper, restraints—a skin-thin membrane tough and impervious as sheet metal.

Gun-shy, licking my wounds, I stayed off the stand for a few nights. Then, with no sign of the marauders' return, I wandered gingerly back, testing the water. On a Friday, a week after my humiliation, I had a good night, winning accolades after my solos, and only Auraline's absence prevented my sense of triumph and renewed self-esteem from being complete. When she came in a little later, I said, "I scored a touchdown, baby, you didn't even see the game."

She regarded me in her glancing sidelong way. "You're not only beginning to play colored, you're talkin' colored."

"Well, you right."

Her look turned reproachful. "Now don't you go cappin' on me with that nigger talk. You be respectful."

"Auraline, listen, I respect you more than anyone I know."

Something cunning infiltrated her expression. The tapering face with its yellowish-mauve tinge, glistening red mouth, and luminous eyes was like an exotic African flower, and my heart slammed in my throat. She grinned at me then—an audacious, violent smile—gave her shoulders a brief, wild shake and, pivoting regally in her satin dress and spike heels, sashayed away down the line of booths.

She didn't seem to belong to anyone. She usually arrived alone and left alone—unless it was with her cousin (or half brother) Wesley—and was no longer working at the Columbus Avenue show bar; I had dropped by to see her early one night and found the place shuttered. Lacking the courage of my infatuation, I never asked to take her home, wherever it was. There was no way I was going to leave the club with her; not in 1952 on the outskirts of Roxbury at four in the morning weighing 130 pounds in my winter overcoat.

But she was right, the rhythms and idioms of the black culture were permeating my speech patterns as well as the texture of my playing. "Ain't that a bitch," I might say, registering surprise, wonder or delight. I no longer departed, I "cut out." A "nickel" was five dollars, and a "dime" ten. I wore a "sky" or "lid," not a hat. Someone trying to get my attention was "pulling my coat," and a musician playing strong and confidently with an element of grandstanding was "showing feathers" or "fluffing out his feathers"; if I were greatly impressed by his performance I "wigged." With reference to women, "ace broad" or "fine bitch" were expressions of the highest approbation, but Charles had better be careful in what context and with what inflection he flaunted the argot.

One night I had my first taste of pot. ("Tea," "Mary Jane," and "shit" were the prevailing expressions then.) I don't know how I'd avoided it for so long, except that its use was nowhere near as universal as it would become a decade later. I knew Wesley and others were lighting up in the john—I had been present once or twice when a joint was being passed around—and this night, by whim, or an accident of timing, I was included. "Try some of this Panama Red," Wesley said casually as the joint came back to him from a youth in a tattersall vest. I'd wondered off and on about the sensation and saw no reason not to indulge; it would be a sociable gesture as well as a new experience, akin to accepting a passed-around jug in the booths and taking a pull without wiping the neck. "It's truly evil shit, señor," Tattersall Vest said in a choked voice. I had watched enough musicians smoke to know what to do. The joint had a rich, powerful aroma, a piney fragrance. I took several deep pulls, holding the smoke in my lungs as long as I could. When I left the toilet I felt a languorous buzz in one ear as if a somnolent and not particularly bothersome fly had lodged there, and moments later an airy, drifting lightness as if my brain had come unmoored and were floating gravity-free around my skull, much like the flakes in a paperweight globe. Well, I thought leisurely, this shit is a gas. I don't know how long I stood by the stage listening to the music, all soft peaks and hollows, watching through a trembling blue curtain of smoke the congenial clusters of Coffee John's regulars, brothers all, smoking and jiving and sipping their spiked coffee. Lucius was beckoning me back to the stand. Grinning loosely, confidently (someone told me later), I spun the vacated stool up and up—for some reason it was imperative that I assume a stratospheric position over the board; it took a long time to reach its summit. The trumpet player, Hardy, called "Black and Blue" and began snapping his fingers in a soft staccato crack, his hand tracing blurred ovals before my eyes. I played a four-bar intro, notes slipping effortlessly off my fingers (petals from a flower). Innumerable languid choruses drifted by, brass and reeds soloing. Someone poked me in the back: my turn. I broke out and away, chords stacking neatly beneath my left hand like rubber coits, the right hand fleet, darting, venturous. After what seemed a half dozen choruses I reined in (not wanting to show too many feathers), looking around for one of the horns to reenter. "Keep goin'," Hardy said. "Enough, six choruses, don't wanna hog," I responded. Hardy was smiling down at me in a puzzled, half-frowning way. "You ain't even reached the bridge of your first yet."

I remember little else of the evening, only of sauntering down the long corridor of booths—the gritty linoleum floor oddly soft and yielding as if I were walking on blankets or cork—a close-up gallery of faces, whites of eyes gleaming at me through the sifting lavender smoke. I seemed to be taking a sinuous path, wandering unwillingly from booth to booth, my shoulders thumping against the wooden supports; it was like promenading the deck of a rolling ship without the accompanying sensation of vertigo. As I lurched for the door someone opened it for me, then someone else was hugging me, someone who smelled like a whole backyard of gardenias; a warm, faintly disappointing embrace, though, one of fraternity rather than romance. "Baby, you feelin' awright?"

"I'm cool," I told Auraline. "Everything's everythin'."

"Had hisself some o' Wesley's Panama Red," a disembodied voice said as the throbbing, pumping music propelled me out the door like a giant hand pushing at my back.

I recall getting in my car and a wall of honking horns behind me, then rolling weightlessly from window to window in the deep swaying backseat of a taxi. I woke at 2:30 the next afternoon in my room on Fairfield Street feeling unanchored, my extremities—fingers, toes, ears—numb and tingling as if I'd been out on a freezing day underdressed and was just beginning to thaw. I drank something cold and metallic-tasting from a juice jar in the refrigerator, dressed and caught a bus to Massachusetts Avenue to look for my Studebaker. It took me an hour and a half, starting at Coffee John's and roaming in widening concentric circles, under sober observation from upper-story windows, the framed faces as fixed, doleful, and expressionless as those in old sepia photographs. The car was parked five blocks west of the club. The right rear wheel was up on the curb and the headlights were burning; a ticket under the wiper flapped in a gusting wind. The key was still in the ignition. I got in, shut off the lights and tried to start the motor, noticing two youths watching from the opposite curb. It whirred thinly, coughed, tubercular . . . faded. I waited a half minute and tried again: a feeble complaint, another quiet cough, and she died like a dog. The two observers were crossing the street toward me, one tall and slim with a thin fuzz of mustache, wearing a poplin jacket; the other much smaller and lighter-skinned, a plumpish baby face tucked in the hood of a bulky gray sweatshirt. I rolled down the window and asked where the nearest gas station was.

"Got yourself some trouble, huh?" the tall youth said. "Why don't we take us a peek under the hood."

Maybe like Wesley he worked with cars; Negro kids, I thought, seemed to know a lot about cars. I got out and lifted the hood, propping it on its stick.

The two silently inclined their heads, inspecting the innards. "Hard to say," the tall boy said after a moment.

"Where's the nearest station?" I asked again.

"Oh, there's nothing for a ways around here," the tall boy said. He stuck his hands in his poplin jacket, regarding me in an unhurried, thoughtful manner.

"We could use money for ciggies," the other said in a piping voice that matched his face, the light brown eyes limpid, vacuous, trusting, hands folded into the gray pouch of his sweatshirt.

"I . . . didn't bring my wallet," I said truthfully, shivering a little though it wasn't that cold, wishing I had brought my empty clarinet case for show.

"Any kind of change will do," the tall boy said reasonably.

"I only brought bus fare, some quarters . . ." I fumbled in my pants pocket.

"That'll get it," the tall boy said, holding out a soft palm as pink as a frosted wafer.

I looked around me, at the afternoon shadows darkening the brick buildings, the sun hanging wan and thin, a pale disc pasted on the rim of the November sky; a gust of wind blew dry papers along the gutter. I played the coins carefully into the pink palm. "I'm a musician," I blurted and knew immediately it was a mistake.

"Oh?" The tall boy pocketed the change. "Where at do you play?"

"Coffee John's. Actually I just sit in nights whenever—"

"Where's that at?" The tall youth's eyes had rolled leisurely upward and away, the mouth compressed and rubbery.

"Over on Mass. Avenue, maybe five blocks—"

"What d'you play?" the small boy asked, respectful.

"Piano," I said, which was my second mistake.

The small boy brought something out of the pouch of his sweatshirt, pressed a thumb to it—there was a faint whirring sound—and drew it carefully along the back of my right hand; I thought I heard a soft tearing, like tissue paper parting. Both youths were racing down the street then, yards apart; the small plump boy surprisingly swift, outdistancing the other. The surrounding buildings were now completely in shadow and a piercing chill had fallen over the street. With a sigh I dropped my eyes. There was a thin red line across the knuckles, the skin parted delicately like paper. I reclined against the fender of the car, watching the blood suddenly bloom, incredibly bright, bubbling and winking like a ruby chain in artificial light.

The wind had risen; it had grown colder. I was glancing listlessly toward both intersections and around at the silent darkening buildings, wondering which way to turn or go, or whether to go anywhere at all, when a car stopped in the middle of the street. "What's up, man, what's the problem?"

It was Wesley, poking his head out the window of a faded-green Chevy, the whites of his eyes flaring as they fixed on the blood-soaked handkerchief. Everett was in the passenger seat beside him. They pulled over to the curb and got out.

Everett took my hand in his and gently peeled back the clotted cloth; I felt nothing.

Wesley's breath expelled as if he'd been punched in the chest. "Oh, man, who did you like that?"

"Couple kids. I thought they were going to help . . ." I motioned my head vaguely in the direction they had fled.

"You jus' never knows anymore, all these weirdies cruisin' the avenues. Why jus' last week I was over Huntington comin' out of—"

"Stop the damn jabbering and let's *go*," Everett said, "we got to get this nigger to a doctor."

Riding between them, my legs cushioned by Everett's massive thighs—a fat man's inadvertent caress—a tangle of emotions engulfed me. Bewilderment and wonder that the locus of the music that was my breath and heartbeat should also be the source of animosity and venom. It would take courage to venture to this part of town again; the barrier had been raised a notch, made more forbidding, fortified . . . But even as the pain took hold of my hand with the car's jounce and rattle, my spirits began to lift, a small glow of assurance warmed me as Everett's words echoed far back in my mind . . . *Let's go, we got to get this nigger to a doctor.* Within the urgency, the humorous play and idiom, was a suggestion of alliance, kinship, acceptance.

I turned to Wesley. "That was some powerful Panama Red last night."

Wesley nodded solemnly. "I can dig it."

A THIN WHITE scar remains, riding the ridge of the knuckles like a badge of initiation, an emblem of battle.

I never scored the big touchdown, never made it all the way through to the other side—few of us whiteys do—but ten years later, when I was house pianist at the hungry i in San Francisco, a middle-aged black man approached me in the bar following an entr'acte medley of Duke Ellington tunes. He said he had enjoyed the music and that I must have grown up or spent a lot of time around Harlem to play like that. I told him I had been born and bred in eastern Massachusetts. "Okay," he said, "but somewhere along the line you must've eaten some okra and sweet-potato pie."

THE PARTING WORDS of William, my twelve-year-old assistant at the Chinatown lawn party, lingered and rang in my mind, striking a doomful note for my continued employment with Rudy. *So long, you guys, see you all later at that big tuning fork in the sky . . .*

The big fork sounded its knell in late May when Rudy's secretary phoned to give me my week's engagements. The last date was for

Saturday night: Clearview Golf and Country Club, tux, eight to twelve. "And wear bathing trunks under the tux," she added. I was sure I had heard incorrectly and asked for confirmation. She confirmed. I said, "Where are we playing, in the swimming pool? A fish pond? Is the club supplying aqualungs?" She testily repeated the information and hung up.

I spent an uneasy week speculating on those bathing trunks. The fateful night arrived. Gladiators and Charioteers was the theme of the party, sponsored by the Junior League. Plaster statuary and colonnades amid the ferns; purple grapes cascading from six-foot papier-mâché urns; helmets and wreaths garlanding the heads of the tuxedoed and gowned revelers. At the first intermission Tommy Tedesco told us to bring our instruments—"Not you," he smiled wanly at me; "Drummer, take two sticks, woodblock and cowbell"—and we followed him to the downstairs locker room. Averting his gaze from us, frowning in concentration, Tommy undid the twine on two large clothing-store boxes, and the enigma was resolved: crepe togas. There was a moment of funereal silence.

"Over the tuxes?" a tremulous voice piped.

"Under. The tuxes come off," Tommy said, removing his coat and slipping off his suspenders.

"You're pulling our legs."

"Let's *go*." Tommy scowled, unclipping his tie and unzipping his pants.

"What happens if we don't," the second trumpet said, appropriating my question.

In his canary yellow bathing trunks Tommy looked at him incredulously. "Wha'd'you mean? You *have* to."

These were family men, with kids in nursery schools and colleges. I was the least encumbered, but we were only seven pieces, three rhythm; without piano the band would go down in flames, and Rudy would do his damnedest to insure that I never played another octave on a rotten tomato in the sovereign domain of the bean and the cod.

"Next week it's high heels and garter belts," someone murmured resignedly, and the mass disrobing commenced, soup and fish shedding like black chrysalises.

Musicians do not often see one another with their clothes off, nor should they. Never would you be likely to encounter a more goose-stippled, pale-fleshed, spindly-shanked motley of bodies; never in a hundred years would you associate that locker room with the playing fields of Eton. The varicolored paper togas reached, contingent on the musician's height, from midshin to midthigh. "Single file behind me, piano last," Tommy said. "We go in with 'Never on Sunday,' three flats."

Upstairs, past the trophy cases, and into the banquet room we wound, a Greco-Roman version of the Chinese dragon snaking among the tables with a clatter and tinkle and bray of horns. An excursion down Nightmare Alley to gargoyle smiles and decadent applause; all that was missing were the geek, the carny's spiel, the barking of trained seals. The piano player in armed-forces parade bands is supplied a glockenspiel or helps carry the bass drum; that night at the Clearview Golf and Country I brought up the dragon's rear banging a cowbell with a drumstick. The nadir of a burgeoning career. Like Fitzgerald's boat, beating on, borne back ceaselessly into the past.

I jumped ship the following morning (a knife between my teeth for severing the lifeline)—leaving word with Rudy's secretary. Goodbye forever, old fellows and seals.

The last news I had of Rudy and his stable before leaving for the road was in a *Boston Globe* account of a dinner dance at the Copley Plaza Hotel. The society-page item concluded, "The scintillating music was provided by Rudy Yellin's Orchestra. Enlivening the festivities were the antics of a member of the band attired in a colorful checkered vest who periodically got down on all fours and howled like a dog. The lovely flowers were courtesy of Baldoni-Heggins."

PART THREE

ROAD

12

Hoary musicians' gag: What's the difference between a trumpet and a cornet? Answer: You can carry more dirty laundry or a larger jug in a trumpet case.

I joined the hard-drinking ten-piece Alvie Drake band out of Providence, Rhode Island, for a three-month summer tour through upstate New York and Pennsylvania. Eleven pieces if you counted Alvie, for which there was small justification. Alvie played a kind of tin-soldier trumpet, achieving a tone that lead trumpet Val Catalona described as having the "carrying power of a bird fart in a Minnesota blizzard." Originally he'd billed the band as

Alvie Drake and His Gentlemen of Rhythm, but one fine day his wife, Estelle, was bitten by the flea of inspiration and the billing got changed to Alvie Drake and His Rhythm Ducks. Estelle sang (to use the word in its loosest sense) and banged the claves on the wrong beat during Latin tunes. She was nineteen years younger than Alvie—who called everyone "dad," though he was the one with the white hair—and a looker in a kind of starved, sleazy way; that is, she had the right weight and lines for a model but lacked the carriage and class. (There was something slightly suspect about Estelle's gauntness; you had the feeling from the way she carried herself—buttocks tucked in, pelvis forward—that she had been a lumpy teenager.) She possessed one endearing habit, which involved the bridge of "Easter Parade." The last four bars go ". . . The photographers will snap us / And you'll find that you're in the rotogravure." Born and raised in Attawaugan, Connecticut, Estelle had never heard of a rotogravure. She'd learned the tune off the Bing Crosby record; her ear transformed the last phrase to "on the road to grandeur," and that was how she sang it. Hearing her rendition for the first time, a new member of the band would try to correct her, explaining what a rotogravure was. Estelle, convinced there was a conspirational put-on afoot (like the summer-camp kid told to fetch the key to the oarlocks or a bucket of steam from the shower room), would smile in a bored fashion and remark, " 'Tain't funny, Magoo." Eventually everyone gave up trying to persuade her—she refused to listen to the record again—and some of us even came around to accepting that her version was at least on a par with the original.

Our transportation was a Buick station wagon and a hearse Alvie bought at auction and converted to a six-seat van with a storage well for instruments. Sidemen took turns driving. Occasionally we'd pick up local musicians in the towns we played to augment the band, if a booking called for more than ten pieces, or to replace ailing or drunk musicians or those who had abruptly departed for whatever reason. It wasn't unusual for someone to split between stops, having had his fill of the rinky-dink towns, Alvie's fart-in-a-blizzard tone, and Estelle's missed cues and wandering vocals. For the faint-hearted there were distinctive travel hazards, depending on who was behind the wheel. Mitch Ajoux, our bass player, loved to drive the hearse; at least I think he did. Mitch was a compact, boyish-looking Frenchman with a pencil-line mustache that barely made its mark; when he embraced his instrument, as bass players tend to do when the music heats and passion takes them, he looked like a stocky adolescent trying to lift a chiffonier by himself. He drove the hearse at a ferocious, meandering clip, enveloping the following Buick in curtains of dust, frequently pounding the steering wheel with his fist and shouting, "I'm going to destroy this sucker!" We never knew whether Mitch was making a gut identification of vehicle with owner, or, considering its original function, was expressing a subconscious dread of his own mortality. But we always knew when he hit seventy-five: the chassis began shuddering. He'd take her up to about seventy-eight, where strangely she ceased shuddering. "Go, you sucker!" he'd exhort, but that was all the machine could give, and he'd have to ease her back down through the vibrating stage to the low seventies. It was like a periodic crossing and recrossing of the sound barrier, and it helped to be either asleep or juiced out in back. It was no secret that Mitch was frustrated by the strict time-keeping sanction imposed on his instrument by Alvie. He loved to solo and stretch out on up-tempo numbers, but Alvie would rarely let him. Once or twice a week at most, catching sight of Mitch's perspiring, pleading face, Alvie would relent, loosen the reins and let him have an eight-bar bridge. Mitch would suddenly be all over the fingerboard, a scrambling double-time barrage of buzzing notes. There was a strange, wiggy kid in the reed section who eagerly awaited these excursions. His name was Purvis Honeycutt, and as the first bumblebee frenzy of bass-fiddle notes poured over the stand, Purvis would twist around, his jutting, angular face cracked in a loony grin, and scream in piercing falsetto, "Mitch Ajoux about nothing!"

THE TOUR GOT off to a shaky start. Alvie's Providence agency had booked us on a Saturday night, eight to twelve, into a ballroom in—we thought—Barrington, Rhode Island. The booker saw Mitch and me and drummer Tubbo Winslow (whom Alvie always introduced to the crowds as "Tubbo on the tubs," in a coffee shop at three in the afternoon in downtown Providence and said, "Jesus, haven't you guys started out yet?"

"For an eight o'clock gig?" Tubbo said. "It's less than an hour drive."

"An hour to *where?*" The booker looked apopletic, breathing heavily through his nose like a trapped animal.

"Chickie told us the other side of the bay," I said. (Chickie D'Alessandro was our trombonist and band manager.)

"Aren't we playing . . . Barrington?" Tubbo added on a plaintive note.

"You're at the Mahawee Ballroom in Great Barrington, Mass.!" the booker exploded.

We got Alvie out of the steam room at his club, and half of us were on the road with most of the equipment by quarter to four. The others would follow with Alvie and Estelle in the Buick as soon as Chickie could round them up. As we barreled west on 44, Mitch shouted with fist poised over the hearse's steering wheel, "This sucker will get us there by eight or be destroyed!" A speeding ticket outside West Springfield took the wind out of his threat.

By the time the six of us had set up and were playing our theme-opener, "Can't We Be Friends?," over half the tickets had been refunded. The rest of the band arrived an hour later. By midnight two couples were left on the floor, one of them falling-down drunk like in a thirties marathon. Val Catalona put a lugubrious capper on the evening, braying taps over our sign-off, "Sleepy Time Gal." Alvie was too depressed to give him more than a glum look. The ballroom manager was beckoning him to the office, where a dismal accommodation would be reached for the abortive evening.

ON THE ROAD I roomed with Val (for Valentine). In those days bands didn't pay room and board, so we doubled and tripled up to save money. (Purvis spent many a night on the floor of the hearse stretched out between the jerry-built seats.) Val Catalona had grown up in Fall River, Massachusetts, had been a varsity track star (220-yard low hurdles) in high school and was still known by an aging coterie of sports fans in that melancholy town as the Fall River Flash. He was a crossword-puzzle nut and a prodigious juicer, addicted to I. W. Harper bourbon. ("Want to introduce you to a dear friend of mine," he said on our first meeting in a bar, "Mr. I. W. Harper, Esquire, on the rocks." I'm convinced his choice of bourbon was dictated by the aesthetics of the overture.) After the fourth or fifth drink his color would turn russet. "Val's got his Florida tan early," Chickie D'Alessandro noted when Val rejoined the band—this was his third time around with Alvie—in mid-June. I had heard him on small-combo records during the forties: a lyrical player with a fat, exuberant tone. Alvie, semiaware of his own musical shortcomings, valued him, as did the rest of us. If there was a distinctive timbre and drive to the band, Val supplied it more than anyone. "Good to have someone back who uses both lungs," Alvie said early in the tour, clapping him on the back, putting aside recollections of past besotted nights. And when he stood bent-kneed on the stage's upper tier, horn aimed at the rafters, taking one of his soaring Berigan-like choruses, the broad-bore, plangent sound ringing clear and true, Purvis would twist around, grinning crazily up at him, pure joy dancing in his eyes, and scream in that shattering falsetto, "Catalona on a clearrrrrr day!"

Alvie got his gigs by hiring good musicians and tirelessly wining and dining management people, showing glossies of the group grinning in their cheesy summertime outfits—white ducks, blue cotton coats cut like mess jackets, and polka-dot bowties (Alvie appeared as our negative image: blue pants, white coat, blue suede shoes)—and Estelle in one of her slinky, cathouse numbers. He paid well, was a lax disciplinarian—juicing was accepted as long as you didn't fall on your face in midchorus—and allowed us free rein musically, a judicious decision since much of the time he didn't know what he was doing. When he kicked off a tempo, there was a tacit understanding in the rhythm section that we would alter it—pick it up or ease it back—until it settled into a proper groove. I doubt that he was ever the wiser.

Those sidemen who had played with name bands appreciated the freedom and flexibility, the respite from fifty-week itineraries. Alvie's tours were fairly short, and during the breaks he kept certain key men on one-third salary so that they would be available to him. This was a boon to those of us who did not care to be full-time vagabonds, and especially to someone like Val who needed a periodic rest from the rigors of the road. But most important—his strictures on bass-fiddle solos, which he claimed put people asleep, aside—he let us *play*. The charts, written mostly by our violinist-saxophonist Shorty Beauregard, were uncluttered and achieved an easy balance between sophistication and spareness. On our best nights, with "Tubbo goosing the rhythm and Val pushing the brass," Chickie said, "we can swing Cincinnati into the sea."

Val's relationship with Alvie had complex threads running through it. If Val had a bad cold or was feeling out of sorts, juicing too heavily, Alvie would call numbers in the book that tested him and stretched him out; it occurred too often to be unintentional. Val acknowledged the challenge, considered it a rightful throwing down of the gauntlet, and strove to rise to the occasion. "Rise to it," he'd say, "and if need be, go right over it."

BANDS TRAVEL AT night for two reasons: (1) There's less traffic, so it's faster and safer (the paradox collapses by day); (2) to avoid the cost and hassles of lodging. Unless a band has national standing and/or a reputation for integrity and decorum, its members will have trouble renting rooms, establishing credit, and cashing checks, particularly in the heartland. Tradespeople regard musicians in the same light as small-time traveling salesmen: both itinerants and slightly disreputable—here tonight, gone tomorrow. (And there are still towns where you would be wise not to tell a cop you're a musician when stopped for whatever violation, because he will infer: unemployed vagabond dope fiend. Nor should you divulge your profession or instrument to the vagrant or potential mugger, as I learned the day after partaking of Wesley's lethal Panama Red. There is always the chance he will go for the essence of you: your hands if you're a pianist, your mouth if you play a horn. I've never known a musician to involve himself in a fistfight, for the obvious reason. A New York journalist once wrote, "Show me a musician and I'll show you a physical coward." We weren't offended.)

If the band was working two or more towns in the same vicinity, we usually sought out rooming houses with kitchen privileges so we'd have a central base from which to operate. This arrangement allowed us to save on food and catch up on our laundry. Tenor saxophonist Nelly (Nelson) Nesbitt was the cook of the band. Which is not to say that he cooked for all of us (though we would occasionally bribe him to prepare an out-of-the-ordinary repast), but that he was the only one possessed of skills beyond the frying of an egg or the opening of a can of Spam. He could make cheese omelets and blueberry pancakes, and fashioned lovely, small individual salads from tomato, garbanzo beans, zucchini, avocado, and bags of shredded cabbage and lettuce, which were prevalent in small-town markets in those days. He'd shape the cabbage-lettuce to a perfect inverted cone and on its slopes arrange the beans and precisely cut slices of vegetable as evenly and meticulously as baubles on a Christmas tree; a fat Greek olive became the crowning star. So beautifully sculpted was the end result you hated to see anyone dig into it; it was like the desecration of an objet d'art. He said he had learned the trade as a short-order cook in southern New York State, but that didn't explain the delicacy and refinement of his concoctions. Nelly was constantly writing postcards home, and much of the time had a slack far-off look on his face that you might take for thoughtfulness or introspection but that most of us were persuaded was an adjunct of slow-wittedness. It was true his

conversation was functional and his reading matter limited to road maps and recipes. (In Rome, New York, the band was interviewed by a radio disc jockey, who asked, during a discussion of creative expression, what images went through our minds while we were improvising. Nelly answered truthfully that he might be wondering how the jar of mayonnaise in his bag was holding up during the current hot spell, or if the bag of cabbage and lettuce he'd left on a motel window sill in Schenectady had wilted by now. The d.j. thought Nelly was jiving him, laughed abruptly, glared, and went on to the next player.) But the frequently absent expression on his face had a troubling, pensive edge to it, and I suspected that something out of the past, perhaps of a family nature, was eating at him.

"WHAT THIS PLACE needs is a couple of punkahs," Val said as we set up in a sweltering hall in Troy, New York, for a convention of automotive supply dealers. He was always studding his conversation with crossword-puzzle specials, studying the faces of listeners for comprehension. If he was in a good mood—a receptive crowd, the band swinging, maybe a chick out front who had eyes for him—he'd raise his I. W. Harper on the rocks to me during the break and say, "Here's to us, man, nothing but green leas ahead." Where others might remark on a patron's odd, funny, or pathetic appearance, Val would observe, "Strange phiz on that cat." And at the end of the job when we started packing up and the general commentary ran, "Next week East Dogpatch" or "Another perfect night—ruined" or "Anyone want to scarf?" Val's valedictory was invariably, "That's it for the nonce."

Chickie, taking in the hall's bare walls, went out front to check the acoustics as we warmed up. He came back muttering, "Unless there're floor-to-ceiling bodies we're gonna rattle around in this cave like loose bones in a tomb."

The automotive people were beginning to take their places at the long rows of white crepe-clothed tables. From the stage, if you

squinched your eyes, the hall looked like an armory with parallel rows of white cots set up for flood victims. Spaced every few places along the tables, Chickie reported, were screw-cap bottles of something called Sundown Burgundy; the wineglasses were water tumblers.

Three couples took the floor for our opening medley. When it was over, a man with a brush haircut, whose crimson slacks hung a half foot shy of his shoes, moseyed up to the bandstand and said with a disarming smile, "Now play something you rehearsed."

It had all the earmarks of a long night.

After dinner (swordfish steak, string beans, mashed potatoes served with an ice-cream scoop) there was an extended break for speeches. Most of us adjourned to a bar across the street. People do not generally care to see musicians juicing at their affairs, particularly in aggregates of ten; besides, the hall bar was no-host. When the last speaker was well into his remarks, Chickie came across the street to collect us. A lot of rounds had gone down in the hour-long interlude. Val went into the can and said he'd see us back at the hall pronto. Ten minutes later the last speaker had finished and Alvie was getting nervous; he told Chickie to go find Val and drag his ass back here. Chickie was halfway across the stage when Val wandered in from the wings, grinning amiably, carrying his horn and a full open bottle of Pepsi-Cola. "Trumpet and trumpeter have arrived well lubricated," Chickie called to Alvie. The Pepsi, I knew, had been one-third drunk or decanted and topped off with I. W. Harper from his horn case. Alvie allowed soft drinks on the stand on warm nights—he wasn't yet hip to the topping-off process—and tonight qualified. Estelle's face had a shine to it like moonlight on a dead butterfish, and swatches of damp ringed the boards around Tubbo's drum set.

Alvie immediately called "Our Love Is Here to Stay," which featured Val. He sauntered to center stage with his horn and derby mute and announced extempore over the mike, "And now a venerable oldie from the prolific pen of George Gershwin and his lovely sister Ira . . ." The gambit fell like a cement kite on the people out front. During his second chorus he hit a couple of uncharacteristic clinkers, and when he returned to his chair to sparse applause, Shorty Beauregard—as was his custom with players who clammed during feature spots—solemnly passed him a Rolaid from the pack he kept in his shirt pocket.

The band's book contained a couple of novelty numbers that we'd throw in when things got slow. One involved gymnastics on Shorty's part. A spry and sinewy bantam at five-four and 110 pounds, he'd hoist himself and his clarinet atop the piano, a towel wrapped around his head, and squat yoga-style, facing down on me. (Visually the bit worked best if the piano was an upright, which this was.) He'd then play either "In a Turkish Bazaar" or an original I'd written for the occasion, "Take Me to the Casbah," while I wove my head in and around like a cobra entranced by his music. (This was the fifties, remember.) In the towel and blue mess jacket, with his spruce little mustache, bony nose, and alert eyes, he looked like a head waiter in a cheapo Middle-Eastern restaurant. The trouble with the routine was that it was funny for maybe eight bars at most, but Alvie insisted on stringing it out for a chorus or more. Another problem was that Shorty's embellishments weren't all that interesting; though arguably the best reader in the band, he was an uninspired soloist. "We're going down in flames," I whispered to him beneath the flailing licorice stick.

An enormous perspiring man in a seersucker suit began pounding the stage with his fist. "Pick it up, pick it up! You're not working a wake. Play 'Pennsylvania Polka'!" Alvie drew a cease-fire across his throat for Shorty and me, and signaled Tubbo to lay down a polka beat. The fat man seized Estelle's arm, pulled her bodily off the two-foot-high stage, and even as she shook her head vehemently *No*, proceeded to whirl her around the floor with that astonishing sureness and agility some fat men have. Alvie, a confusion of emotions swarming across his sweating face, watched his slender bride spinning helplessly in a vast maw of damp seersucker. "Play a couple more!" the fat man bellowed when we finished. Estelle broke from his grasp and fled, tripping up the side stage stairs in her tight sheath, sinking into her chair, and rapidly fanning herself with a tambourine. We followed with "Beer Barrel," "Rain Rain," and "Helena." Below us the floor exploded, pinwheels of prancing, jerking marionettes yanked about the room by the strings of our ricky-tick two-beat. Mitch leaned over his bass toward me. "I don't mind playing boleros, guarachas, beguines, whatever you want, but I draw the line at deliberately crapping on music."

The frenzied, tireless couples—ties pulled askew, mascara melting—kept clamoring for more. As they cantered and careened around the floor, loosing hoots and strangled animal cries, a distinctive aroma wafted up to us, which Shorty would later identify as "Abyssinian locker room after a hard soccer match."

Val detoured around the piano bench on his way to the mike—where Shorty was hoking it up on fiddle, his bandy legs performing a rapid little jig like a country shitkicker at a hoedown—bending to my ear to deliver a confidence through the yowling din: "Know what I'd rather be doing than this, man?" I shook my head, providing him the opening. "Selling neckties on a street corner in Jackass Flats, Idaho, during a blinding snowstorm."

At 12:58 A.M. our bow ties began to come off even before the last strains of "Sleepy Time Gal" had faded. Tubbo had sweated completely through his blue coat. There was a weary exhalation of breath and drifting for the jugs in the horn cases backstage. I put my charts in order, watching Val, slumped in his chair, the worn, flushed, almost handsome face sweat-bathed under the yellow stage lights. I noticed for the first time how deeply the permanent half-moon was grooved into his upper lip from fifteen years' big-band blowing. Catching my eye, he lazily hoisted the two-thirds empty Pepsi bottle at his feet and raised it toward me. "That's it for the nonce, man."

AS OUR TWO-CAR cavalcade rolled into the outskirts of town a little past noon, there was a dull thud on the hearse's windshield and something gray and rubbery fluttered off.

"We hit a pigeon, man, that's ominous," Val said.

"This place looks like the yard in a max security joint," Nelly said.

"Get a load of the sign," Mitch said, turning left, lightly bopping the horn at a middle-aged blonde in shorts and halter. A twenty-foot-high theater-style marquee over a truck stop said GET GAS—LUNCH HERE.

A patrol car slowly passed us from the opposite direction, the officers glancing with interest at the battered, dusty hearse and its nonfunereal occupants. Val lowered his beer can between his legs and smiled genially at the cops. "It's beginning to come in on me," he said, "that every town outside the Apple is Steubenville, Ohio."

Chickie had arranged for us to play a half hour in midafternoon at the local zoo. This was a promo stunt to hype business, as we'd be working for a percentage of the door that night. Chickie had got the idea from one of Tommy Dorsey's former sidemen, and he and Alvie persuaded us that if Dorsey's boys had gone along with it we could as well, particularly as it was in our own interests: bonuses might be forthcoming if the hype took, boosting admissions. We had to admit the idea had flair and was more inspired than the usual door prizes and lotteries.

The gimmick, as the Dorsey band had worked it, was to determine which animals reacted to sweet music, which to hot. The press and TV were invited, and a spinet piano rented, which I would play from the back of a pickup truck; we set up in the bright sun on the gravel walk outside the cages. A pair of ocelots and a platypus appeared to close their eyes when we played "Deep Purple." A mandrill clutched its privates during the opening bars of "Yacht Club Swing," and in the midst of Shorty's snake-charmer turn a lemur relieved itself. The monkeys chattered through it all, and the other residents remained sublimely indifferent. (Purvis said later we should have warmed up the menagerie with a couple fast choruses of "Buffalo Gal, Will You Come Out Tonight?")

Back at the hotel we tuned in the six o'clock news, but we'd been bumped by an afternoon bank holdup and a developing municipal railway strike.

Two hours later Chickie despondently watched the straggling admissions to the tarnished, once-ornate ballroom. "A couple more nights like this we'll be eating the berries off the wallpaper."

A girl on the floor was interested in Val. (There was a shadowy childless marriage somewhere in his past; most of us were either divorced, separated, or single.) An eighteen- or nineteen-year-old raven-haired looker with vermilion lips and wide green eyes. She kept shyly batting her eyelashes at him over the shoulder of her date, whom she continually maneuvered close to the stage. I had thought only movie actresses of the Marie Wilson school did that, but here were the lashes going for real, a mile a minute, on a June night in upstate Oneida County. Val directed all his solos to her, horn aimed like an arrow at a bull's-eye. During intermission he passed up his usual ration of I. W. Harper to hustle her in the hallway while her date waited in line at the soft-drink counter.

"This is it," he reported back happily to me, "it's all set for later. The big streetcar ride, green leas. Her name's *Heather*—you ever hear anything so *right?* I hate to ask this of you, man, but do you think you could double up with Tubbo or someone tonight?"

A sizable crowd of high-school kids came in after the first break, raising our spirits. We were sounding good—Val, in anticipation of after-hours activity, swinging the brass into next summer. Sometimes Alvie kicked off the tempos so far from where they should have been that there was no compensating, and every tune came out sounding like "Yaka Hula Hicky Dula." But tonight the tempos settled and drove like Citation down the backstretch at Hialeah. When you swing you swing, and there's no explaining it. But it's almost an axiom of the trade that when a band achieves a deep and effortless groove, some outside force will materialize to deflect it: the older folks asking for a Viennese waltz, an insistent request for "Saber Dance" or "Moonlight Sonata," or management asking us to tone it down before someone calls the cops. Tonight the potentially malign force appeared in the guise of a freckled kid in round-toed shoes and a green suit the shade of a freshly painted park bench, lips moving on some vapid request, preparing to suck the wind out of our sails. "Five bucks says it's gonna have *bayou* in the title," Tubbo called out.

"What can we do for you, dad?" Alvie said in his accommodating, chirpy manner.

"I bet you fellas can do a real good job on Ellington's 'Mood Indigo.' "

It's such unexpected reprieves that make all the hassles bearable.

WE SIGNED OFF at 12:30 and I watched Heather of the raven tresses saunter out arm-in-arm with her date, sending Val a lingering promissory glance over her shoulder.

I wouldn't see Val again until shortly after six the next morning. I'd hardly slept, and understood now why Tubbo roomed alone. We'd shared a double bed, head to toe. He slept on his back, floundering and spluttering like a beached whale, but the intermittent sonorities that issued from his mouth and nose were no sweet song of the humpback. I got up finally, dressed and left Tubbo's one-man concerto. On my way to the coffee shop I saw Val in T-shirt and slacks pecking Heather's cheek through the open window of a taxi. It was a buttery summer morning just before sunup, the sky along the horizon tinged with violet and rose. Val came over to me, rubbing his hands, a high color to his face. "C'mon, I'll pop for coffee." There was a little outdoor terrace with tables bordering the highway, and we sat and waited for someone to take our order.

"You know when I was last up at this time of morning?" He didn't wait for an answer. "I don't mean to be uncouth or anything, man, and I know this kid's somebody's daughter, but Jesus, a stray fresh young piece like that makes up for a lot of things. It was like . . . the first breath of spring. I'm turning the corner of forty, man, I don't know how many more lucky accidents of this quality I can count on . . ." He was grinning at me in a wistful boyish way, the taut, lean face I remembered from an album jacket going to flesh, suffused with the semipermanent "Florida tan," the eyes still direct but milder, reflective, the fires banked. I could smell the faint, sour reek of booze through the limey after-shave lotion. Val had more than fifteen years on me, and I thought of all the road time he'd put in, the 300-mile hauls between gigs, the unrelenting night-to-night juicing (which he claimed, and I think half believed, was the energy equivalent of fuel, consumed cleanly by his heart and muscles and mind and therefore incapable of affecting his playing), the tumbledown factory towns and starchy-greasy food and dirty laundry, catnaps in jouncing backseats, the drafty halls and nonfunctioning PA systems and indifferent-hostile-hayseed crowds. Now an eighteen-year-old All American long-stemmed beauty bred in the wilds of Oneida County had for a few hours breathed a breath of spring into his life, making it all worthwhile.

"Damn, man, I feel good!" he near shouted, warming his hands together, muscular forearms rippling, the torso beneath the T-shirt thickened but still powerful, limber, despite the lapse of twenty-three boozy years since he'd won the Fall River high school city championship in the 220-yard low hurdles. "I'll tell you something, man"—the exhilaration turning him garrulous—"remember the letter you showed me last week from your mother, all the home-front news, your brother and cousins and guys you went to school with locked into their eight-to-five gigs, raising their little families and joining the PTA and the lodge and the country club? Well, when those cats wind down and retire on their pensions, they won't even have the presence of mind, the . . . *perspective*, to look back at their lives and weep, man. What they'll be doing is sitting out on their front stoops, just a-settin' and a-rockin', watchin' the parade go by . . . '*Hey, Lucy*,' " Val megaphoned in a cracked miming voice, " '*two cars from Virginny just went past in succession* . . .' But we'll still be on the move, stretching out . . . hitting new towns and turning folks on. Know what I'm saying?" Val slapped his palm resoundingly on the metal table. "I feel *good,* man!"

He was suddenly up and moving briskly to the shoulder of the road—the shadows falling away and the first pale rays of sun lighting him. He dropped down, butt high and fingers splayed, test-rocking on the balls of his feet, body tensed in a coiled crouch. I shaded my eyes as the eastern sky flared. A whoop escaped Val, the coil unsprung, and he was sprinting down the macadam border, shoulders low, charging . . . now the legs lithely scissoring like a ballsy ballet dancer, another whoop like a bird's exultant cry at dawn and the legs neatly slicing air again, taking the banked hurdles in memory. The whoops grew fainter, the figure smaller and more precise, etched on the horizon, diminutive, stalwart, the Fall River Flash kicking up cinders, hurtling into a blood-red sky as the ghostly cheers crashed his ears like drumfire.

13

Mitch's unceasing threats to destroy the hearse as she buffeted through the 70 m.p.h. barrier were making me jumpy. I switched places with Chickie and drove to the Finger Lakes with Alvie and Estelle. We'd be playing an outdoor pavilion on the shores of Lake Seneca. Tubbo was driving, and Alvie was in a charged, loquacious mood. He'd been expounding on the competition—the territory and name bands who occasionally followed or preceded us on locations, and whose paths we constantly crossed. The more he talked, putting down the other bands and building up ours, the more impassioned he became.

Saliva collected in tiny pools at the corners of his mouth and his cheeks grew ruddy. "James, Kenton, Les Brown, what've they got we haven't? I'll put our charts and first men up against theirs anytime," he fumed. "Hell, James isn't fit to empty Val's spit valve. Why we aren't getting that exposure is the goddam mystery of the decade. It's just an unfair, goddam shame. Thornhill, McKinley, any of those groups making top dollar—they aren't fit to launder our shorts! God willing," Alvie thundered—slamming his fist on the back of Tubbo's seat, causing him to bounce a little like a chunky baby in a buggy going over a curb—"I'll fuck 'em all!"

The peroration was greeted by total uncomprehending silence.

A half mile later Nelly, who was writing his daily postcard home (I'd looked over his shoulder on occasion; the tiny print was encircled by rudimentary graphics, stick-figure hitchhikers, road signs, railroad tracks, and telephone poles), reiterated something that had been on his mind for the past week: "Alvie, why can't we skip Elmira Friday?"

"Dad, will you knock it off about Elmira?" Alvie was just coming down from his tirade, wiping the corners of his mouth with a handkerchief. "We're going to Elmira 'cause we got a booking in Elmira. If you want to contact the convention management there and cancel out, then pay off me and the boys and the booker, then we'll skip Elmira. Otherwise we're going to Elmira. Jesus K. Christ . . ."

Estelle said in a sudden panicky voice, gazing at an overhead sign, "What are we doing back in Cazenovia?" I'd suspected for some time she had vision problems—the way she'd make a show of studying the charts on which she had a featured vocal, pondering and squinting a lot, then handing them back to Shorty with a remark like, "Why don't we just wing it?"

Alvie said patiently, "That's Canandaigua, dear."

"Casanova's just wishful thinking," Tubbo interjected.

" 'Tain't funny, Magoo," Estelle said.

THE PAVILION, A broad, converted pier on the lake's shore, was strung with hurricane lamps and varicolored bulbs woven through a partial overhead latticework. It was a gorgeous night, and there was a good turnout. A South Sea Island moon hung in the black sky over the dark water like a fat Japanese lantern over a mirrored tabletop. Only two aspects marred the idyllic setting: a ship's bell that clanged sporadically throughout the music—we discovered later it was rung by the bartenders whenever a tip of a dollar or more was forthcoming—and a Galápagos-variety of insect life, drawn by the pavilion and bandstand lights, that attacked with fearless abandon. Moths, June bugs, gnats, mosquitos the size of daddy longlegs. Once I glanced up from the music—my eye caught by swarming shadows—to see the entire brass section flailing their horns in unison (it looked almost like a slick band routine), trying to ward off a marauding cloud of gnats. Alvie complained to management. Management said they'd never seen it this bad. Shorty squirted valve oil at the interlopers, and Purvis pulled his coat up over his head, shrieking, "It's all-out fucking war!" We finally turned off our reading lights and faked the rest of the set, playing blues and old standards.

At intermission, most of our jugs depleted from the night before, we homed in on the bar, ten strong, like a pack of thirst-crazed dogs on a backyard pool.

"Sorry, gentlemen," the head bartender said as we called out our orders.

"What are you sorry about?" Mitch said.

"I'm not supposed to serve musicians. I have my orders."

"You have your orders?" Shorty said. "Hey, the war ended a couple years ago . . ."

"If you'll step aside, please, people are waiting . . ." He was actually fluttering his hands, shooing us away like pigeons from a doorstep.

"It's drawn épées," Val muttered darkly.

"Pour the damn sauce, man, or I'll zap you," Purvis cried, crooking a finger. "You ain't nothin' but a cowpie."

Alvie came over to see what the ruckus was about.

"All we want is a little taste," Shorty said. "The supply sergeant here, acting on some *macher*'s idiot orders, is shutting us off."

"Treatin' us like damn mangy dogs in a junkyard," Tubbo said heatedly. "Hey Buster," he shouted, "I spent fifteen years learnin' how to drum, how long'd it take you to figure out how to add soda to a scotch?"

"Back off, Ducks," Alvie said, "let me see what I can do." He approached the manager, who had been pussyfooting around the perimeter of the scene, and talked to him for half a minute; the manager stared out at the lake and kept shaking his head.

"It's no use," Alvie said, returning. "The last band they had out of Watkins Glen overdid it and some of the boys went into the lake."

"All's we want is to wet our whistles," Nelly sulked.

"Let me borrow the keys to the Buick," Mitch said to Alvie.

"Town's a couple of miles," Alvie said, "you won't have time . . ."

"Alvie," Val said, "you got ten ass-dragging bone-dry cats bein' attacked by every bug in New York State, and there are three hours to go. You're gonna hear a mess of clams up there . . ."

"Now, Val, I won't be intimidated by you or—"

"Alvie," Chickie said, "let Mitch have the keys. If he isn't back we'll start the set without him."

Alvie looked around him, gauging the overall mood, sighed and reached into his pocket. Mitch collected a couple of bills from each of us and left at a fast jog for the parking lot, while the rest of us wandered down the grassy bank to the lake to cool our heels and pray for his safe and unimpeded return.

A quarter hour later Alvie called over the pavilion railing, "Let's go, Ducks, rise 'n' shine!"

"Quack, quack," Tubbo honked weakly and we straggled to our feet.

No Mitch.

There was a curious, lemony fragrance on the stand that became more pronounced as I slid onto the piano bench. The insect hordes appeared to have thinned out. Alvie dragged the mike over to the piano and called "Beat Me Daddy, Eight to the Bar," which featured me. It was a judicious call: the boogie-woogie bass would compensate for Mitch's absence. Tubbo laid down a four-bar rhythm intro, and suddenly I found myself floundering over the keys like a kid trying out his first pair of buckle-on ice skates; simultaneously the lemony scent hit home. Alvie was looking at me askance. I held up my oily fingers. "Some goon sprayed the keys with citronella!"

Shorty bounced a Rolaid off my head as I went at the keyboard with a handkerchief.

"Jesus K. Christ . . ." Alvie blew the breath out of his plump cheeks. "Estelle, sing something . . . 'Easter Parade.' "

"In July?"

"Sing it!"

At which point Mitch came around the back of the stand lugging a bulging paper bag. A lusty greeting rose from parched throats. At the far end of the pavilion the ship's bell chimed an inadvertent welcome. And Estelle sang " '—and you'll find that you're on the road to grandeur . . .' "

AFTER THE GIG we drove back to Penn Yan, where we were billeted—a few to sleep, others to seek an open bar or coffee shop or simply to unwind from the hectic night. Shorty and Chickie and I were strolling down the deserted main street, enjoying the quiet and the lake smells mingling with the fragrance of hedges and trees, when the strangest episode of the evening occurred. I'll have to back up here to explain something about Shorty's childhood. His real name was Morris and he had stammered badly as a kid. A natural leftie, his mother forced him to use his right hand for schoolwork, and the resultant trauma, coupled with an inferiority complex—he was always the shortest kid in his class—brought on a severe case of the yammers. Doctors and dentists were consulted (one suspected

Huntington's chorea), batteries of tests administered. Finally an elocution teacher was employed; Shorty suffered innumerable indignities—warm honey poured down his throat, strips of cardboard inserted behind his back teeth prior to recitation, peanut butter pasted to his palate and marshmallows tucked into the pouches of his cheeks (layering a chipmunk complex onto the inferiority)—before he arrived at his own haphazard self-cure. He discovered that if he *sang* the words he could not utter, he was able to soothe the tumult in his throat and chest and achieve a continuity of sound. Another device he stumbled on, which produced even greater fluidity, was to press his ear to the trunks of young trees and sing nonsense syllables in concert with the trees' imagined vibrations (growth, sap flow, insect life). This bit of business had to be conducted with the utmost secrecy, he confessed, because in Lowell, Massachusetts, in those days, you could get locked up for much less. He eventually overcame his afliction and was convinced that these self-cures he happened on were the beginnings of his passion for music.

Now some twenty years later on a midsummer's night in a small lakeside town in upstate New York, sauntering along the fragrant moon-drenched street with his spry, feisty, Chaplinesque strut, feeling exceedingly mellow, not drunk, but not sober either, flinging his arms wide and crying, "Ambrosia! It's positively Adriatic out tonight!"—he was inspired to reexperience the piquant vibrations that molded his childhood, utilizing a succession of Penn Yan trees, bounding ahead of us to lean his ear into the wood and emit his personal immemorial call of the wild, a crowing, exulting sound like an animal's or child's ecstasy borne on the wind. To the two officers in a passing patrol car—our furtive cries of warning to Shorty drowned in his own primeval howl—the tableau presented an open-and-shut case. They pulled him, bug-eyed and sputtering, into the car, our frantic explanations of a childhood stammer and dingdong trees nearly triggering our inclusion in the dragnet.

It was five in the morning before we managed to bail him out. Collecting his belongings at the station counter, Shorty vented an impassioned harangue on an unheeding officer: "This the, uh, special brand of justice you lads serve up for the summer trade? Believe me, buddy, I'll take Germany 1939. Have a book burning on the village green every July fourth, do you? Toss the Constitution and Bill of Rights on first? Hey, I'll tell you guys this much, you sure know how to make the tourists feel welcome . . ." He raved on in this vein, beginning to stutter a little—a spooky throwback. When we finally pulled him outside, he was still berating the bored cop over his shoulder.

The sky had begun paling in the east. Chickie had the keys to the hearse, which we had parked blocks away, envisioning: *Subjects inebriated and semi-coherent, commandeering out-of-state mortuary vehicle.* We trekked three abreast down the lightening main street of this time-passed town, Shorty calmer now but moving stiff-kneed, arms close in to his body, clenched on himself like a fist. "I counted five roaches," he was muttering, "one the size of my goddam thumb . . ." But for all that it was a sweet time of morning, the air cool and perfumed with wet smells, lake marsh and dewy leaves and mown grass.

Chickie's arm was around Shorty's thin shoulders as we moved unhurried under the elms. Then with the lifting darkness, the first flesh pink glow on the sky's rim, Shorty slipped into a wistful, philosophic vein: "Nobody should have to suffer this much to make music. Know what we are?" he said, his voice lifting with the wonder of proclamation. "Casualties on the road to truth. Sometimes I think we'd be better off heaving our instruments in the lake—open a dry-cleaning business or a string of delis."

"Forget it," said Chickie, whose family operated pizzerias in Waltham and Somerville. "Our friends'd all freeload on us and we'd go belly-up."

ELMIRA, NEW YORK, if you can believe the AAA Tour Book, derived its name circa 1828 from a little girl who wandered away from home so often not a day would go by that you wouldn't hear her mother calling over meadow and across stream, Elmira, Elmira . . .

Val, Shorty and I banged the brass knocker on an old gabled house with a shingle hanging off the front porch that said Morpheus Arms Guest House—Mrs. O'Doul. We were free to find our own lodging if we could beat the price Chickie had negotiated and were reasonably close to the others. Along with kitchen privileges, Shorty and I were always hoping to find a place with a parlor upright; I tried to get in as much practicing as possible and had begun writing arrangements under Shorty's tutelage. A tall, raw-faced woman of indeterminate age came to the door.

"Three trustworthy travelers seeking board, room, and hospitality for two nights, ma'am," Shorty said in the courtly idiom he employed for dealing with provincials.

Wiping her hands on a print apron, she looked us over, taking in the bags and horn cases. "You salesmen?"

"Musicians, performing this very evening at your most prestigious downtown ho—"

"I'll want the money in advance. Three-fifty a night apiece, three for a double."

"Would you perchance have a piano?"

"If I did you couldn't use it."

"And the three-fifty includes—"

"I can sleep ya but I can't eat ya," said Mrs. O'Doul.

The three of us grinned at each other. A winning example of local hospitality and patois.

We'd already looked at two other places and it was getting late. Mrs. O'Doul showed Shorty a room on the second floor and Val and me the only available double at the rear of the third. Twin cots, a clothes pole, a narrow dresser, and a ceiling canted at 45 degrees. Tubbo standing dead-center would have been hard-pressed to make a 180-degree turn unscathed.

"This is it?" Val said, looking around for some sign of closet or bath.

"Everything you're lookin' at is it," Mrs. O'Doul said. "Toilet's in the hall." An odor of frying potatoes floated up the stairwell.

"Let's fall out, man, I'm beat," Val said.

I handed Mrs. O'Doul twelve dollars for the two nights while Val rolled onto one of the cots, lacing his hands behind his head and staring up at the overhanging ceiling. "It's what I've been saying all along. Every town outside Gotham is Cross Fork, Pennsylvania."

I drew the shades, leaving Val to sleep off a rough previous night—"Bring a six-pack back with you," he called after me—and walked into town with Shorty to join the others at a prearranged bar and grill.

There isn't a whole lot to do in these towns if you arrive early. Eat a western sandwich at Larry's Diner, drink a few brews, sit in the park and look at the cannon. A first-run movie house or well-stocked music store is an unexpected boon, and Shorty spotted one of the latter now opposite the Mark Twain Hotel, where we'd be playing that night. We'd been getting requests for a new tune we'd heard Sinatra sing on the car radio, "In the Wee Small Hours of the Morning," and Shorty wanted to write an arrangement of it to replace "Sleepy Time Gal"—which we were all heartily sick of—as our sign-off tune. I went in with him and he asked the clerk for the sheet music. When it was produced, Shorty walked to the end of the counter; I watched his rapid eye movement as he scanned the music three, four times. He then returned the sheet to the clerk saying, "Sorry, it's not quite what I was looking for." We went outside. Shorty took a small music-manuscript notebook from his pocket and scribbled down a lead sheet—melodic line and chord symbols. What he had done in a little over a minute—what I had admiringly watched him do a half dozen times before—was memorize the music and beat the store out of seventy-five cents. As I said before, musicians are funny about loot.

We joined the others at the bar-and-grill counter. I took a stool beside Nelly, who was scarfing a ham-and-cheese, and ordered an ale. Suddenly Nelly broke off his complaint to the counterman—he'd got boiled instead of baked ham in his sangwich (his pronunciation)—

his eyes locking on the mirror above the beer and ale bottles. I glanced up. A burly cop in short-sleeve uniform had come in and eased into a booth diagonally behind us. He doffed his cap and scanned the backs along the counter, his glance stopping momentarily at the stool on the other side of me—Purvis in the red deerstalker hat he'd picked out of a Goodwill bin in Utica—before coming to rest on Nelly. The two pairs of eyes fixed like lodestones on each other in the dusty oblong mirror. "What's the matter?" I whispered. Nelly's mouth, full of sangwich, was agape like a kid at his first sight of a flying squirrel. Now the cop replaced his cap, rose, took a leisurely sip from the water glass in front of him and strolled out. Nelly slowly pushed his plate aside; his face was the color of turned milk. I asked again what was going on.

"All of a sudden I ain't too hungry." He got up and walked out with the careful stiff-legged gait of a man with shin splints.

"Who's paying for that?" the counterman said, pointing to Nelly's unfinished ham-and-cheese. I pointed a finger at my chest.

A half hour later five of us started on a walk around town to see the sights, such as they were. I mentioned to Chickie the staring match between Nelly and the cop and their closely spaced departures. He chewed a corner of his lip, seemed concerned, but didn't say anything.

"We could always go check out Mark Twain's grave," Mitch suggested. The AAA Tour Book had mentioned this landmark.

"That poor sucker," Purvis said; and a moment later, "Any you guys believe in God?"

"Only when I'm sight-reading," Mitch said.

"That buggy reminds me of one of Estelle's gowns," Shorty said, indicating a mud-flecked pink convertible stopped at a traffic light. "Pepto Bismol gone bad."

"I'll tell you something about Estelle," Mitch said. "If she wasn't servicing Alvie she'd be lucky to have a gig baiting fishhooks in Skaneateles."

IT WAS SUNDOWN by the time Shorty and I got back to Mrs. O'Doul's. I gently woke Val. He came out of it with a start, the whites of his eyes stark, glancing around the little shade-drawn room. "What is it? Where are we?"

"Elmira. Hour and a quarter before the gig."

He released his breath with a drawn-out sigh, rubbing his eyes. Sometimes when I woke him in the dark like this, there was a moment of dislocation, shadows and unfamiliar shapes looming, when he was not only unsure where he was but at which end of the day—early morning or evening. He had told me that when he roomed solo and woke in the dark not knowing whether it was evening or predawn (and if the former, had he missed the gig?), the way he got his immediate bearings was to note how he was dressed: pajamas (or naked) and between the sheets, or street clothes and on top of the bedding.

I lit the lamp and took our band uniforms down from the pole.

"You bring the brew?"

"I forgot."

A groan. "Every once in a while," he said, staring up at the stained plaster of the pitched ceiling, "I wake up like this, hundreds of miles from home, and almost wish I'd listened to my old man and was back there punching the clock at the paper mill, scarfing my noontime cheese sandwich and apple with the rest of the yokels." His puffy face broke into a wan grin. "Notice, I said *almost.*"

WHEN WE GOT to the hotel, a stranger in a well-worn, tight-fitting blue suit was unpacking a variety of reed instruments. Chickie introduced us. "Meet Austin Fiske, Nelly's replacement."

"Wha'd'you mean, replacement?" Val said.

"Replacement. How clear can I get? Nelly cut out. I'll explain later."

I knew it had to be connected with the encounter in the bar and grill that afternoon.

"Howdy," Austin Fiske said, shaking our hands. There was no

way he was going to fit into Nelly's band uniform. He was a big, fleshy guy with thinning, sandy hair, and moved like a 250-pound lumberjack with bad knees. He had set out clarinet, alto, tenor, and soprano saxes on individual stands alongside his chair.

"Quite an assortment of axes," Val said.

"Well, I'm a doubling fool. Been working mostly weekend gigs, which is all there is in this area outside resort work. Irish weddings, beer busts, an occasional Elks Lodge dance, and if I'm really pressed for loot the spring hootenanny down by Seely Creek. I may not be Charlie Parker but I'm a versatile son of a bitch." He gave us a grin as wide as Canandaigua.

"Lively-looking bunch," Val said, watching the guests beginning to fill the ballroom. "Jesus, check the big dude in the racetrack sport coat . . ."

"They usually manage to feel their oats," Austin said. "I've played this gang a few times before."

"Who are they?"

"Tri-city morticians. They always hold their conventions here."

"You're joking," Val said.

We hadn't been told, but often we didn't know whom we were playing for until we arrived on the stand. They were unlikely-looking undertakers, dressed to the nines: plaid pants, white buck shoes, bright blazers with outsize name tags, and paper hats, the ladies in chiffon, matching pastel shoes and handbags.

"How was it the other times you played for them?" I asked.

"Like crossing Grand Rapids, Michigan, in a rowboat," Austin said happily.

The baby grand looked ominous: a scattering of ivories missing from the keys, exposing rough, raw wood, and cigarette ash and other debris caked in the corners. I ran an arpeggio and whimpered like a dog in pain. The notes jangled with the toothache sonority of an out-of-tune harpsichord. Val came over to commiserate. "Listening to that all night is gonna be like running on a barbwire track."

I played another arpeggio using different notes, soliciting a miracle.

"I ain't tunin' up to that," Purvis said.

"Alvie," I called, "this box is brutal."

"Do the best you can, dad, we're going to have our hands full out front," he said, sizing up the milling back-slapping throng seeking their place cards at the pink-clothed tables.

SHORTY HAD WRITTEN a new chart, an original composition he called "Southland Suite." We'd rehearsed it off and on over the past week, and for some reason Alvie chose this unlikely occasion—a new tenor man and a high-energy crowd—for its premiere performance. The music had had an intriguing genesis. Shorty had a distant cousin whose great-grandfather had fought in the Civil War. The cousin inherited a Confederate flag that had been carried by cavalry into one of the great battles. Faded and frayed, the Stars and Bars had been kept in various trunks and bank vaults through the years. By a complicated progression, greased by an exchange of monies, it had finally come down to Shorty. He carried this proud, tattered banner as a kind of talisman on his travels, tacking it to the walls of countless hotels and boardinghouses, and a few months ago, spurred by the golden vein of postbellum melody that had emerged from the Southland in praise of New Orleans, Memphis, Mississippi, Georgia, Alabamy, etc., he had been inspired to compose his suite. It was a dramatic and stirring piece of work, weaving subtly distorted strains of W. C. Handy, Stephen Foster, and Hoagy Carmichael through an intricate structure rich with the fervor and flavor of Dixie. As Purvis had said when we first played it through, "I can see the riverboats, Shorty, and smell the magnolias—I can almost hear them darkies singin'!"

We gave it a fairly proficient reading with a minimum of clams during the serving of the opening fruit-salad course. The sole reaction came from a portly woman in a wide-ribboned hat who tottered up to the stand on spike heels and said to Alvie, "I'm having an argument with the gang at my table. Was that 'Oh! Susanna' you just played?"

"So much for the accomplishments of genius," Shorty said ruefully.

It was a sign to Alvie, if he needed one, that we'd do better sticking to the tried and true standards and golden oldies. Serving up music of any distinction for this crowd would be like feeding caviar to a family of chipmunks.

They were a spirited bunch, you had to say that much for them, leaping up from their chicken leg/lima bean/boiled potato dinners to dance every dance, forming arm-linked clusters to sing raucous grade-school harmony to the nostalgia tunes, and peppering Alvie with hokey requests: "Can you guys play 'Far Far Away'?"

Austin played well on all his instruments, sight-reading the charts flawlessly. I was becoming more and more impressed by the competence of substitute musicians we occasionally picked up in towns like Elmira, recommended by Alvie's contacts in the various union locals—guys with a little of the bumpkin about them who subsisted on two or three nights a week augmented by nonmusical daytime gigs (Austin, I discovered, delivered mail), yet had solid command of their instruments and could read or fake with equal proficiency. It made you proud of the far-flung fraternity; at the same time you were saddened by the knowledge that so many, by accident of locale or the dictates of a perennial buyer's market, were unable to fashion a livelihood from their passion and their craft.

I was trying to block my mind and ears to the tuneless atrocity under my fingers—the crown prince of all the bad boxes I'd encountered so far on the road. Playing gingerly, backing off instead of digging into the keys, my hands and arms were cramping like those of an oarsman stroking incorrectly. The harpsichordlike jangle reminded me of famed conductor Sir Thomas Beecham's professed aversion to that instrument. "The harpsichord," he'd said, "always sounds to me like two skeletons fornicating on a tin roof."

"Put your arms around me, honey, hold me tight . . . ," Estelle sang, and the three-hundred-pound embalmer in the loud sport coat Val had pointed out earlier bounced up on stage and suited action to words, cranking her back and forth across the boards—a virtual reprise of the polka-crazed fatso who'd seized her in Troy—while Alvie bestowed on this striking duo the full beneficence of his shit-eating smile.

Austin leaned over to me and said, "If you could guarantee me I'd be in this crew's hands when it comes time to be fitted for the wooden overcoat, I think I could go happy."

As the waiters trundled in the sherbet and cookies a workman began setting up a mobile movie screen against the far wall, and shortly thereafter Alvie called a break. The band moved en masse to the instrument cases backstage; the lesson of the lake pavilion shut-off had been well learned, and full jugs were in plentiful supply. I hung behind, telling Tubbo I thought I'd see what the movie was about.

"I'd join you, but I want to hold onto my supper," Tubbo said.

I lingered long enough to hear the keynote speaker's introductory remarks concerning the "burgeoning summer-resort trade." When I realized he was referring to the drownings and fatal auto accidents endemic to the season, I wandered out into the balmy night and joined the others on the sidewalk; some had carried their booze out in paper cups. A lean and bony man with a name tag pasted to his red blazer was inspecting our converted hearse with avid interest.

"Somehow that gives me the shivers, man," Val said.

Tubbo waddled over and solicited the man's professional opinion. The mortician turned with a toothy grin and said, "It's sacrilegious—like converting a Rose Bowl float to a sanitation truck."

Shorty cupped his hand to my ear. "You'll never see that gent crying in his b-i-e-r."

I saw Chickie standing alone and went over to ask him about Nelly, who had been on my mind.

"This is confidential because that's how it came to me. Remember he told us he worked as a short-order cook upstate? Elmira was one of the places. He got caught on a bad check charge and did ten months at Ossining."

"So the cop who was looking at him funny this afternoon—"

"Was in on the arrest. Nelly panicked and split."

"Will he rejoin us?"

"He was too nervous to discuss it. I don't even know which way he headed. Remember those fancy dishes he prepared, the elegant technique, salads in particular?"

"What about them?"

"What do they tell you?"

I thought of the perfect cones of chopped lettuce and cabbage, precision-sliced vegetables colorfully adorning the flanks like a child's yuletide treat. "They seemed out of place in a short-order cook's repertoire."

"He was cook-houseboy for the warden at Ossining."

"And the warden was a gourmet."

"You got it."

Ten minutes later Alvie came out of the hotel to collect us. "Out of your corners, Ducks, round two. Hey, you guys missed a choice flick inside."

On the stand Austin lowered his considerable bulk to his chair, and a loud vulgar noise erupted. He slowly rose, pink-faced. At the side of the stage two morticians were bent nearly double, convulsed, clutching each other in mindless glee. Austin picked the trick cushion gingerly off his chair, and, carrying it in two hands before him like a wet baby, dropped it offstage at their feet. "Evenin', fellers . . ." He came back past me. "What'd I tell you, Grand Rapids, Michigan, all the way. These jokers give crematoriums a bad name."

By midnight Val had made a prodigious dent in a fifth of I. W. Harper and cracked badly on the high F-sharp on the final bars of "Sleepy Time Gal," bringing a reflective look to Alvie's face and a Rolaid popping over Shorty's shoulder into the brasses.

"Catalona on a cloudy day!" Purvis piped in a fluting Butterfly McQueen voice.

Alvie's face darkened. He called to Chickie, "I want a meeting directly after. Things're getting out of hand."

"A sawbuck," said a rasping voice out front, "you guys can't play 'The Old Gray Mare' in the key of three flops."

IT WAS ONE-THIRTY before I got Val home from a town bar. Climbing past the second floor we heard a ruckus coming from Shorty's partly open door.

"If you need to hang up something what's wrong with the Stars and Stripes?" Mrs. O'Doul's voice said.

Val lurched on up the stairs while I paused to listen. Shorty's patient, convoluted explanation of a family keepsake, the heritage of the South, and divine inspiration wound down on a note of futility.

"My second husband drowned in a muddy river in France," Mrs. O'Doul said, "makin' it easy for fellas like you."

A SUMMER STORM broke in the early-morning hours: fitful rolls of thunder, and shutters banging in swift lashes of rain, the room bleached by flash-bulb flares of lightning pinning the narrow dresser to the wall. Val's white band pants were sprawled on the only chair in the room, the legs trailing over the edge so they looked as if they were dancing in place. Two feet from me, flat on his back, arms slack across his chest, Val slept the sleep of the dead. Little danger tonight—even with this storm's light-and-sound effects—of his waking, crying out, "What is it? Where are we?" . . . *I'm turning the corner of forty, man*, I remembered, *I don't know how many more lucky accidents I can count on.*

I tried to look ten years ahead into his life and gave a shudder. And ten years into mine? I wasn't even sure I would last out the tour.

The uncertainties of the road and this talented, jokey, perpetually polluted band were wearing me down. I was saving a little money, picking up experience and a few nonacademic credits in human psychology, but the reins were too loose; I missed a sense of orderliness and progression: scheduled meals and lessons and practice sessions . . . The dilemma might be resolved without a decision on my part. In the short meeting after the gig, Alvie had threatened to completely turn over the band's personnel. This was the wettest tour he could ever remember. We were goofing off and growing sloppy, not taking care of business, he said, looking squarely at Val. From now on there'd be no more pranks and jugs backstage, and he was on to the phony Pepsi and Coke bottles, so don't try to pull that over on him. Any questions?

"Can we wash our hands after takin' a leak?" Purvis said.

Envisioning Val, Mitch, and the others without access to their intermission jugs was like contemplating a drive across the Mojave with no air conditioner and a leaky radiator. But we were already in sight of August, and two weeks at a resort lake in the Adirondacks at the close of that month promised, if nothing else, a respite from the baked ribbons of interstate highway we'd been locked onto like fading horses on a rusty merry-go-round.

WE DIPPED INTO northwestern Pennsylvania.

The crude-lettered sign held by the unshaven kid in army fatigues said YOU NAME IT.

"Sorry, kid," Mitch yelled out the driver's window, "we're goin' everywhere but there."

Along the bleak asphalt stretches the towns were beginning to fuse in their sameness. Approaching the rubbish-strewn lots, the clutter and decay of the next town's outskirts, I found if I squinted my eyes and indulged in a fantasy of miniaturization, the squalid contours took on ghostly, childhood shapes, looming like the shelf of old oil cans, scattered bricks, and dusty bottles spied through the wired cellar window of the house across the yard from where I grew up in Worcester. On the resource maps of my grade-school geography texts, the country had been laid out in immaculate, colorfully labeled segments: textiles, dairy products, chemicals, sorghums, poultry . . . They gave no hint of barren lots or tumbledown blocks of paint-peeled houses and dingy brick piles of buildings encrusted with a half century's grime; nor did the pages carry illustrations of listless knots of men milling on corners and leaning against storefront windows, shifting their feet and rubbing their noses. Were we driving consistently through the wrong parts of town? I thought of Nelly, wondering if he might be living in a cubicle behind one of these ruined facades, cautiously practicing his horn (a cloth stuffed in the bell) after a day of frying eggs and pork chops in some flyblown diner.

There was occasional relief, blue-green lakes glimpsed strobelike through stuttering groves of trees, and lovely stretches of weathered barns and rolling green farmland, the workers and grazing animals—viewed from a distance—as motionless and immemorial as figures in a frieze.

We worked our way across southern New York and western Pennsylvania in two weeks. A three-hundred-mile limit between successive engagements, imposed by the American Federation of Musicians during World War II (when dilapidated buses and threadbare tires took a lethal toll), was ignored by Alvie, just as we evaded his new restrictions on booze, employing various subterfuges: filling lubricant-spray bottles with the hard stuff and switching to gin drunk from paper cups backstage, swearing in all innocence (aggrieved when confronted!) that these cups had been filled at the water cooler or dressing-room sink. Now the drinking was virtually out in the open again as it became evident that Alvie had neither the patience, energy, nor disposition to enforce sanctions.

From Altoona I sent my mother a picture postcard of the Horseshoe Curve, assuring her I was eating well, sleeping soundly, seeing fantastic sights. (In a recent phone call she'd complained, "For all the news I get you could be stranded in the prairie with the deer and the antelope," and then had filled me in on home-front developments: My older brother, a chemical engineer, had paid "four thousand dollars in federal taxes alone" last year; my cousin Alan had been appointed director of physical education at an expensive private school in Hartford. "And you, you're throwing your life away. You might as well be jumping on freight cars with the rest of the tramps.")

In a roadhouse café outside Harrisburg where we stopped for lunch, we saw a garish machine the size of a bungalow enclosed in bottle-thick rainbow-hued glass; it looked like the monstrous offspring of a church organ and a jukebox and featured a sign in Old English lettering:

THE FABULOUS CONCERTIZER
I Play Marimba & Mandolin Accompanied by Piano
To watch me play is fun to see
For I am quite a novelty

"You're looking into the dim dark future, boys," Shorty said. "Contraptions like this are going to make us as redundant as bats in Transylvania."

I slipped a quarter into the metal slot.

"She's out of order," a busboy hollered.

"Somebody up there's lookin' after us," Purvis said.

AS WE APPROACHED Reading in the hearse after a short, violent downpour, the clouds lifted and the sun's dying rays laid a cinammon shawl across the distant hills.

"How about slowing it to seventy around the curves, Mitch," Chickie said.

"Hey, man, I'm an orphan. I got nothing to lose."

Beside me Val tilted his head, draining a can of Carling's ale, belched and tossed the can rattling onto the highway.

"There's a hefty littering fine in this state," Chickie said.

"Believe me, man, that can'll improve the vista in this particular area." Val reached into the bag between his feet, brought up another ale and popped it.

"Drink up, Valentine," Austin said cheerfully. "Drink till you git ashamed of yourself."

In front of me Shorty was recounting his brief marriage for Tubbo. ". . . It was only our second time in the sack so I was trying to prolong things. You like to give your old lady pleasure at the beginning, right? I said, Baby, don't worry, I can stay with you as long as you want . . ." Shorty moved his pelvis rapidly to and fro, making panting-grunting noises. "She said, Morris, you already have."

Ahead, the iron-and-brick contours of Reading loomed in the fading light.

AT LOEWS THEATER we would play two days of four-a-day stage shows, filling in for a band that had run into road problems. The union classification for the theater was twelve pieces. As we were only ten, we hired an alto and trombone through the local union. The trombonist, Norton Bemis, turned out to be blind; the business agent had not indicated this; all he'd said on the phone was, "We try to throw as much work Norton's way as possible." It wouldn't matter that much. Our charts were written for ten, so the added players would merely be duplicating parts. It was an unalloyed case of featherbedding. As for the show—jugglers, an animal act, and a comic—the addition or subtraction of a horn or two would hardly be noticeable. A rehearsal was called for 11:00 A.M., an hour preceding the first show. As luck would have it, the theater manager, a lumpy man in a badly fitting plaid suit, saw Chickie leading Norton to his chair.

"Excuse me, but is that man blind?"

"Beg pardon?" Chickie had on his face the look of a kid whose hand is deep in his mother's purse just as he is being assailed by a stern voice behind him, "What is your hand doing in Mother's purse?"

"I said is that musician blind?"

Norton's head tilted up and away as if he were sniffing something unusual and trying to place the scent.

"As a matter of fact, yes," Chickie said.

"And he's going to play a *show?*"

Chickie's eyes were blinking like crazy: what to say to Mother? "Mr. Bemis's contribution will be of an improvisatory nature."

"Improva—what? The acts have music, the music gets passed out. How in hell is he going to read the music?"

"It . . . would be difficult," Chickie conceded.

The manager lumbered off, muttering to himself. I caught the phrase ". . . expecting me to pay for basket-weaving courses . . ."

A dancing, whistling Negro comic named Ollie Gayle opened the show. The centerpiece of his act, an undistinguished mélange of soft-shoe and lascivious one-liners, was an astonishing tour de force—the whistling of flawless three-part harmony on a chorus of "Bye Bye Blackbird." It seemed an impossible feat, comparable to centering, passing, and catching a football at one and the same time. We suspected trickery, inspected the comic's body for protruding wires—some concealed miniature electronic marvel—and found none. After the rehearsal we badgered him for the secret. Gayle obviously relished the excitement and consternation aroused in musicians wherever he worked and gleefully parried our questions with frivolous, evasive responses: "Ain't no secret to it, I'm a split personality," and "What I do in front that nobody gets to see is swallow three referees' whistles."

A juggling act followed, and the show was closed by a pair of roller-skating chimpanzees in striped suits. Between acts we played a production number. "Southland Suite" garnered meager applause and scattered hoots from the sparse matinee audience. "Let's retire the poor son of a bitch," Shorty said in self-deprecating disgust. "But I can still smell them magnolias, Shorty!" Purvis cried.

The juggler's pièce de résistance consisted of juggling a pair of bananas and a pair of oranges and "shaving simultaneously and at the same time"—he announced, backing away from the mike and lathering his face with a spray can. He tossed the can into the wings, whipped out a small safety razor, and between tosses of arcing fruit slashed at his face with rigid perpendicular strokes while we played a way-up version of "Zip-a-dee-doo-dah." Halfway through the turn, a bright crimson streak bloomed through the cream on his jaw, spreading like strawberry syrup in a vanilla sundae. The band—with the exception of trombonist Bemis—cringed.

The skating chimps' names were Peter and Polly. To the strains of Leroy Anderson's "Sleigh Ride," they zipped around the stage and back and forth under the piano. A slim, preserved blonde in a purple leotard called out indecipherable instructions; the chimps seemed to pay her no mind, shooting here and there in apparently random fashion. On one sweep beneath the piano Peter (or Polly) ricocheted off my right foot without acknowledgment (perhaps mistaking the limb for a piano leg); the other, careering past Alvie—forcing an evasive little backward skip from the maestro each time—kept grunting in an assertive manner. Austin said later it sounded like, "Faster, faster." We had been onstage close to two hours without a break. As the indefatigable chimps continued their erratic itinerary I saw Mitch, who had been squirming and grimacing in discomfort for the past ten minutes, furtively bend and lift Val's derby mute from the floor alongside his chair, then straighten and spin his bass, himself, and the derby around so that his back was to the stage; he seemed to fumble at his clothing and his torso grew suddenly rigid—necessity, as always, spurring invention.

Our intermission ran for an hour and a half. Some of the guys stayed to watch the movie, a Crosby–Lamour–Hope road epic; the rest of us went out to look for a bar or coffee shop. It was an overcast, humid afternoon. We saw Ollie Gayle in the alley behind the stage-door exit, smoking. "Five bucks," Val said, reaching in his pocket, "for the 'Blackbird' gimmick." Ollie's smooth oval face split in a wide grin. "Actually I cheats. What I do is use three or'fices. The two lines come out my mouth and nose, the other out my bum."

Val said ruefully as we wandered down the street, "I could make a lot of loot in Fall River with that routine."

"Boy, them chimps were somethin', weren't they?" Purvis said, a high, reflective shine in his pale eyes; I'd noticed that in a certain light they had the slippery half-mischievous look you see in storybook pictures of elves and gnomes. "Just zipped around free as baby pigs on ice."

"Jesus, dig the name on that old building," Val said, nudging me.

The four-story gray-brick tenement was fronted by a rusted fire escape; beneath a torn green shade in a second-story window an elderly man gazed down expressionlessly. The flyspecked sign, murky in the leaden daylight, was formed of unlit light bulbs.

"Sincere Hotel," I read aloud.

"Send a couple chills down your spine?" Val said. I nodded, experiencing an unfamiliar pang. "Story of our life, man. When we've played the last cadenza and they ask where do you want to go to die, say, Sincere Hotel . . . Hey, there's a bar in the next block."

THE HOUSE REMAINED sparse through eight shows over the two days.

"SRO. Sitting room only," Chickie said.

Backstage closing night the manager drew a roll of bills from his pocket. "I haven't included the cost of your trombonist's seeing-eye dog." He gloomily counted out the band's wages into Chickie's hand. "You know what the worst three weeks of the year are in show business?"

It was an antiquated gag and Chickie reeled off one of the versions he knew: "Christmas, Easter, and a week in Red Bank, New Jersey."

The manager vigorously shook his head. "Hanukkah in Berlin, nineteen forty-one, and two weeks in August at Loews Theater in Reading, Pennsylvania."

Ollie Gayle presented Alvie a plastic bag containing a dozen narrow black ties as a token of his appreciation for the band's backing, and we left town no closer to the secret of the trifurcate whistle.

14

Baggio's casino, a sprawling barnlike structure, extended over the water on massive pilings and was separated from the main road by a tall stand of pines. It was the end of the tour, which some of us welcomed and others—with nothing lined up for the fall—regretted. But without exception we were happy to reach this pastoral spot. Most of us were city-bred. The prospect of two stationary weeks on the shores of an Adirondack Mountain lake after our long string of tank-town one-nighters was like emerging on the borders of Shangri-la after a forced march through unrelieved swampland. Not even the spartan accommodations—double-decker bunks in pine-board cabins in a marshy tract behind the casino (for sidemen; Alvie and Estelle had wangled a private bungalow off in the woods)—and backbreaking hours, 9:30 P.M. to 3:30 A.M., seven nights a week, could detract from the idyllic setting: the tall, sun-warm pines and perfect blue lake nestled in the hollow of deep-wooded hills like a sapphire in a teacup.

But small drawbacks almost immediately began to materialize, like spots of damp on freshly laid wallpaper. A heat wave arrived with us, and Alvie refused to let us take off our coats on the stand. (For what he considered good reason: Baggio's was a new account; he had been vigorously cultivating management, aiming for two weeks at the resort every summer, and this initial booking was his foot in the door.) Even with the water lapping directly beneath us there were barbarous nights on the stand—nights when Tubbo would come off-stage looking like he'd just emerged from the deep, a benign dripping monster in funny clothes; during breaks he'd go outside on the deck, peel off his coat, and wring it out over the water like a wet dishrag. On Sunday nights Alvie dressed us in red-and-white striped coats with string ties and red straw boaters that made us look like a phalanx of barber poles (Tubbo excepted). I don't know where Alvie found these outfits; we were in the middle of nowhere, though Mitch remembered passing a costume-rental shop around Lake George on our way north. Some of the coats bore unidentifiable stains and none of them fit; for every guy who had to double over his too-long sleeves to form cuffs, someone else saw his hairy wrists protrude like a farmboy hitching to town on Saturday night—and trading off only seemed to raise problems in other areas. Sunday was Roaring Twenties night. Patrons gained admittance by passing through a crack in the door a piece of paper that said "Eddie sent me" or "I'm a friend of Joe's." Employees wearing boxy suits and fedoras stood around the crepe-hung walls wielding cardboard tommyguns. Management strung balloons and streamers through the rafters and set free platters of sliced cheese and sausage, jars of pickled eggs, and boxes of el-ropo cigars on the bar. Schooners of beer were priced at a nickel that night and business surged. Management compensated for the giveaways with hyped-up sales of the hard stuff—people who normally wouldn't, drank boilermakers all night, thinking they were getting a bargain. On a warm evening with the crush of people juiced way up and dancing their brains out to our simulated ticky-tack two-beat—whiskery twenties tunes like "Peggy O'Neill," "Stumbling," and "Rose of Washington Square"—an essence would rise off the floor that Val described as "the fragrance wafting from a Louisiana abbatoir on a ninety-eight-degree day." To complement our barber-pole outfits Alvie dressed Estelle in one of her slinkier cathouse numbers—a midnight-blue sheath studded with rhinestones, and a red velvet headband that I had to admit looked pretty sexy against her lank, bleached-out hair.

THE CASINO DREW its clientele from the lodges, motels, and little housekeeping cabins around Cluett's Landing. Schoolteachers and stenos from Queens and Brooklyn; mechanics, beauticians, bank tellers, county clerks from the upstate towns. Many of them were wizard dancers, and we were bombarded with a wide range of requests: mambo, polka, jitterbug, rumba, beguine, hora, Viennese waltz, samba, Mexican hat dance, tango . . . It crossed my mind, watching these expert performers—looking like they'd been entering contests, and winning some, since they were teenagers, the women in light cotton dresses or pedal pushers, the younger men stripped down to T-shirts and chinos—that musicians, despite their ingrained rhythmic skills, are notoriously poor dancers or nondancers (which may have as much to do with the divorce rate among us as lonely Saturday nights, daytime schlepping around the house, and extended road trips). I think I know why. The simplest and most certifiable fact is that many of us never learned how. When our classmates were attending the spring hop, the junior and senior proms, we were either working the saloons or, if our talents had smoothed out and taken on a society sheen, playing for those same hops and proms. Our inside knowledge of the intricacies of rhythm and tempo renders those of us who have mastered the rudimentary steps self-conscious and cautious when we venture onto the floor. Though we may indulge in daring flights of invention in our playing, we are not adventurous off the stand. We won't dance in a manner that we think makes us appear absurd—a fast jitterbug, the trickier and more demanding of the Latin rhythms, and (over the last three decades) the rock and disco crazes, which, as we watch middle-aged patrons turn spastic and endanger muscle and bone in their misguided attempts to emulate their kids, arouse in us simultaneous feelings of dismay, amusement, and pity.

Beyond all this lies an even more complex set of mind: I suspect we sometimes feel a half-conscious superiority bordering on disdain toward the people for whom we're playing. From the stage we see how subservient they are to our bidding. We're the puppeteers, they the puppets—and how easily we manipulate them! No sooner do we release the oom-pah Bavarian cadences of "Beer Barrel Polka" than our charges are sent prancing and skipping across the floor. We bless our good fortune in sitting coolly up here making music rather than romping and sweating down there. Occasionally when we know we sound rough and disorganized—hung over and/or listless, a tempo badly set, an inexperienced sideman pulling us down—we'll be effusively complimented. It almost seems a perverse rule of thumb: the audience's enthusiasm in inverse proportion to the quality of the music. We wonder if everyone out there has a tin ear. (A corollary of a sort holds: unschooled or inexperienced musicians backing professional performers may not comprehend their own inadequacies.) Our attitudes and perceptions can at times be indefensibly cavalier. We feel our tastes are parochial but impeccable. If jazz-oriented we'll not often attend conventional musical comedies, unless coerced by family; for myself, I don't care to listen to nonswinging pit-band music. If there's a choice between hearing "On the Street Where You Live" rendered by a theater show band and the same tune transformed on wax by a George Shearing or Oscar Peterson, I'll sit home by the stereo. Regardless of what cultural era we were nurtured by, we have a general aversion toward certain dance rhythms. Specifically: polkas, horas, and tangos. The first two because they are harmonically, melodically, and rhythmically barren. Some beautiful tangos have been written and somewhere I'm sure there are musicians who dote on them, but most of us would prefer not to play them. Despite their lyrical lines they seem stilted—mannered in an unpleasing fashion—and do not easily lend themselves to embellishment. (Austin, with his wide-ranging experience playing beer busts, Irish weddings, hootenannies, et al., would groan aloud when Alvie called one: "I can't do any damn justice to those fool things.") To this day I don't play tangos well and do not care to learn how, nor do I like to watch people dancing them; it most likely has to do with my distance from the culture that begot them. If my livelihood depended on mastering their execution I would probably change professions; it's myopic of me, I know. I feel something of the repellent mystery the mystic Argentine writer Jorge Luis Borges must have experienced when he remarked, "There's something infamous about the tango. How can I put it? Something brutal and at the same time sentimental. Like Wagner . . ." All this drifted across my mind as I watched a couple who looked as if they had been born in each other's arms swagger and glide through the arrogant, sinuous formalities of "La Cumparsita"; he an uncomely, hard-breathing Valentino, she a smoldering Pola Negri with a sunburned nose.

Along with the night shift I had to work a solo Happy Hour stint in the bar from 5:00 to 6:30 every afternoon; this paid me an extra twenty-five dollars a week. The sorry little bar spinet had a Solovox attachment—a short keyboard clamped to the upside edge of the piano; you played it with the right hand for organlike effects while the left accompanied on the spinet. Management had purchased it at considerable expense and naturally wanted it used. Beneath the Solovox keyboard, at knee level, was a metal lever that adjusted the volume: for *forte* (loud) you nudged it to the right, for *piano* (soft) to the left. It was a highly sensitive little gizmo responding to the minutest pressure. I'd never worked one of these contraptions before, and because of my unorthodox keyboard posture I had the damndest time coordinating my right knee movements to produce the desired volume, particularly as the same foot was needed to work the piano's damper pedal. My knee would tremble in anticipation as it approached the lever, turn spastic on me, and there'd be a sudden blast of volume followed by an equally sudden hush as I drew the knee back in alarm. The effect was that of a small child at a grown-up party fiddling with the knob on a radio or phonograph—it startled patrons when they were least expecting a change in mood; many literally jumped, and martinis and highballs sloshed over the rims of glasses. The third time it happened in the space of a half hour, a local lodge owner strolled over with his drink, crouched, peered under the piano, and glanced up at me quizzically. "Just wondering who the gremlin was working the controls."

ON OUR SECOND day at the lake a slow-moving stray dog attached itself to Tubbo; its muzzle was gray and featureless and its patchy brown coat had the nap of a moth-eaten rug. Tubbo called him Zero. In the canteen where we ate our first meal of the day the waitress would bring a mini-plate for Zero—the crusty hind end of the meat loaf and some tailings of potato and vegetable. If Tubbo was still hungry after scarfing his own lunch—which was usually the case, as we rarely rose before noon, and missed breakfast—he would furtively reach under the table (checking to see that the waitress was occupied), push Zero's muzzle out of the plate and gobble the remains. Austin, observing this performance the third time around, smilingly shook his head in a kind of stupefied admiration. "Go on, Marvin," (one of Austin's idiosyncrasies was to address everyone by their formal names), "do it all, scarf till you git ashamed of yourself." Later in the day, remorseful, Tubbo would pop back in the canteen with Zero and buy him a couple of cupcakes, a bag of pretzels, or an apple turnover.

Tubbo not only had a dog, he had a woman. She hung around

the bandstand a lot, performing little solo dances, and called him her "Paradiddle Joe." Bovine, perfumed, she came scratching at the cabin screen at quarter of four in the morning, wrenching Tubbo from a shower, a game of hearts, or imminent sleep, and dragging him off into the wild mountain night. She was a Swede of bubbling energies and heroic proportions: saucer blue eyes, throw-pillow breasts, and a mouth, Shorty said, "you could stuff a whole bagel in." Tubbo would roll in by dawn's early light, bushed and bedraggled, moist leaves and twigs and pine needles clinging to his clothes. He was the only one who connected during the two-week engagement. The glamorous lure of instrument, spotlight, and band uniform is overrated and mostly illusory. Sailors, marines, and cops probably do better. All we have to offer is our late-night availability and we don't/won't dance. The sole overture that came my way at the lake was made by a slender middle-aged woman who wore her silver-blue hair in a towering beehive (that sent my mind reeling back to a childhood carnival and my first cotton candy) and drank her martinis, wreathed in cigarette smoke, on a corner bar stool during Happy Hour. "I suspect," she said to me in a cultured, husky voice one afternoon, "that you have more profound things in you than 'Chattanooga Choo Choo.' "

If the night was especially warm, and sleep difficult, Val and I would go out on the lake after work to unwind. There were a couple of dilapidated rowboats moored in the marshes behind the casino that didn't seem to belong to anyone. We'd drift, talking or not talking, the mood pensive because of the time of morning, the impermeable darkness folding around us like a robe.

"I'm hitting forty next month, man. September twelve."

"One step from the glue factory," I said.

"I feel my body beginning to tell me something. Like, get off the treadmill, find a location gig or a couple nights a week steady back home."

"So, do it."

He didn't answer directly. I let one oar trail in the water; the stillness was so deep you could almost hear the shadows shifting in the near woods.

"I start to see how guys can get turned onto junk," he said. "Friend of mine, tenor man from New Bedford, good player, told me when the stuff's right it's like wearing a warm coat with a fur-lined collar and belt in the back. You feel together, you feel . . . *spruce*, was the word he used. Nothing bothers you. Sorry-ass little town in the middle of nowhere, funky club, cold audience—no sweat. You're totally relaxed, confident, unafraid . . ."

"If you have to use, you're better off with bourbon," I said carefully.

"No, no, I wasn't considering . . . I'll tell you, man, I used to be able to snap back much easier. You know how when you're soloing and moving out to the edge, taking big chances—you can be on the verge of fluffing but if you're thinking fast enough you can anticipate the clam, deflect it, turn it around, shoot off in another direction. Like the counterpart in life itself, man, learning from your mistakes and near mistakes—bounce off, change course. But you have to be flexible and, what's the word—*resilient*. Like an athlete in condition. I used to be able to pick off those clams in midair and turn 'em around so easy, like a kid skipping rope, rolling a hoop . . . just like *that*." I heard Val's fingers snap in the dark. "But lately, I dunno, I've lost the split timing. They just lie there, Clinker City . . ." I felt suddenly, profoundly depressed. This superb talent, whose reputation for booze and abrasiveness had blunted his development and shortened his tenure with major bands, leaning into middle age, losing—or thinking he was losing—touch with himself, his confidence slipping away. And nothing I could say was going to help.

Something turned the mood, a stirring, almost a trembling in the air. And with it, my concern began to ebb. The first pale light tinged the eastern sky. Spirals of mist crawled over the wooded slopes like a giant gray centipede, then the pinnacles of trees appeared, lit by a pure, unearthly light. In the next instant I was strangely buoyed and tingling, the hair rising on the back of my neck. Washes of mauve, lemon, and rose banded the sky's rim, loosing streaks of color racing over the glassy surface toward us. A crescent of sun flared like a diamond, and the woods stood out from the shadows.

The spectacle lifted Val out of his self-absorption. "Think if you could capture this in a concerto, man. You'd be right up there with Ravel, Bartók, any of those heavyweight cats."

IN THE HEAT of early afternoon we'd wake groggily, eat our lunch in the canteen, and wander down to the dock to swim or paddle a canoe around. But mostly we just fell out in whatever shade we could find and watched the chicks.

On Chickie's birthday we chipped in for a magnum of champagne and brought it to the lake in a pail of ice.

"You spend much time thinking about dying, Chickie?" Purvis said while Val, scuffling on his knees, poured bubbly into outstretched paper cups. We were sprawled in one corner of the massive dock, spattered by the cool spray raised from people diving and splashing around us.

"Hey, I'm only forty-nine . . ."

"Flaubert," Shorty said, giving the name an exaggerated French twist, "said he could never see a cradle without thinking of a grave."

"Who's Flaubert?" Purvis said.

"Okay," Shorty said patiently, "you know the name Emma Bovary?"

"Why're you answering a damn question with another question?" Purvis said, upset.

Tubbo's girlfriend, mammoth in a pink one-piece suit, clambered dripping onto the dock to collect him for a swim. "Not now, sweetheart, a little later—" Tugging him to his feet, no mean feat, then pushing him relentlessly from behind down the short dirt path to the pebbled beach and into the water, leaning patiently into the job like a sturdy tug nudging a torpid freighter.

"Watch this," Shorty said. "True theater-in-the-round. Man Mountain Dean frolicking with Mother Earth."

"Check the fine bitch stage right," Mitch said sotto voce. At a corner of the dock a long-legged honey blonde in a black suit was bent like a forklift, entwined arms pointed to the water, held from behind by a beefy, freckled man with a walrus mustache and old-fashioned, knee-length trunks. "Man, if I ever paraded something that fine down the main street of Woonsocket on a Saturday night all the cats' tongues would be hanging out of their faces and their dicks wagging like Ferdinand the bull's."

"To Woonsocket, the tar pit of New England," Val said, sitting crosslegged, his raised cup of champagne winking in the bright sun; alongside him was an auxiliary paper-bag pint with which he'd been chasing the wine. "I'll tell you, man, one of the greatest highs you can encounter, and I'm talking now, ahem, from a quarter century's experience in the business, paying heavy dues right down the line and carving asses from Boston to Kokomo"—I always knew when Val had a heat on: that rushing, verbose, half-caustic half-put-on way of talking, blood staining his face like blight—"one of the all-time *acmes* in life, is catching the eye of a young chick out front, knowing you're turning her on and playing right to her, man, getting jacked way up, your energy high and burning, ideas crowding for space in your head, coming out the bell through your fingers and chops, easy as a kid running in the early morning, up hill down dale. You're rising to the occasion and playing right over it, and the reward is she's waiting outside for you after the gig under a lamppost or in the shadow of some trees, ditched her date, and then . . . then everything goes *swimmingly*, man, you perform like a champagne—*cham-pi-on*, and you wake in the morning to spring sunshine streaming in and the chick's bare back nestled into you and there're tears of gratitude, tears of happiness in your eyes 'cause you know the music did it for you and it was worth it, all those years of scales and clammed notes and the first rat-hole joints you played with out-of-tune pianos and bad-cat proprietors—you've put all that behind you, you're finally making music, and if only this one pretty chick heard you and got turned on and you connected, then fuck it, it's all been worthwhile . . ." Val trailed off and took a deserved pull from his paper sack.

"Well stated, Valentine," Austin said at the same time that Chickie murmured, thinking of tonight, "Slow down to sixty, fella . . ."

Val was back up on his knees, maneuvering like Jose Ferrer in the Toulouse-Lautrec flick, pouring the dregs from the magnum. "Down the hatch, jocks, good to the last blub."

"Steady there, Valentine," Austin said as Val lurched to leeside, the wine missing the cup.

"Watch out, folks," Mitch intoned with a barker's inflection, "he walks fine, he talks fine, but he's liable to pitch forward on his face at any moment . . ."

"Some birthday," Chickie said as champagne cascaded into his lap.

FRIDAY WAS AMATEUR night. Austin looked over the contestants and said, "We're gonna be climbing Battle Mountain tonight, boys." But the best of the talent turned out to be no worse than the cutthroat juggler and the skating chimps at the theater in Reading. Both Alvie and Estelle had caught colds, which must have been hard to do under that scorching sun, and Chickie would be fronting the band.

The first act, a ballroom dance team, requested a medley of tangos. A concerted groan rose from our ranks. "We'll give you two choruses of 'Jalousie,' " Chickie said; and to us, "Piano take the verse, brass and saxes unison on the chorus." The woman wore a peasant blouse and dirndl skirt, her partner a red silk shirt, silver pantaloons, and midnight-blue cummerbund. "Wouldn't mind a couple pair of drawers made out of that guy's outfit," Purvis said, as they moved into professional lockstep to my opening bars. "I hate this fool piece," I heard Austin mutter. "It's like pullin' out a man's toenails one by one." Val called down exuberantly, "Dance, dance, dance, babies—Mama needs a new shawl!" and hoked up the chorus with an outrageous hand-shake vibrato, undeterred by Chickie's shouted warning, "Take care of business, Val—"

A small, extremely fat accordionist in Bermuda shorts and a rugby shirt came on next and played with considerable verve and expertise a medley of "Lady of Spain," "Tico Tico," and "My Adobe Hacienda."

"I thought those tunes went down with the Titanic," Shorty said.

Four nondescript acts followed.

In the seventh slot was a tall, gaunt woman with girlish gray bangs who handed me a scrawled lead sheet of an aria from *I Pagliacci:* no way the band was going to be able to fake this. Shorty brought his alto to the piano and tried to read over my shoulder while I chorded. The woman sang in a howling soprano, her head constantly swerving from the audience to us. The penciled notation was barely legible, and Shorty and I floundered all the way. The woman was near to tears at the end and told Chickie she intended to register a formal complaint with management. Austin leaned cheerfully toward us. "You guys sounded like you were trying to cross Fall River in a kayak."

A young Negro vocalist closed the program. I had seen him off and on through the week, dressed in polo shirt and pressed white ducks, wandering alone about the grounds, occasionally hitting a tennis ball awkwardly against a backboard (the only nonwaterfront facility provided by casino management). He never came to the dock and no one understood what he was doing in the area. On this humid night he wore a dark blue suit with a starched white shirt and silver tie. He sang Duke Ellington's "In a Sentimental Mood"—oversang it: too much deep throbbing baritone, too many florid hand signals—but the pitch was true, and the voice, I suspected, professionally trained. The audience listened raptly, as if in the spell of some exotic tent-show evangelist, and the applause that followed was respectful and sustained. The judges—Chickie and the resort owner's plump wife, Margie—went off to the bar to compare notes as a buzz of excitement filled the hall. They returned shortly with the prizes, and Margie read the winners over the mike. First prize (a bottle of California champagne) to the ballroom dance team; second (a quart of Mr. Boston gin) to the accordionist; third (splits of New York State red and white wine) to the Negro.

Chickie announced that the band would be back in a few minutes to play for dancing, and we headed for the bar. The accordionist, buoyant at having won his first prize in six successive tries that summer, bought the band a drink, though only Mitch and Tubbo had provided accompaniment. "I'll pass," I told the bartender; it was still early, and on a six-hour gig you need to pace yourself. Val swung around on me. "Are you crazy, man—it's a freebie." And to the bartender, "He'll have an I. W. Harper on the rocks." I thought of what Austin had said during a break the previous night, one of his homespun upstate insights: "Valentine can no more refuse a drink than he can sneeze with his eyes open." The Negro was standing alongside us, waiting patiently for a bartender to acknowledge him and perspiring heavily in his woolen suit. "Good show, man," Val said, "but they gave out the prizes wrong. You should've got the gin, right?" A tiny frown etched the Negro's forehead as he tried to correlate the remark with the loose, genial grin on the trumpet player's face. "How's the Count, by the way?" Val persisted.

"Beg pardon?"

"Basie. I heard he was doing some one-nighters in the area, I figure you gotta be his band boy."

"Val . . ." I tried to pull him away; when he was tanked up on a steamy night, I was beginning to learn, his demon could assume antic guises.

The Negro drew himself perceptibly erect and cleared his throat. "The mere fact that one is colored does not necessarily guarantee employment with Mr. Basie . . ."

"Just jivin', man." Val threw a fraternal arm around his shoulder.

"C'mon, have a drink . . . Barkeep, a double gin here. Uh, on second thought, make it another I. W. Harper over . . ."

AFTER THE NEXT break Val failed to return to the stand, and Chickie sent me out to look for him. He'd been nodding off in his chair during the previous set, so I thought the ground a likely place to reconnoiter. The thunder that had begun a half hour earlier continued its distant rumble—a welcome sound, presaging a break in the heat. I found Val stretched out on his back some fifty feet from the casino, head propped awkwardly on a gnarled tree root. I shook him awake.

"Where are we?"

"Lake Laramee, New York. Three sets to go."

He blew out his breath and pulled himself forward like a tired athlete doing sit-ups; his head dropped between his knees. "And so to Bled, as they say in Yugoslavia."

"Come on, we're late." A loon's cry sounded downwind. We had heard them occasionally, an eerie, piping, almost human sound—half scream, half laughter.

Lightning raced around the sky, then a barrel of thunder rolling close by; the first drops pattered down. I reached out my hand and he used it to yank himself up. "Thanks, man, you saved me from a watery grave." We walked quickly across the patchy grass, pulling up our coat collars, the rain rustling the leaves and beginning to hiss.

"I'll tell you something, man, the nights in this place are getting to be as long as a Sunday in Keokuk, Iowa."

It was a long, slow bend around midnight to half past three, a steady downpour pelting the casino roof. The dismal evening was partly salvaged by Shorty's just-completed arrangement of our new sign-off tune (the melody of which he'd lifted in the Elmira music store). At 3:25 we gave it its premier performance. Shorty had done himself proud, imparted loving care to this lilting and fragile ballad, a sweet threnody of parting that would always fill me with yearning and set my scalp tingling whenever I heard it. Even today, almost four decades later, the slightest prompting—a slant of moonlight on concrete, a lonely drumming of midnight rain, the curl of smoke from a girl's cigarette in a semidark café—can send it humming through my mind: "In the Wee Small Hours of the Morning." Only one thing marred its debut—a missing horn on the out chorus: Val, chin on chest, trumpet cradled tenderly in one arm, worn by the long night and lulled by the gentle strains, nodding off in his chair like a weary businessman at a road-show musical.

That night I had an odd, disjointed dream. I was accompanying a famous vocalist on the stage of a prestigious showroom, opening night, the room packed and stifling, the huge audience resplendent in black tie and gown. The star's complex musical charts were spread on the piano rack before me. I was nervous—we had had the briefest of talk-through rehearsals. Eight bars into the up-tempo opener an air conditioner mounted overhead began blowing a strong blast of chill air on the piano. The music shivered, the notes blurred. Distracted, I temporarily lost my place and fell behind the beat. The star, a burly man in a white dinner jacket, half turned to me, still singing but fierce-eyed, scowling. Suddenly the airstream lifted the accordioned chart from the reading rack; it rose like a wounded bird and fluttered to the stage at the star's feet. I tried to fake the tune and got hopelessly lost. The star broke off, facing me with a brutal, pitying smile. The shocked audience's murmur rose like a sea roar. The star turned back to the microphone. "Ladies and gentlemen, I apologize. Management apologizes. I am not accustomed to this caliber of accompaniment." There was no place to hide. I crawled under the piano and huddled on my side on the floor, imploring the curtain to come down. The star's placating words were drowned out as the sea roar grew louder, more threatening. Humiliated, I curled into a ball and willed myself to sleep . . . Much later I opened my eyes. The piano and stage were gone. I was alone in a bare-walled room, lying on my side on a cot without sheets or blankets. Faint daylight shone against a drawn shade. I got up and crossed to the window, feeling weightless, airy, and indescribably sorrowful. I drew the shade—it was a sunless day—and looked down into a deserted street rutted with trolley tracks. Just above the window and angling out from the building were the massive rusted struts of a sign. The lettering was backward: I patiently worked it out: ⅃ƎTOH ƎЯƎƆИIƧ.

THE RAIN CONTINUED intermittently through the next day, and Happy Hour was more crowded than usual. I'd been playing the Solovox less and less, growing to hate the beery organ-grinder sound and the Saint Vitus' dance my knee did at the controls. Finally I got around to asking Margie (her husband was rarely visible, and it was her hand that seemed to be the controlling one on the tiller) if she'd mind my dispensing with it entirely. She said she was glad I'd brought that up, as she'd been getting numerous complaints from jumpy people.

It was during these Happy Hour sessions that I became aware of a peculiar distortion in the public's perception of musicians on summer-resort gigs. Seemingly intelligent people would ask me during breaks what I did during the "regular season" or what I did for a living. It must relate to the vacation aura, the inability to connect a person apparently having fun playing fine old show tunes and standards—the sparkling sea or wooded lake within view through the picture window—with a means of livelihood. Yet they hear a professional sound emerging from the music box, they see my hands moving with dexterity, they must assume that years of work prepared the hands to function at that level of competency.

For most of the week my main support during the daily afternoon grind had been my silver-haired friend with the beehive hairdo, who had detected in me something more profound than "Chattanooga Choo Choo." Her name was Mrs. Danvers, and she had taken to carrying her martinis to the piano, leaning her elbows across the top and listening intently, eyes averted, considerately blowing smoke in staccato puffs over my head or off to the side. Occasionally she'd make a request—vintage Porter, Kern, or Gershwin—commenting on the lilting quality of a passage, humming lightly along or singing a fragment of lyric in a wavering voice just a shade off-key, her worn, refined face fixed in a remembering smile. When the bar voices rose too harshly or a noisy group began singing some barbershop or boola-boola tune against what I was playing, she'd cast me a long-suffering, compassionate look as if to say, What can you do when philistines are in charge of the world? At 6:30 she'd blow me a kiss from her fingertips as I closed the piano lid, the sad, pensive smile lingering on her face, and I wouldn't see her again until the next afternoon.

Once a stocky man in a yellow porkpie hat came over in the midst of one of Mrs. Danvers's requests and asked for a mossbacked ole-boy tune—what we called moldy-fig or dogpatch specials. Letting my fingers run secure hold patterns, as is their habit when someone converses with me in midtune, I said I didn't know it. He asked for another of the same genre; again I drew a blank. "Son," he said with an unpleasant smile, walking away, "as a piano player you make a great peach picker."

Mrs. Danvers shook as if a sudden fever had taken her; she expelled a violent plume of smoke at the man's retreating back. "You insufferable clod," she called after him in a trembling voice, "you poor, gross philistine. He's a highly skilled musician, a fine, fine artist . . ." She turned to me, her color vivid. "You must dismiss such incidents from your mind, my dear. People of that ilk are beneath disdain, they are the lower primates. You mustn't let them shatter your spirit . . ." It seemed a propitious time to take a break; Mrs. Danvers's voice had carried and eyes were converging on us. She looped her arm protectively through mine and walked me to the bar.

She had frequently offered to buy me a "well-deserved libation," which I'd always gracefully refused, explaining the long night ahead and the need for musicians who valued their livers and pancreases to be alert to the occupational hazards. But we often chatted about music and other impersonal things (I enjoyed her courtly old-fashioned locution; it passed the time) as she smoked and sipped her gin, only a slight thickening of the tongue toward the end of the afternoon betraying the extent of her consumption. Only once had she broken through the civilized veneer of small talk, launching a rambling, impassioned account of a recent divorce, greedy attorneys, and ungrateful out-of-control children that startled me with its unexpectedness and vehemence.

Today with the rain finally slackening and a pale luminous light infiltrating the bar, she told me she wouldn't see me for a few days, as she was leaving to attend to "imperative business in the city." I wondered, which city, what sort of business, but did not press her. She seemed more detached and drawn than usual; she did not come to the piano but watched from her private corner of the bar, soaking in an endless stream of gin, head tilted in a self-absorbed, half-listening way. I asked if I could buy her a farewell drink, as a token of gratitude for her support during the week. "I accept graciously and gratefully," she answered, her voice slurring. "It's more than some would have done." She turned her worn blue gaze on me and said with a misty smile, "As you may have surmised I'm very drawn to the finer things in life, particularly to young persons of artistic leaning . . ." Her gaze widened perceptibly and became fixed. She then bent her head supplely and resignedly, like a swan in a siege of melancholia, and vomited copiously onto the bar.

"There," a woman's voice said beside me, "but for the grace of God go I."

VAL WAS IN a wistful looking-back mood that night. He and I and Purvis were sitting out under the trees on our second break, watching a full, bloated moon silvering the lake. It was one of those velvety, breathless late-summer nights, an Indian-summer night out of season, that can trip a million memory cells and send your mind swarming in as many directions.

"Every club we played," he said, speaking of earlier, better days, "I used to think, Any minute now the president of RCA, or Columbia, or Decca is going to walk in the door and change my life. None of them ever did, but it didn't stop me from looking. I figured if one of those wheels of the industry didn't show, then a pretty chick might and turn me around . . ."

"That ten-inch you cut with a quintet on Contemporary was one of the first jazz tracks I ever listened to when I was a kid," I said. "You were *good* . . ."

"Oh, man, that was long ago and far away."

"Now there's a pretty tune," Purvis said.

Val was staring out at the water, picking at pine needles. "You know what I was thinking about today? That hotel we saw across from the theater in Reading."

"Sincere Hotel."

"That's it."

It seemed too much trouble, too complicated at the moment, to tell him of my dream.

"Well, I've been a gypsy a long time now, man. I can hardly remember anything else except the hurdles . . ."

"I used to think gypsies came back to earth as wolves or bats," Purvis said, off on a track of his own.

"Funny what can set your mind off," Val said, unheeding. "When I was in town getting my laundry this afternoon there was a crack in the pavement where it had been pushed up, a jagged line with little branches running off and weeds poking through, and I swear the crack was identical to one on the sidewalk in Fall River on my way home from school. I'd run all the way to get changed for track, my head down, watching the sidewalk speed under my feet like railroad ties in a movie . . ."

"Calling all Ducks"—Alvie's fatuous voice splintered the soft night.

"Alvie got on my case again tonight," Val said as we dragged ourselves up.

I knew Chickie had reported him for his Amateur Night hijinks, and I had seen them talking in the bar earlier: Alvie still sniffling from his cold, face flushed, taking the glass out of Val's hand—an enterprise normally fraught with peril, comparable to wrenching a bone from the jaws of a German shepherd. Tonight Val had submitted meekly. Had he begun to acknowledge to himself that Clinker City was showing up too frequently, that the booze was no longer mere fuel for his heart and muscles and mind but had begun to leak corrosively into his horn? We started back, the astonishing moon lighting the way.

"Maybe the president of RCA will walk in tonight with Count Basie," I said. "Or at least a pretty chick."

"Oh, man, I don't even bother looking anymore."

THE NEXT DAY, Sunday, the heat returned with a vengeance, and the simmering end of summer came to a fast boil; it was a Sunday I wish I could forget. A group of houseware conventioneers from Glens Falls had rented the casino and grounds for an afternoon cookout, and management asked us to do a double session, afternoon and night. There would be twenty bucks extra for each of us. It turned out to be nowhere near enough.

The conventioneers began their partying early, just before noon. It was already in the high eighties and moving up, sun blazing in a hazy, white sky and not a breath stirring. Picnic tables had been set out under the pines along with charcoal grills and kegs of beer. We'd moved our instruments onto the outside deck; the waiters had dropped one end of the piano while moving it offstage, jamming the damper pedal and putting it out of commission, which presaged the kind of day we were in for. Our only protection from the sun was the straw boaters we wore with our sad-sack barber-pole blazers. Alvie wouldn't let us take off the blazers or ties, and within fifteen minutes of the opening up-tempo medley there was a wide circle of damp saturating the planks around Tubbo's drums and his face had turned the color of a spoiled turnip. The houseware folks, most of them in their middle years, went into high gear right off and stayed there, dancing up a storm—more frolic than dance actually, cavorting and sliding over the pine needles, the men stripped down to their undershirts with their pants rolled up, and the women barefooted, fanning themselves with their orange-and-white cardboard hats and hiking their dresses, both sexes letting out lusty whoops and hollers into the smoky, breathless heat. It seemed like the faster the hamburgs and hot dogs disappeared from the grills and the lower the beer dropped in the kegs, the more abandoned and frenzied they grew.

Alvie kept the tempos up, digging old flagwavers out of the book, Model-T numbers that bore the notation Brite 2—Boom Chick. By two bells the temperature had climbed to the low nineties, and the heat and insects were bedeviling us. Estelle had already retired back to the bungalow in the woods, and no one begrudged her her haven. The more bedraggled we grew, the higher the picnickers' spirits soared; it was as if some uncanny transference of energy were taking place. Though they had some benefit from the shade, none of them were spring chickens, and jumping around half-undressed on full stomachs amid the soot and smoke rising from the charcoal fires, they looked like revelers leaping at high noon in the pits of hell. With all that brew and cheap, greasy food sitting in their guts I don't know how they managed it. Mitch said maybe they were possessed. I kept expecting to see them totter and drop, one by one. Nor would I have been surprised to see our wilting brass and reeds slump and slowly topple from their chairs, both ranks at once, like shriveled stalks cut down by an invisible thresher. We were taking the sun head-on now, and the deck was a blast furnace. We pleaded with Alvie to let us get rid of the blazers, but he was looking toward next summer, and he'd always maintained there was no more unprofessional sight than a bunch of hairy-armed musicians in different-length short-sleeve shirts—though how a hairy arm or two could have mattered to those carousing half-naked conventioneers I couldn't have said. The only way we could get any relief was to move inside between sets and guzzle brew. Alvie watchdogged us, trying to tighten the reins, warning us not to get sloppy as we had a long way to go, and casting emphatic looks at Val. But we mostly ignored him; it was close to open rebellion. He had been pushing Val most of the afternoon, calling numbers that stretched him out and tested his endurance; and Val, growing more glassy-eyed as the gruelling day progressed—but with a combative fire burning behind the glaze—bore up valiantly, meeting, if not especially enjoying, the challenge. It was like a semi-sadistic coach driving his star halfback, about whom he has ambivalent feelings, to the limit under brutal playing conditions. The more brew we put away the more we sweated, and by late afternoon we all looked like we'd fallen into a community tub in a Bulgarian town square.

We played straight through to six-thirty (the piano's bollixed-up pedal a constant irritant, like walking with a pebble in my shoe), leaving those crazy picnickers clamoring for more. I remember the sun hanging big and low in the sky like a copper frying pan. After a break for supper and a fast shower—Tubbo couldn't wait, just stripped off his ducks and blazer and dove straight off the deck—we moved back into the casino and started in again. The heat had hardly let up at all. Most of the conventioneers had stayed on, and the place jammed up early with the Roaring Twenties crowd. Hot nights always bring people out; the motel rooms and little housekeeping cabins had been baking in the sun all day and weren't fit for human habitation. By ten o'clock, even with the doors and windows all open, the casino was a steam bath, moths thick as leaves beating on the screens and flicking around the hurricane lamps, and fly swarms going to work on the bar buffet. During our breaks we got brews and took them outside under the trees to try to cool off—the reverse of the afternoon's procedure. After the second break Alvie told the bartenders to shut us off. Those of us who had jugs went for them. Half the band was wasted and the music was growing rougher and more strident by the minute. Not that it mattered with all the noise and frenzy out on the floor.

It was during our third break, getting on toward midnight, and the crowd showing no signs of thinning out, that the roof caved and the fecal matter (as Austin fastidiously phrased it) struck the fan. We were flaked out in our wet monkey suits under the pines trying to catch a breath of air, talking fitfully about our plans when the tour ended the following Sunday: some of us had gigs lined up; others would be scuffling again, an ever-renewing process.

Val had been unaccustomedly silent for some time, sitting with his back against a tree trunk, his face sunken in thought and weariness, staring out over the water. We'd been playing almost steadily since noon, so allowing for the supper break we were going on our tenth hour. Alvie came out looking at his watch and called in that mock-cheerful tone that by now worked on us like sandpaper, "Rounding the homestretch, Ducks, up and at 'em." Tubbo let out a weak "Qua-a-a-ck," we straggled to our feet, and that's when the material hit the blades. Val, instead of joining us, strolled casually down the incline to the side of the casino and rested his head and arms against the wall: it looked a little like the stance someone assumes when the cops are patting him down, except every bone in Val's body seemed to be sagging. Now this was the basement level of the casino, where there was a row of small dingy windows sloping from the deck in back to the front entrance. We started dragging ourselves in, some of us watching Val with varying degrees of curiosity and concern. Alvie turned and called, "Val, you coming?" And Val answered, his voice muffled but calm and matter-of-fact as if he'd been asked if he wanted to go for a swim or needed a lift into town, "No, I don't think so, Alvie." Alvie stopped dead in his tracks and called back, a tiny tremor to his voice, "What'd you say?" What Val did then was to push himself off the wall like a boxer pushing off his opponent, step back a short way, cock his right hand, and drive it clean through one of those little windows. It made the same pleasant, tinkling sound you hear when the wineglass gets smashed at a Jewish wedding. He held his hand up to his face—even in the semidark you could see the blood beginning to pump—and said in that same eerie calm tone, but with a tiny note of triumph or satisfaction in it, "Looks like I won't be playing any more horn tonight." We stood stock-still in a row like a dumbstruck Greek chorus when something goes wrong with the script.

"For goodness' sake, Valentine," Austin said in a breathy voice, and Shorty murmured, as if delivering an epitaph, "It's all part of the via dolorosa, boys, we're casualties on the road to truth." I shook myself out of it and started down the bank—slowly, trying to put off what I had to see. "Val, what'd you want to do a crazy thing like that for?" The hand looked like it had just come down off the cross. "We've got to find a doctor for this," I said. He watched his own blood drip onto the pine needles with a kind of detached interest and said, "I think your instinct is correct, man." I took out my handkerchief and wrapped the hand as best I could. We walked around to the front of the casino—Alvie's voice calling after us, "Onstage, let's go!"—and into the packed bar that was like a Dutch oven, people making way pretty good when they saw the blood-soaked cloth. One woman let out a stifled scream, her hand flying to her throat as if Godzilla himself had stepped off the silver screen onto the beautiful shores of Lake Laramee. I cupped my hands, calling as loudly as I could—despite the urgency, you feel kind of silly shouting a tag line in a crowd—"Is there a doctor in the house?" The head bartender worked his way through the crowd, glanced at the bloody handkerchief and said, "Oh boy oh boy." "Where's Margie?" I said. "Asleep. How'd it happen?" "It's complicated—where do we find a doctor?" "I'll scout around. I don't think our insurance covers that," he said over his shoulder. I hollered again for a doctor, my voice ringing idiotically in my ears. "I have some mercurochrome in my car," the lady who had screamed said, backing off. "I don't think we need any more red," Val told her. I was about to give it up and try in the casino when a small man in a rumpled Palm Beach suit pushed through and identified himself as a doctor. He unwrapped the handkerchief and said, "Looks like it went through a window." We were both impressed by the instant diagnosis. Val grinned wanly at me. "I think we're in good hands, man." My hand, I thought, I would have been sobbing like a baby. The doc told us to go into the john and wash it off while he fetched his bag from the car.

When he returned he examined the hand, said it could be worse, applied disinfectant and bandaged it with about ten yards of gauze and tape. "No more drinking tonight," he said, glancing briefly into Val's eyes, and told me to have someone look at the hand first thing in the morning, that it might need suturing. I said, "We've got three more hours of music to play." He looked at our outfits for the first time and asked, "What does he play?", putting the question to me as if Val weren't there at all or his brains were scrambled, which for the moment may not have been far from the truth. "Trumpet," I said. "Right-handed?" I nodded. Val was glancing interestedly back and forth between us. I watched the doc's right-hand fingers move at his side, depressing imaginary valves. "He can no more play the trumpet with that hand than he could run the hundred-yard dash with a broken ankle," he said, uncannily touching on Val's past glory. Then he closed up his bag and left the john before either of us could think of offering him money.

Val studied his hand, wrapped like a mummy's except for the fingertips sticking out, and said, "I could *try* playing"—having his regrets now, probably thinking of the impact on the rest of us as well as on his standing with Alvie. The tour was almost over—I couldn't help wondering if he would have indulged in so theatrical a gesture earlier in the summer; most likely he had closed the door on any future work with the Rhythm Ducks. I saw the slackness and exhaustion in his face now, the distant focus of the eyes, and told him to forget it, red valves weren't in style this year, and to go back to the cabin and sleep it off; I'd try to smooth things over with Alvie.

I pushed through the casino crowd stomping their feet and hollering for music, and told Alvie that Val wouldn't be coming back tonight. Before I could offer excuses—the sliced hand, the heat, the long day—he began fuming and sputtering about drunken musicians and prima donnas, his face under the snow-white hair twisted and an angry color like a dish of uncooked chicken livers. We started up again, reaching deep into our Roaring Twenties bag—"Toot Toot Tootsie," "Nobody's Sweetheart," "Mary Lou"—Alvie taking over Val's lead, which was like sending in a Little Leaguer to pinch-hit for

Ted Williams. It didn't much matter, what with the bedlam out front, but most of us half-consciously raised our volume so that Alvie would get drowned out in the general clamor. We were all pretty well wrecked by now and just honking away, trying to get the nightmare over with. We didn't know it at the time, but Godzilla wasn't through for the night—a second fright was in store. I was alerted first by a blast of sound ringing from the far end of the casino, then by Estelle breaking off with a kind of strangled cry in midvocal on "Back Home Again in Indiana" and pointing to the floor. Alvie turned, and his face collapsed like a bad cake.

Val had come back in wearing only his yellow bathrobe and was advancing through the crowd, horn canted to the rafters—the rolling, broad-bore tones meshing with the band—his fingers partly free of the bloody bandage, which was playing out like line off a fishing reel and trailing along the floor. A couple of women screamed seeing the gore, and people were shoving at each other, backing out of the way. It was a little like Moses, in the guise of Gabriel, coming through the Red Sea. There was a three-foot stone parapet separating the floor from the bandstand, stairs on one side. Val didn't bother with the stairs, vaulting onstage using his left (unbloodied) hand without dropping a beat, then advancing on the mike, prudently vacated by Estelle. His eyes swept briefly over me—the fire back in them, a crazed gleam tempered by a playful, flickering humor. The horn began to soar as he bent his knees and got his torso into it, a big dense shoulder of sound—Alvie, a confused half smile on his face, laying a gingerly hand on his arm ("Easy now, dad"), which Val flicked off, a muscle's reflex to a fly's landing, as people began yelling up from the floor to let him play. A few couples were still dancing, but most had pressed in toward the stand, suspecting they were hearing something they weren't likely to hear again—some perhaps less transfixed by the music than by the yellow robe and dusty bare feet and the flapping bloodstained bandage that danced around the stage with the movement of his body like a nervous snake molting.

With everyone laying out but piano, bass, and drums, Val entered his second chorus of "Indiana," and entered it grandly, a wayback, joyous belling of sound, layer on layer, a carillon that filled every chink in the room, bounced off the rafters and shook the joint. The pyrotechnics were formidable: broad, tumbling cascades of notes interspersed with leaping broken-field spurts (Val taking the 220 hurdles again in his die-hard imagination); it was showboating, no question of it, but showboating in a classic mode, with authority and license, all the proper credentials on display—sure, grand-tour performance, the drive and propulsion so irresistible all you could do was sit there with your mouth half-open and say to yourself, Goddam, what good music! . . . But maybe the wildest part of all was hearing that thrilling sound and realizing it was coming from a wounded, half-crazed, half-drunk, gifted artist in bare feet and a yellow bathrobe, and watching the grisly bandage whipping around with a life of its own in a frantic danse macabre.

"Catalona on a clearrrrr *day!*" shrieked Purvis with his moonstruck grin and a high shine of madness and glee in his pale eyes.

I stole a glance at Alvie. His expression was rapt, but it was a complicated face to read: Either he was caught up in the music and spectacle the same as everyone else, or he was temporarily paralyzed by this first-of-its-kind breakdown in his authority. He'd faced insubordination before, but nothing quite as dramatic or inspired, and had no tools for coping short of picking up a music stand and crashing it over Val's head. While this conceivable thought was crossing his mind, Shorty stealthily insinuated himself, the sinewy upper-register clarinet as spry and pesky as its player, skittering above, under, and around Val like a light-crazed moth circling a brass lampshade. Within moments trombone had followed suit—Chickie joining the renegade, disavowing his second-in-charge authority—the broad tailgate slide supplying foundation and springboard that, in union with the goad of Shorty's feisty clarinet, catapulted Val to new heights, the whole casino ringing like a big brass bell as he stormed into yet another chorus, setting off explosive cries from the floor . . . But not even Val's lip could hold out forever. His face and throat were slick with sweat, his eyes had a ragged shine as he flicked his glance to me, signaling he was ready to take it out. I signaled the others and Val banked the fires, the heat draining from his horn as swiftly and subtly as the warmth slipping from an autumn afternoon when the first shadows fall; the pitch dropped and the tone swelled, grew vibrant and smoky, and on the tune's plaintive closing bars a keening melancholy infused his horn, it slackened and softened—we softened with him—and drifted out of tempo, the beat imperceptibly melting away as he placed a jeweled cadenza into the space above the crowd, a dying fall of supple notes as precise and shining as the first pale stars in the evening sky.

The applause and shouts lifted below him as he matter-of-factly emptied his spit valve. At which point Alvie broke out of his trance and moved in. Smiling uncertainly (the same quizzical, wavering smile he'd conferred on the three-hundred-pound mortician who'd shuffled Estelle around the boards in Elmira), he placed a careful arm around Val's shoulder and tried to lead him offstage, the way you might handle a seriously disturbed person who has to be taken into custody because he could be endangering himself or others. Val shook him off—not angrily, but just as he had earlier, as you'd twitch your shoulders to shake off a gnat or fly—and something in the gesture stifled the applause. The crowd quieted, absorbed in the two men above them. (Mitch would say later that the abrupt silence was appropriate, that the mood was similar to what must have come down after Lincoln gave his famous address. I respectfully pointed out to him a few nonparallels, such as: Lincoln hadn't been wearing a yellow bathrobe or trailing a bloody bandage after him.) Val walked down the side stage stairs and onto the deck, not looking at anyone, a kind of far-off satisfied smile playing at the corners of his mouth as if he understood this was his swan song and he had carried it off in style—moving with that sure, limber, athlete's stride, a small swagger to it, while Tubbo supplied a humorous martial roll and rat-a-tat-tat. For a few choruses the booze had become pure fuel again, burned cleanly, leaving no residue but an honest, earned film of sweat; for a few choruses it had all come easy again, like a kid rolling a hoop or the pavement cracks reeling underfoot on the run home from school . . . *just like that.*

The last I saw of Val, beyond a shadowy glimpse at dawn, was the yellow robe and mucked-up bandage gliding off through the pine trees like the raiment of a valiant wounded ghost.

He wasn't in the cabin when Alvie came back with us at three-thirty, but his bag was packed and standing beside his bunk. "Looks like he's read my mind again," Alvie said.

It must have been just before dawn, the light gathering in the screened window, when I heard the cabin door open, and half waking saw a silhouette moving. "Val . . . ," I called, or thought I called; the door softly clicked shut . . . And just before drifting off again I heard a faint, sorrowful, not quite human sound that I thought at first must have come from Purvis in the bunk over me, snared in some unfathomable dream; but a far, still-wakeful corner of my mind told me it was much more distant—the desolate, piping, childlike cry of a loon.

It wasn't until late morning that I woke again and found the note on my blanket: "Can't hack it anymore so I guess that's it for the nonce. I was good last night. Val."

IT WAS A humdrum week without Val. Eat, play, sleep; watch the chicks on the dock. It was as if he had sucked all the band's energy out with him that final night. Alvie got a replacement up from Albany, a steady, dependable ex-studio player who read the charts as scrupulously as a CPA and blew careful, risk-free choruses.

We talked on and off of Val's farewell performance, agreeing that the "Indiana" choruses possessed some of the verve and magic of Berigan's choice solo work with Tommy Dorsey and even Bix's clarion excursions three decades earlier. Shorty said the trailing bandage had put him in mind of the crimson banners that unfurled from the horns of heraldic trumpeters in the Middle Ages, and Chickie said it evoked for him a vision of Isadora Duncan's scarf, which if nothing else served to emphasize the span of years separating Chickie from the rest of us.

One afternoon in midweek a half dozen of us drove to the race track at Saratoga Springs in the hearse. Mitch very nearly racked us up as he'd been threatening to do for months, screeching to a stop at a railroad crossing bare seconds before the barrier descended, scraping the hood, and a fifty-car freight train plowed past.

Purvis was the first to speak. "I just saw my whole family walkin' slow and singin' low behind me."

"You almost took us through the pearly gates that time, Mitchell," Austin said.

"Well, we got the right vehicle for it."

My heart still hung in my throat as we entered the outskirts of Saratoga Springs, where a gaudy illustrated billboard announced

PIPING ROCK INN

Sophie Tucker *Parisienne Follies*

In between races Shorty picked up an Albany paper, his attention caught by an article at the bottom of the front page: Entertainer Killed. We huddled around and read, "Comic-dancer Ollie Gayle, a notable Negro entertainer, was stabbed to death last night in a brawl outside Harvey's Paradise Lounge, where he had been headlining a show for the past week. Three unidentified men were reported fleeing the scene at approximately 1:55 A.M. Mr. Gayle, who was noted for his whistling prowess, had been on a tour of upstate theaters and show bars and was slated to appear on the Ed Sullivan Show in late September . . ."

"Maybe they asked him how he did the 'Bye Bye Blackbird' bit," Tubbo speculated, "and he wouldn't tell."

"That routine's locked in a permanent safe deposit box now," someone else said.

I remembered Val trying to bribe him in the alley behind Loews Theater, envisioning the killing he could make in Fall River.

"Maybe he'll come back as a bird," Purvis said.

We all lost money except Austin, who didn't bet, and on the drive back saw—strung like glorious sentinels along the roadway—a scattering of statuesque showgirls with lifted skirts: the cast of the Piping Rock Inn's "Parisienne Follies," I guessed, parted from their week's wages and catching rides back to town.

We watched their smiles fade as our dusty, battered black hearse approached, their thumbs wavering and skirts drooping like becalmed flags.

The next day a postcard from North Conway, New Hampshire, arrived at the casino. "Cooking up a storm and blowing occasional gigs," it said, and along the bottom and up one side was a pencil sketch of a highway winding between barren hills. A signpost at the far left said "Elmira," and the highway trailed off to a mere ribbon along the side, disappearing into a shadowy mass, an outline of looming city towers, perhaps, or a formation of peaked clouds—it was difficult to make out. The card was signed "Lookin down that lonesome road, Nelly."

On Saturday I asked Margie where Mrs. Danvers, my civilized martini-swilling friend from the Happy Hour, was. I missed her attentions and solicitude, the courtly way she blew kisses from her fingertips to me at the close of the afternoon, and her sorrow that the world seemed to be ruled by philistines; she had promised to return by midweek, but I imagined that her mortifying exit that last afternoon may have caused her to change her plans.

"Oh, she won't be back," Margie said.

"She told me she had urgent business in the city."

Margie gave me an odd, glancing look. "I suppose she also told you about her dreadful divorce, kids running wild—one in a reformatory—lawyers gouging her?"

I nodded, recalling that wandering impassioned outburst.

"She's never been married. She's the sister of my attorney. You wouldn't guess she's spent the last three years in the nuthouse, would you?"

SUNDAY WE PLAYED our final Roaring Twenties night. Employees in gangland costume, flaunting their cardboard tommyguns, simulated a raid, two hundred balloons dropped from the rafters and exploded like a prolonged Gatling-gun burst, and the summer was over. I had planned to take the boat out to see one more of those majestic sunrises, but just after midnight it began drizzling, and a quiet soaking rain continued into morning. In the impenetrable mountain darkness, listening to the dripping branches and eaves, I thought of Val coming awake in Fall River, wondering whether it was twilight or dawn.

By noon we were packed. Tubbo put down a double lunch for Zero in the canteen, slipping the short-order cook a few bucks to ensure his being fed at least through mid-September when the resort closed, and our little caravan took off on the wet macadam under low, shifting clouds for Providence (the most misnamed town in America, Val once said).

"Here we go again, folks," Shorty spieled, "the big boat ride on the River of No Return." Some of us would disembark in Albany and go our separate ways. And some of us during the lean weeks ahead would, in Chickie's phrase, be eating the berries off the wallpaper. Alvie told us he had signed a contract with Margie for the entire month of August the following year, and "God willing" we'd all see one another again.

Heading south on Route 9 Mitch's foot turned brutal on the accelerator, his fist pounded the steering wheel. "I'm gonna destroy this sucker—once and for all!"

As we crossed the Mohawk River a few miles outside Albany the color left Shorty's face, and he fell back against his seat as if slammed in the chest by a giant invisible hand. His cherished talisman and fount of inspiration, the proud tattered Stars and Bars, was still tacked to the pineboard cabin wall on the lyrical shores of Lake Laramee.

IN BOSTON I resumed my studies in piano, theory, and composition (if I wasn't destined to be an Art Tatum or Bill Evans, and the portents were growing every day, then I would be in need of backup talents) and played club dates in the area. It's easier for a pianist: there's always solo work—the cocktail lounges and piano bars, if you have the stomach for them.

Val had been on my mind; I had given his name to several Boston contractors looking for lead trumpet players. We had talked about getting together after the tour, and I had been meaning to call him but kept putting it off. Another foreboding perhaps. Finally, in mid-October, I phoned.

"That's strange, man, I been thinking of calling you."

"How're you doing?"

"Fine. Okay, except my head's bandaged."

"Your head?"

"You aren't going to believe this but I was coldcocked by a gate in a bank parking lot. I'd parked my short and was walking back through the entrance. Another car must have just come in, and the gate, you know, descends each time. I never saw the sucker. Next thing I'm on my ass with stars in my eyes. I got a lawyer working on it."

"Then you weren't seriously hurt? . . ."

"Just an egg on my head and a few residual stars is all."

"I got your note the night you left. You were right, you played good."

"Yuh, you might say I rose to the occasion." I could see him smile, the remembering light in his eyes.

"The guys talked about it for days afterward. Where were you from the time you split the casino until you came back for your bag?"

"I took the boat out and goofed around. Waiting for the sunrise like the rest of the world."

"I was half-asleep when you came in. I called to you but you didn't hear me."

"That's the story of my life, man."

I took a breath and said, "Are you working?" knowing he would have already told me if he were. "I gave your name to some people up here."

"I've called a few cats here and in Providence, but they've heard about the, ahem, problem. I'll tell you, man, there's a vicious grapevine operating. I wouldn't be surprised if Duckhead [Alvie] leaked word about my sign-off at the lake. The stigma's wrapped around my neck now like a wet noose."

He was hardly exaggerating. The contractors I had spoken to who had heard of him responded in almost identical fashion: "Last I heard he was hitting the jug pretty hard."

"So why don't you cut down?" I said, and got the answer I deserved.

"Why don't birds fly in a T? Even the times I've been on the wagon and tried to pass the good tidings around, the melody lingers on. Meanwhile it's Checker time."

"What?"

"I'm driving a cab—buddy of mine owns a half interest in a company. Just for a couple weeks till things pick up. Believe me, it's no worse than playing thirty choruses of 'Hava Nagila' in a synagogue basement and they're pouring only Mogen David . . . Hey, I heard the Detroit Symphony here last week. There was a solo pianist, famous cat, Argentine, I can't think of his name. He played a Brahms concerto the program said he'd played a hundred or so times, and, man, there was one passage that was like a blizzard of flubbed notes—I mean clinkers dropping like change out of a wino's pocket. It made me wonder how one of these wizard cats who's taken a year to master a piece, turned it inside out and stuck it in his back pocket, can still clam during a performance. I've been giving it a lot of thought and

I think I've come up with an answer. They have time to get *nervous.* They think, uh-oh, here it comes, the string of sixty-fourth notes or the left-hand four-bar trill—maybe they had a heavy lunch that didn't set quite right, the stock market took a dive, the old lady phoned from Palm Springs that Archie the dog got the mange—their concentration wavers for a split second, they blow it and there's no recovering. It just lays there, Deadwood, South Dakota. But when *we* solo we're thinking the stuff virtually at the same time we play it, so we don't have time to get nervous. And even when we're feeling frisky and taking risks that maybe we shouldn't be taking—like I said that night out on the lake, if you're in control and got your wits about you, you can see the goof coming and throw a hand up, deflect it, even turn it to advantage. Anyway, I thought of some problems I was having in that respect, and hearing this cat made me feel better—But listen, I'm running on and this is costing loot . . ."

"Ollie Gayle got killed," I blurted, wanting to prolong the call.

"Who?"

"The comic in Reading. 'Bye Bye Blackbird' in three parts."

"Oh, that dude. Well, life and talent are cheap, man. I was thinking today, musicians and entertainers are like athletes or cabbies or anyone else. We're all after the same things—perfection, fame, loot, fantastic chicks. Own a Caddie, shack up in a mansion. Like I used to hope a record company president would come through the club door. Driving a hack, you hope Sinatra or a TV scout or Gina Lollobrigida will flag you down—don't ask me what those people would be doing in Fall River—and you make a few right moves and score . . . But I'm sorry about that spade. Lots of good cats are either scuffling or keeling. Fortunately there's longevity in my family. I still do some running, try to keep in shape. The days are getting cooler, though . . ."

My mind darted to the motel terrace alongside the highway in Utica. A golden summer morning. Val crouched on the road's shoulder, butt high, fingers splayed—then loosing an exultant cry in the air like some joyful, delirious songbird and sprinting for dear life down the macadam, legs blithely scissoring, taking the 220 hurdles in memory, the cheers crowding his imagination, roaring in his ears. That's how I wanted to remember him, the Fall River Flash at the top of his bent, in his prime on a very clear day hurtling down some sleepy early-morning roadway *just like that*, nothing but blue skies, green leas ahead . . .

I shook my head to clear it of another vision—indistinct, oppressive, taking shape down a dwindling avenue of years—and said quickly, inconsequentially, "How's the hand, by the way?"

"What hand?"

"The one you put through the casino window."

"Oh, fine. Funny . . . the things that slip your mind."

15

I read that Art Tatum was booked into New York on Fifty-second Street, that close-packed strip of canopied bandboxes that had long been a mecca for jazz musicians and fans and would in time acquire the dimensions of myth. Whenever the master was within a half day's driving distance I found myself irresistibly drawn. By now the bebop revolution was in full throttle, but it did not interest or deter Tatum; he went his own godlike way. His renown was international and his artistry had reached supernal heights. Pianists tried like mad to mimic him and fell back gasping. The notes could be superficially duplicated, lifted with enormous difficulty from records and read off transcriptions, but the velocity and verve and soul were missing. Cavalier critics launched flea-bite attacks on the fortress of his style: the music could not breathe, he inundated the keyboard with florid geysers of notes. Never!—not for my money. I was thirst-crazed, insatiable. You play what you hear, and he heard more than any of us, a universe of sound, purls, and shouts.

At the Three Deuces I wanted badly to speak to him, to tell him, without fawning, that he had filled my life to brimming with his magic; to hear his voice (the *other* voice, suspecting it would be as earthbound as the music was ethereal); to look at the hands close up (I had heard he sensitized his fingers by constantly working through them a particular-sized filbert). I could not gather the nerve. How do you approach a deity?

It was after two in the morning, the final set just finished. As I was agonizing, he rose wearily from the bench and turned toward the back room. A girl at the table behind me was suddenly galvanized. She was about eighteen, dark curls under a beret, her face flushed with the joy of what she'd heard. She was pushing toward the bandstand against the flow of departing customers.

"Mr. Art . . . Mr. Tatum," she called, her eyes glittering with excitement. I imagined her an aspiring concert pianist, studying at Julliard, making her pilgrimage from that other world. He turned slowly, gazing around, up, sight only in the corner of one eye, the heavy face gleaming with sweat. The girl stopped a few feet from him. She caught her breath. She said, "I wanted you to know . . . You do it better than anyone does it!"

Yes, that was what I had wanted to say.

A few years later, when I heard on a newscast that he had died of uremia at forty-six, I thought, How can it be? The loss was stupefying, too much to bear. Such a talent comes along once in a century. And I wondered what there is about the music that strikes some so early and exacts such a terrible toll. Charlie Parker had bowed out at thirty-four the previous year, and in the coming decades more young giants (Wes Montgomery, John Coltrane, Hampton Hawes) would fall, barely into the summertime of their lives. Our brothers on the other side, the Horowitzes, Heifetzes, and Rubinsteins, seem to endure into their ninth and tenth decades. Is it the tensions implicit in the more spontaneous, less contained craft—perilous improvisational swings out to the edge—that dictate a baleful lifestyle? Something pernicious slipped into our mothers' milk, as the Boston critic had suggested to me? Or simply the saloon stamping grounds offering temptations not afforded by the concert hall?

Pianists keep trying to capture Tatum's elusive pulse, simulate the daring trapeze work, tune into the grave. We weep at his early departure and are joyous he came our way. He led us a merry chase, this lionheart roaring down the Route 66 of American classical music, and his death put permanent distance between us.

But there are rare moments during the rendering of compositions associated with him—"Yesterdays," "Sweet Lorraine"—when a curious vibrancy charges us, and for a half chorus or so we take wing, soaring above our land-bound selves. A new dimension, an altered emotional and rhythmic edge enter our playing. We interpret pieces in a way and with a spirit we never have before. We can't explain it, even to ourselves. It's as if there is the breath of someone else in us.

MY LAST GIG in the Boston area was probably the longest night of my career, surpassing in both longevity and angst the nefarious Chinatown lawn party. I was booked for the month of December as a single at the Terrace Bar and Grill. Business had been slow from the start and turned dismal during Christmas week. Victor, the boss—a pudgy sad-eyed man who looked a decade older than his thirty-five years and had inherited the restaurant-club from his father the previous spring—was glummer than usual and kept making nervous, hackneyed jokes to the employees: "One more couple and we can play four-handed pinochle . . . Anyone looking to make a few bucks tomorrow night bring a five-gallon can of gas and a book of matches." He reminded me a lot of Morty Gelb, the proprietor of the Foxes and Hounds on the Worcester–Boston road—the same gallows humor and mournful, self-defeating air; I was beginning to think it was characteristic of club owners. Victor apparently owned but one suit, a heavy-duty, drab, gray number that retained its sharp creases through night-in-night-out wear and tear, and that he wore with a viciously knotted crimson tie pulled askew. I thought of him, in a lugubrious way, as the Man in the Iron Suit. On Christmas Day he took out a newspaper ad: "New Year's Eve Gala. Ring in the Year with Cocktails and Choice Cuisine in a Select Atmosphere. Dancing to the Don Asher Trio. Noisemakers." Victor took it upon himself to provide me with a horn player and drummer. The inadvertent juxtaposition of the ad's final word would prove prophetic.

New Year's Eve affects the musician and the reveler in contrary ways: The patrons' growing excitement as the clock hands march toward twelve is the musician's relieved awareness that the job is mercifully nearing an end; their nostalgia and sentimentality match his apathy and indifference; and as the melancholy strains of "Auld Lang Syne" ring out he experiences an ennui tinged with annoyance at having once again to pound out innumerable choruses of that bulky, graceless refrain. Mingled feelings of compassion and dismay overtake him as he observes the solitary couples in their best suits and dresses, paper hats at a jaunty angle, nursing watery highballs and flat champagne, watching their watches, waiting, waiting, the plaintive bray of noisemakers signaling a dwindling of conversation. The prime ribs and filet mignon and fresh champagne-for-two arrive at eleven o'clock, and the frequency and fervor of the dancing pick up. Finally the magical minutes of countdown before the hour strikes the anvil—then the bright balloons released like fabulous soap bubbles and the fleeting moments of tumult and elation on a heavy stomach and a light head like a rushed orgasm on the heels of an uninteresting buildup.

Though an integral part of the activity, we feel ourselves actually outside it (and are pleased to be), as the veteran captain of a cruise ship functions outside what must appear to him the organized, ritualistic, and hence synthetic pleasures of his passengers. Two benefits do accrue to us on this longest night of the year: Union scale is considerably higher than on any other night, and as demand invariably exceeds supply everyone gets to work, from the old-time palsied trap-drummers with illustrations of exotic sunsets on their bass drums to the rankest amateur capable of playing a C Major fanfare without dropping his horn. But for the professional thrown in with such a motley of neophytes and hacks, it can be a night when every tune takes on the timbre and cadence of "Wagon Wheels."

I had caught cold shortly after Christmas and then lost or misplaced my only pair of gloves, adding to the burden of the cheerless week. On top of which my funds were precariously low, depleted by a valve job on the Studebaker and the purchase of a new tux. I kept hoping the gloves would show up. My unprotected hands began to chap in the freezing weather, and soon the skin was cracking and shredding around the nails where the constant snagging on the ragged Terrace Bar and Grill ivories had opened tiny fissures. It became painful to play. I took to soaking my hands in warm salt water before sets and wrapping the sorest fingertips in Band-Aids. It was time to dig into my last few dollars—with business as brutal as it was I dared not ask Victor for an advance—and replace the gloves. In a department-store basement two days before the New Year I was rummaging through a display of mixed lots when my eye caught something intriguing on the adjacent women's table: a sale of fur muffs. I remembered an account I had read of European concert pianists who arrived for recitals during the icy fall and winter seasons with their hands snugly ensconced in these sensible accessories; one was a world-famous Russian, whose muff was electrically heated and discarded only moments before he stepped onstage. I bought the cheapest one, a rather ratty-looking job with a rabbit's-foot tassel hanging from the zipper. A half hour later I was picking up my key at the desk of the residential hotel where I was staying (I'd had to give up my apartment when I joined Alvie) when a stout man with a briefcase, checking in, glanced sidelong at my green Alpine hat, then at the muff. He grinned at the clerk and leaned forward, shielding his mouth with his hand but speaking quite loudly, "Put me anywhere but on this guy's floor. If that isn't possible, make sure I have a double-bolt lock." Slowly turning, he cocked his head at a sly angle and gave me an exaggerated wink.

That night, leaving the parking garage and walking to the club through the bone-chilling cold—imagining that I was the renowned Russian strolling to the Concertegebouw in Amsterdam and that the muff was sable and electrically heated—a passing elderly man in thin shoes and a fur-collared coat smiled coyly at me and said, "Hello, dear." The next day I exchanged the muff for a pair of knitted gloves.

It began to snow on the afternoon of the big evening—the second storm of the week—tapering off around dusk. Victor had waited too long to hire auxiliary musicians. The best he could come up with were a semiretired former vaudeville drummer in his late sixties (the sergeant-at-arms of the union local) and his trumpet-playing nephew, whose total professional experience consisted of eighteen months with his high-school marching band.

By quarter to nine the room was not quite two-thirds full, well below expectations. As the drummer (in a moth-eaten tuxedo and brown loafers) set up, Victor stood by the bandstand, wringing his hands, awaiting last-minute reservations that would not materialize. My cold had worsened; Victor forlornly watched me blow my nose into a cocktail napkin and said (as Morty Gelb had remarked on a parallel occasion ten years earlier), "I'm the one should be weeping."

The music began: it was an acute embarrassment. Gary, the high-school kid, knew but a handful of standards that we had to keep repeating, camouflaging the tune each time around, at my suggestion, in a different rhythm. Thus "Jeepers Creepers" became alternately rumba, waltz, beguine, samba. It was a reprise of my Blue Marlin days; you like to think you've left those Cro-Magnon times behind. Gary kept a tight mute in his horn—also at my behest—to soften the clinkers that dropped in every bar like jelly beans spewing from a malfunctioning vending machine. His uncle used a maximum of cowbell and woodblock, regardless of the character of the tune, as if he were accompanying a dog act or livestock show, both of which he had undoubtedly been exposed to during his active years. At 10:15 a party of six told Victor the band was "unlistenable, undanceable, and unprofessional" and, as they were leaving before dinner, demanded a refund. During a break Victor said with a tight smile to the union sergeant-at-arms drummer, "You guys are costing me my shirt. Can I bring you before your own board?" The drummer removed his soggy cigar and tapped ashes onto the floor. "There's no precedent for it." The bartender from whom I ordered—entreated—a double brandy said, in the way bartenders have of adopting their employers' locutions, "I've heard of bands packing 'em in before but never one that packs 'em out." "Do you know what I'd rather be doing than this?" I said to him and sifted through a number of possibilities, settling on the occupation of the hard-luck father of a junior-high classmate of mine, whose part-time gig had taken him three mornings a week, attired in overalls and fisherman's boots, to the county dump, where he spread dirt on festering mounds of garbage.

We tried "My Blue Heaven" as a waltz; my sense of meter should have told me in front it wouldn't work. My eyes were streaming from the smoke and my throat felt as if I'd unsuccessfully swallowed a cupful of ground glass. But exceeding the physical discomfort was the abject knowledge that this Spike Jones–in–earnest parody of music was a profanation of my heritage and far worse than no music at all. Two more parties departed early, and at eleven bells a well-done roast beef/baked spud dinner was served. Throughout the meal Victor made repeated trips to the bandstand exhorting us to "Pep it up, pep it up!"—the club owner's traditional rationale, which equates fast tempos with perspiring dancers with an immoderate desire for cooling, high-proof beverages. Resorting to a dwindling stack of cocktail napkins, I periodically lifted my right hand from the keyboard to wipe my eyes and blow my nose, striving to sustain a bass continuity in rough approximation of the fabled Harlem rent-party stride pianists of yore, whose heroic left-hand facility enabled them to chew a pig's foot or slug down a brew without missing a beat.

Finally, blessedly, the dessert plates were cleared, coffee was served, and the lights dimmed. I said to Gary, "You're sure you know 'Auld Lang Syne'?" He assured me again that he did. "You'll have to take out the mute," I said apprehensively. Six dozen balloons dropped from the rafters, Victor shouted hoarsely in my ear "Now!" and a sustained barrage of noisemakers commenced like a furious herd of lowing cattle, mingling with lusty halloos, rebel yells, and someone barking insanely over it all like a crazed seal. As we pounded chorus after chorus of the midnight anthem, Gary's spent lip clamming notes with the regularity of an Ethiopian slave beating a gong, couples lurched about the floor in death-grip bear hugs, mouth to mouth—their monstrous shadows whooshing around the walls like Neanderthals cavorting in firelit caves—yet somehow the noisemakers maintained their racketing din and the seal-person never let up his or her deranged barking. Cigarette ends skittered like glowflies through the darkness, and a new staccato sound now layered itself into the dissonance—the machine-gun crackle of punctured balloons. A burly cask of a man in a houndstooth jacket, whipping a birdlike woman around the floor, caromed off the piano and crashed into me, knocking me from my stool as neatly as a clay pigeon banged off a shelf—and swung away, oblivious. (I have always suspected that there exists a class of people who consider musicians as functional furniture—that is, they fail to distinguish the instrument from its operator—and a collision with the piano-pianist produces no more neural reaction or inclination toward apology than if the person had bumped into a coatrack, booth fixture, or bus table.) I sat on the floor where I'd landed, head reeling, elbows on knees, the toy-soldier rattle of drums and tinny, ridiculous trumpet above me scarcely making a dent in the dense vortex of noise. And it was then that I understood something definitive about the musical essence of these annual witching-hour rites: it made not a particle of difference that my hands were holding my head and were not a foot higher, pumping ivory. I reached up for another cocktail napkin. The evening was beyond redemption.

AN HOUR LATER I sat in the back office while Victor opened the safe and removed a metal cash box. My four-week engagement was at a close; the contract stipulated a two-week option, which Victor, needless to say, declined to pick up.

"When my old man passed the business on to me," he said, easing into the cracked-leather chair behind the desk, "he failed to mention that involuntary bloodletting went along with the responsibility."

My head was pounding with the vestiges of the anvil chorus and what I was sure was by now a raging fever. I regarded him compassionately from red swollen eyes. "You would have been better off with me alone tonight."

"I tumbled to that early in the evening, but in this town when a high-up union guy books himself into your place for a one-nighter you go along with it." He unlocked the metal box with a sigh and lifted the lid. "What's an intelligent kid like you doing in this dumb business anyway?" he said from the vantage of five years' seniority.

"Applause, bright lights, free days," I said. "A good-looking chick once in a while asking me for a pretty ballad."

Victor began counting out my last two weeks' wages in worn one- and five-dollar bills. It took the better part of ten minutes: I had to stuff the limp currency into three separate pockets among the sodden cocktail napkins.

Outside, a muffled barrage erupted like the clamor of a distant war: some confused celebrant setting off firecrackers in the snow.

PART FOUR

SHINING CITY

16

A Boston-based restaurateur with West Coast connections, who had heard me at several of the Yellin-booked Back Bay parties, was moving his operations to San Francisco.

"Come on out and play for me," he said. "It's a party town. Your tips will be bountiful and you'll drink and dine like a king."

"What kind of music would you want?"

"I'm calling the first place Casablanca. Ceiling blade fans and Persian rugs. Blowups of Bogie and Bergman and Dooley Wilson. Continental cuisine. A small white piano. You get the picture."

"The good old songs, then."

"Of course."

"Too bad I'm not black—and my name's not Sam."

"In my middle years I've learned to make accommodations."

There was nothing to hold me in the East. One thing about making a living as a piano player, the only requisite is a concentration of hotels, restaurants, country clubs, and bars. Deposit your union card, sit in around town, have a few belts with the boys. And if your credentials are in order, as sure as tadpoles emerge from the toad mother's mouth the grapevine will do its invisible work and jobs will materialize. So even if the Casablanca didn't work out—the wrong-named, wrong-colored guy playing the white piano—other lanes were bound to open. I wouldn't be going off the bridge.

Tales of the hoyden queen dowager city had infiltrated my childhood and adolescence. Gold. Romance. Caruso at the Palace. Foghorns in the night. Treasure Island. Flower Drum Song. Jacks London and Kerouac . . . Columnist Herb Caen had dubbed it Baghdad by the Bay, and on rare days when the temperature dared to rise above eighty, streams of cooling fog poured through the bridge towers like chilled chardonnay.

I sold my Studebaker to Duke Goldman and told the restaurateur, Charles, "I'll play your small white piano."

I DON'T INTEND to write a travelogue of San Francisco; it's been done. Except to say it's a white high-up city that shines with a watery light, and the living is bracing and easy. Also it shares with Worcester a conspicuous topographical feature: both are constructed on seven basic hills.

My second day in town I phoned a former Boston musician whose number had been given me by a mutual friend. Oscar was a gifted arranger and guitarist and had played with me the night I got slapped by the corporal in dress uniform. As he was my sole contact on this side of the continent, other than the Casablanca proprietor, I eagerly looked forward to seeing him. He invited me to drop by his place late the next morning. His voice on the phone sounded languid and incurious, which was strange; he'd been a gung-ho, no-time-to-waste, suit-and-tie kind of kid in Boston. In a small, stucco hillside building I found his name (one of six) in a rank and cluttered lobby, climbed to the second floor, and knocked on door number 3. "Come," a voice sounded somnolently from within. The room was square and barren, the walls calcimined; no other doors led from it. Oscar was bare-chested, in drawstring pants, seated yogi fashion on the bare wood floor. An open cigar box reposed at his side. In truth, I recognized only his nose, a distinctively sharp and narrow prow. A scarecrow's strawlike hair fell over his ears; long, wispy chin whiskers were inexplicably tied with a yellow rubber band. He had never been robust, but his thinness now was startling, the collarbone riding his sorry chest cavity like miniature moose antlers. From his gray eyes came a strange gleam, a micalike sheen. Well, I thought, it's supposed to be a partying town . . .

We talked for five minutes and came not even close to rational discourse. It was almost noon and I suggested we go out for lunch. He said in his drowsy unfamiliar voice that he had already eaten, indicating by the merest nod of his head the cigar box alongside his thigh. As politely as I could—I was leaning against a wall all this time—I craned my neck for a view of the contents. I think it was birdseed. During two subsequent encounters with Oscar, on a street and in a park, I observed nothing that would alter this impression.

ONE DRAWBACK I had not anticipated in working a restaurant tagged with the Casablanca cachet: "As Time Goes By" would be requested a dozen and more times a night—often after I'd immediately finished playing it. It is one of those tunes that everyone adores but musicians. The meter is hobbled and the harmonic structure unwieldy—there's little you can do with it in the way of embellishment. Other beloved tunes musicians generally dislike are "The Impossible Dream," "When the Saints Go Marching In," "Bill Bailey," "New York, New York" (ricky-tick), "Tie a Yellow Ribbon 'Round the Ole Oak Tree," and "Mack the Knife." Conversely, people will often apologize when requesting songs that they imagine musicians will consider hopelessly cornball or sentimental, an insult to their sensibilities—"Someday My Prince Will Come" or "Over the Rainbow" ("Would you mind terribly? It's for my husband, his birthday"); and the seasonal standards, "Easter Parade" and "Santa Claus Is Coming to Town." But musicians love to play these tunes. The melodies lift and dance, the flexible chord changes intrigue; there is space in which to breathe and embroider—though I can never play "Rainbow" without remembering what a mortician in Elmira told me: the old Garland weeper is by far the favorite selection at cat and dog funerals. (The Grand Guignol of all requests, if request it was, occurred at the funeral of the mother of country-rock singer Hank Williams, Jr., when a colleague of Williams stood over the open coffin singing "Hey, Good Lookin'.")

But "As Time Goes By"—to this day the tune's mystique and staying power mystify me. It is the Maria Ouspenskaya of popular song. People ask for it with smiling, fatuous expressions on their faces. They call me Sam and command me to—I wince in expectation and silently implore them to desist—"play it again" (though Bogart never said "*again*"). A resonant hush falls over the room as the first strains unfold; wives nudge husbands and lovers lovers; ecstatic whispers and rapturous looks are exchanged. Of course the movie holds up remarkably well, and the restaurant's re-creation in lighting and appointments helps fuse wistfulness to fond memory. If only the theme song had the lilt and grace of "Long Ago and Far Away" or "All the Things You Are," I would happily, indefatigably repeat chorus after chorus into the lilac dawn.

Tourists, cosmopolites, middle- and upper-Americans, the civil and the mean-spirited beat a nightly path across the sumptuous rugs to the white spinet with its brandy-snifter tip receptacle. A dollar, more or less, for dreams reproduced or fashioned like new; a green offering to quicken the foolish heart.

"I can tell from your cultivated expression," said the ruddy-faced man with the bandido's mustache, popping a bill in the glass, "that you must know 'Roses of Picardy.' " His voice was heavy with drink, but he had a look about him of intelligence and humor. I said that I hadn't played that tune in almost ten years, that I feared I would stumble on it, and suggested, since he had already fed the kitty, that he supply me with an alternative. His eyes flared, he glowered at me; he leaned over the piano and shouted in my face, "There *is* no alternative—it's 'ROSES OF PICARDY' OR DEATH!" I played it, stumbling all the way; my volatile friend smiled distantly and raised his glass to me. On his way out a half hour later—it had been a restrained evening with little conversation or response to the music—he dropped another dollar in the glass and said, "The only way you're gonna get a rise out of this crowd is to strip to your shorts and parade around the tables playing 'I'm a Ding-Dong Daddy' on a Jew's harp." Like the quarks of physics, bar-restaurant clientele can prove both strange and charmed.

When I first started playing solo and received a request whose title rang a bell but whose melody eluded me, I would ask how the tune went. This is a mistake. There is no way you're going to get an idea of a melody from a nonmusician who hums or sings a few bars; what you get is an approximation of Tourette's syndrome, a rare and curious ailment wherein the victim twitches, grunts, and barks. To say flatly you do not know the tune is an occasion for disbelief: "Of course you do—" followed by the indecipherable grunts and barks. The only way out is to suggest an alternative (at risk of death) or, if the request is formidable—say, "Liebestraum" or "Minute Waltz"—to equivocate, "That's one I don't know without the music—it's in my piano bench at home. I'll remember to bring it next time." "But you don't need the music, it goes like this—" I suppose the reason a person will accept the lawyer's or accountant's evasion, "I don't have the figures at my fingertips, but I'll get back to you," but not the pianist's prevarication has to do with the immediacy of gratification:

the food is on the table, the wine is flowing, the lover is waiting, shadowed in candlelight, across the room.

Most nights at the Casablanca I played a set of ragtime pieces. I love the Joplin rags, have put in a lot of time on them, and feel I play them with authenticity. The week following the "Picardy" death threat an elegantly coiffed woman in her fifties approached just after I'd finished "Maple Leaf Rag." She said, "I made a bet with my boyfriend that that was 'Chopsticks' you just played—or a souped-up version of it." "Which way did you bet?" I said. "I say it's 'Chopsticks,' " she said. "You lose," I said. Was this a quirk of mind, I wondered later, or a hopeless tin ear? If I had played Gershwin's "Fascinating Rhythm" might she have confused it with "Too Fat Polka"? Would "Malagueña" have merged with "Indian Love Call" in the labyrinths of her cochlea?

A straight male solo pianist working in San Francisco and not looking for offbeat involvement should be alert to the immaculately groomed middle-aged man with hand-carved or gold-headed cane and a passionate love of vintage show tunes. Morton DeVere had flaxen hair, wore tailored suits and monogrammed striped shirts and carried a slender cane with an intricately carved head, which he hooked on the piano whenever he pulled a chair alongside me. (His strong resemblance to a former film star drove me mad for a week until the look-alike appeared fortuitously on my TV screen early one morning in "Foreign Correspondent": my mother's old heart throb and brother Herbie's namesake, Herbert "Bart" Marshall.)

"Your music is an unexpected treat, particularly the version of 'I Concentrate on You.' I cannot get enough of Cole Porter. He is mother's milk to me, mother's milk. If you feel the urge come on you, anything else by him will not go unappreciated."

"I know a lot of Porter. Just a matter of jogging my memory. I'll do another medley next set."

"You're exceedingly kind. I couldn't help noticing the tablecloths—for comfort's sake, I presume."

"I prefer to sit up high when I play." Restaurant linen, I had discovered, because of its folding potential, provides a more adaptable perch than pillows.

"Up high when you play. Ah! . . ."

And so on, as my hands let go of the melody and ran their secure holding patterns. He was a regular patron, I couldn't very well shun him. I know very few pianists who are capable of playing and talking at the same time; I've often wished I could invent a counterpart to trumpeter Hal Harganian's synchronous maneuver. It's a strange thing: I can be playing a tune I've played a thousand times—"My Romance," whose impeccable melody is as ingrained in me as the way I move and smile—and if someone attempts to talk to me, even a simple request requiring but a "yes" or "sorry," I immediately lose my way and the melody under my fingers trails off into a series of meandering runs or random chords. If I'm in a room where a pianist is performing I can always tell, even blocked from his view, when someone is trying to converse with him: the rhythmic structure instantly collapses, the melody fades and runs every which way like molasses on a hot stove. A semblance of music still emerges, for pianists and guitarists—by virtue of their many strings—are able to dissemble, covering the lost melodic tracks with aimless chord progressions and arpeggios. And we take solace in the knowledge that most patrons of restaurants and non-sing-along bars are according us but a fraction of their attention. (Some old-time piano-bar masters develop the hand-mouth facility—a kind of verbal dexterity—after long experience. On my way to work I would occasionally drop into the Geary Street bars on the edge of the Tenderloin and marvel at the pianist's ability to carry on an articulate conversation about a horse race or ball game and simultaneously play strong, defined melody; or, even more impressive, to play melody with one hand and conduct a singalong with the other, cuing the patrons on the lyrics a half bar in front like Ray Bolger in "Once in Love with Amy.")

Morton fed the tip glass with embarrassing generosity and frequency and would usually be waiting for me at the bar during breaks. He told me a little of his life—mornings spent looking after investments in a downtown office ("Unconscionable amount of paperwork, damned nuisance")—and divulged a deep, dark family secret: a sister who had gone to college in Tennessee and married a mulatto dentist. "Imagine my lily white sis drilled by an artisan of that persuasion," he remarked, smiling his dry, effete Bart Marshall smile, fingers fussing with the rim of a brandy-alexander glass. He paid me effusive compliments: "To the Duchin of the Casablanca," raising his glass; and when I refused his repeated offers of a drink (urging him to save his money, as I drank free), he'd often tuck a bill of sizable denomination in my suit-coat pocket, overriding my protests: "Nonsense, I rarely get to hear the master played so sensitively—I don't want to hear anything more about it. If he were here I'm sure he would want to sweep you off to his Manhattan town house for a sumptuous evening!"

"That's an offer I wouldn't turn down."

"I should say! I knew Cole slightly. He was two classes ahead of me at Yale. You know he—"

"What was he like?"

"Elfin, gracious, ebullient, charming. You know, of course, he wrote the famous fight song . . . 'Bulldog, bulldog, bow wow wow—' " Morton sang the refrain loudly and tremulously, balled fist rhythmically drumming the bar, his face suddenly roseate.

I wondered about the cane—if it were mere affectation, since he seemed physically sound, or mimicry of his fellow alumnus and idol, who, I recalled, was never without one following grievous injury to his legs in a horseback-riding accident. (I had once seen a news photo of him: an impish, tuxedoed man being carried throne-style into a theater for one of his openings; his expression, frozen in flashbulb's glare, was a grimace of mingled glee and pain.)

Of course I knew what Morton's game was (Worcester isn't *that* parochial), but I didn't contemplate having to pay the piper. I didn't feel I was stringing him along. He was a steady and valued customer; I thought he'd be content listening to Porter, conversing, feeding the kitty (a largess I admit I didn't want to see cut off). Above all, I assumed he was aware of my persuasion, to use his word, as I had made a point several times of remarking on a female customer's attractiveness, silken hair, luminous eyes, zaftig figure.

I was wrong. Some three weeks after our initial conversation Morton made his move. He brought me a gift, a record album of the musical *Kiss Me Kate*. It would have been futile to protest. "I'll play it as soon as I get home," I said, thanking him.

"Or you could drop by my place one day—or after work. Even tonight. At your convenience," Morton said, running a finger around the rim of his brandy alexander.

"My schedule's a little tight right now. Let me take a rain check."

Morton didn't bring the matter up again. But later that week this item appeared in a column on the *San Francisco Chronicle*'s entertainment page:

> If you have nothing better to do these cool fall nights you could do a lot worse than drop in for a drink or dinner at the Casablanca (2323 Polk Street), a smart re-creation of Rick's Café replete with many-splendored gilt-edged mirrors. But the true gold may lie beneath the fingers of the piano player, who holds forth nightly on the world's highest piano bench from 8 to 12. You'll hear the tried-and-true standards rendered in vintage style along with a smattering of what sound like original compositions. He may not be Sam, or even Son of Sam [eerily foreshadowing the lurid moniker by some two decades!], but this scribe detected a decided Negro rhythmic influence in his lively excursions.

Morton was ecstatic. He bought a half dozen papers and that night presented me the clippings in a ribbon-tied manila folder marked "The Duchin of the Casablanca." "For your scrapbook! Look how people are streaming in—we'll have a full house tonight! How delicious that such a talent as yours should be recognized. It makes one almost believe in God and justice—in the Muses at the very least! We must celebrate. I'll cook us a late supper—a spinach salad and

French omelet, peaches and cream, sparkling champagne. 'Wunderbar' on the turntable! My dear boy, this is a night to remember!"

It was time to puncture Morton's pipe dreams, pull the Persian rug out from under his beautifully shod feet.

"Morton, you know I eat here every night."

"But for an occasion such as . . . Surely you could make an exception."

"I can't, Morton."

"Can't? What. Why not."

"I'm . . . not of your persuasion." The witless phrase slipped out of my mouth.

"Persuasion. What persuasion." His head had tilted stiffly, and his eyes studying me from that awkward angle had a clouded, harried cast.

How much clearer? "I don't go that route," I said gently. (If he insisted what route, I would say Interstate 69-A, damn him.)

"Route . . . But I never see you with—surely you don't think I . . ." His cheeks quivered with indignation. "This is unconscionable."

People were staring. "I have to get back."

"Go. Play your little piano, Sam. 'Ol' Black Joe' would be most appropriate," he sputtered and stalked away.

He came in only once more that week but did not speak to me. A few nights later he was in again with a plump, youngish man as his dinner companion. I was playing "I Get a Kick Out of You" when he sauntered over in a careless manner, not quite looking at me, a wry, almost insolent smile on his face that had the touch of a smirking child about it. Without a word he dropped a ten-dollar bill in the glass and strolled away. There was an attached note; I didn't read it until my break, and by that time he had left. "Some night when you're sad or lonely or blue come by my place and fuck. Always true to you in my fashion. M." The poor old queen, I thought. His poise ran out with his patience.

He came in less frequently after that, and always kept his distance. Never again would the chair be pulled up for a cozy, urbane chat with Son of Sam, the slim cane slung with limpid grace from the white piano. I preferred to think that he'd at least been partially drawn by the music. But every now and then, playing one of the master's tunes, I'd look up and see the charming old-world face across the room, the mild, intelligent eyes fixed on me with a gentle, terrible yearning.

I filed the experience in a journal I'd begun keeping, along with notes for a future composition to be titled "The Toy Terrier of New Haven" or "Poodle, Poodle, Bow Wow Wow." The melody, which I had conceived as a jaunty-melancholy line in alternating major and minor strains, fought me all the way, and I eventually discarded the project. Perhaps the frivolous titles, with their taint of disrespect and derision, strangled the muse. If so, I suppose it was a form of poetic justice.

The *Chronicle* accolade hyped business for a few days—I would look up to see people staring alternately at me and at the blowup of Dooley Wilson behind me—but by the following week it had fallen back to pre-item level.

I said to the bartender, "I guess they just came in to see the world's highest piano bench."

CHARLES WAS BUSY with his other operations, and I saw him only occasionally. But as he had promised, I drank and dined like a king. Veal in Champagne Sauce. Salades "Rick" and "Ilsa." Steak au Poivre. Brochette D'Agneau à la Marocaine. And at the bass end of the keyboard my constant amber companion, a double Johnny Walker Black on the rocks (I'd kicked the Southern Comfort habit and was drinking in a more civilized manner as befitting my advancing years), which I sipped between medleys. By the end of the evening I'd have imbibed three or four of those babies, but I was handling it like a champion, a mensch, never getting sloppy or tanked or even hung over like I used to on the road when I was trying to keep up with Val and the other lushes (an endeavor that might have done me in had it continued for another year), never going beyond the fuel-combustion stage; taking in only what the engine required, achieving a clean burn and maintaining a lucid perspective. Sure, every now and then I admitted, You're kidding yourself; but I was greatly buoyed to read a medical item in a responsible journal offering convincing statistical evidence that males of Jewish extraction possessing substantial body hair rarely contract cirrhosis.

I was stretching out. Driving an almost-new, baby-blue Falcon, writing combo charts and original compositions—premiered each night for unsuspecting captive audiences—and studying with a crackerjack seventy-year-old jazz-loving concert pianist, who numbered Dave Brubeck among his pupils, turned me onto Debussy and Scriabin (was turned on in turn to Nat Cole), and would smoke himself to death within two years. Enjoying this airy, buoyant, anything-goes city, the high energy and raffish style of the beats and pungent commentary by the vanguard satirical comics—Mort Sahl, Lenny Bruce, Tom Lehrer, Professor Corey, Lord Buckley, et al.—who nightly transformed a brick-walled hole-in-the-ground theater-café called the hungry i into a crackling galvanic cell.

I DON'T KNOW why it should be, but people seem to lose their wits around musicians. In the same room where a pianist is performing they will drop coins in a jukebox or turn up the volume of a game show on the TV set. These are not necessarily crude or heartless people. I have had friendly, intelligent patrons attempt to shake my hand while I am playing and persist until I abjectly break off and press the flesh. On my off-night I used to visit my friend Lois Cantor, who played classical and semiclassical music nightly in the Redwood Room of the Clift Hotel. One Monday I was listening to her play a Chopin nocturne on the Mason & Hamlin grand when a distinguished-looking man approached her. Lois, a handsome woman of regal bearing, wore an elegant black gown while working this posh room. She was impeccably rendering a timeless piece of music as the man bent over her. "Where's the men's?" I heard him say. Frowning in concentration, Lois could not answer. The man bent lower, repeating loudly, "Where's the men's?" Grimly hewing to the Chopin lines, Lois blurted a deft, extempore response: "I'm a woman!" Puzzled and irate, the man sought out the maître d', presumably to obtain the answer to his question and/or register a complaint. I watched the silver-haired captain briefly hear him out, smile faintly, and turn away. As I was leaving, I asked the captain what had transpired. "The gentleman's comment was, 'The service in this joint is the shits.' "

At the same time that I commiserated with Lois, I smugly reflected that though that sort of transgression may be common in expense-account rooms like the Redwood, it was a much less likely occurrence in my cosmopolitan boîte with its lower-keyed ambience. My conviction lasted less than a week. The following Saturday a portly businessman thrust his face into mine. Anticipating some mildewed request, a dogpatch special, I looked up and smiled my inquiring smile, hands on hold. But something was wrong with his expression, and his request, like the one Lois received a few nights earlier, was of a nonmusical nature. "Do you have to do what you're doing?" he said. I had noticed him and a colleague at a table near the piano, briefcases at their feet and papers spread between them—a work session while awaiting the entrées. Still, his phrasing was odd; it suggested that what I was doing was generating amorphous noise, an impossible distraction. I said, "You mean play the piano?" He nodded; his face was red with anger. I said, "I'm employed here. I'll play more softly if you like." He turned away without another word. I had been made to feel like a recalcitrant child, scolded for banging a spoon on a dishpan. I underplayed for the rest of the night, the recent *Chronicle* paean reduced to ashes under a moment's blazing crudity.

We're vulnerable up there, sitting ducks in black tie, and we long for dignity and respect. After the years of dedication, care, and passion expended on the mastering of our instruments, we would like to feel we're entitled—if not for ourselves, then for music's unalloyed, sweet sake.

But the overall vibes were good at the Casablanca. Having just crossed the crucial border into my fourth decade, I was looking more to the comforts—the delectable entrées and Johnny Walker doubles—and to security, which I seemed to have found in this congenial home away from home. But this last assumption should have been instantly suspect, for security is as alien to the profession as a duck to a desert. The innovative Charles could decide he had milked the Casablanca theme dry, change the name and motif, bring in a strolling violinist, a classical guitarist on a stool—or sell out to a new owner who preferred Kostelanetz on tape. We founder in adverse economic weather; the winds of cultural change are forever blowing (a cyclone would strike in the sixties), acts of God waiting in the wings. An accomplished pianist and new California friend, Danny Hall, who had been drifting from bar to bar years before I arrived—appreciated, more or less, but never quite finding his niche—had a sobering experience that sent sympathetic shivers through the community of keyboard players. A proprietor-benefactor along the lines of my Charles had offered him five nights a week, at excellent loot, playing for dinner in a newly renovated yacht club fronting on San Francisco Bay. His hours were 7:30 to 10:00. He played his large repertoire of vintage standards on a magnificent Baldwin grand in a softly lighted, paneled room; the appreciative club members plied him with choice food and wine, and expressed the hope that he would not desert them for greener fields (he chuckled to himself); beautiful women hovered about him making requests; his tips were exorbitant. The third week on the job he said to me in a daze, "It's hardly believable. They let me play whatever I want in this gorgeous room on a piano that belongs in a concert hall. I scarf like Henry the Eighth, make out like a bandit with the chicks [my sole point of envy so far], the night's over with before I know it—and they're paying over scale! I keep expecting someone to take the candy away." Someone did: inappropriately, the day after Thanksgiving when the wiring on an improperly installed

Christmas tree shorted and the club went up in flames. But while the gig lasted Danny was like a grateful kid at a surprise party.

THROUGH MY CONTACTS with Casablanca customers I was picking up lucrative outside work. Offers to play solo for anniversary parties and poolside cocktails, to put together combos for bar mitzvahs, wedding receptions, club dances. Charles had called the right shot; it's a convivial, going-out town, and he graciously allowed me to bring in substitutes whenever the gigs fell on Casablanca working nights.

A Mrs. Albertine asked if I'd play for her husband's early-evening surprise birthday party. I quoted her a fairly substantial figure (greed beginning to exert its insidious pull), which she accepted without a quiver. She told me to come a half hour before the guests were due so that we could go over a list of requests she had compiled. I arrived at the appointed time with my props, which I am never without on private-party dates: the pair of cushions and a wad of paper cocktail napkins for bringing flat notes up to pitch. Mrs. Albertine served me a glass of wine and excused herself briefly to go across the street to borrow more glasses from a neighbor. At which point everything that could possibly go wrong, went. I heard a key rattle in the front-door lock. One of the guests arriving early? But why a key? . . . The man who entered the living room had a lumbering proprietary air about him. I knew beyond any glimmer of doubt that it was, inexplicably, the husband who was supposed to have been detained at the office by business colleagues until the magic moment. He confronted me, a stranger in a blue suit sitting on his divan, drinking his wine, with two cushions on my lap. *Surprise* had been drummed into me by the hostess; there was nothing I could say. He looked from me to the cushions; he could not take his eyes from them; they must have represented to him evidence of a direct sexual threat. I watched bewilderment, hurt, fear, and anger struggle for dominance on his flushed face. In a raging second it all burst out of him: "Okay, buster, who're you and just what the hell is going on?"

Many engagements took me to hotel banquet rooms and suites, where the pianos were all on rollers to facilitate their deployment from room to room. This maddening accessory not only raises the keyboard level a few more notches but lifts the pedals free of the floor. A piano's pedals, unlike a horseman's stirrups, require a heel-to-toe action, and the heel must be grounded. So along with the cushions I was now lugging a three-inch-thick telephone book as a floor for my feet—and inexorably acquiring a Willy Loman persona.

Arkansas Diesel, Incorporated, hired me to play in their hospitality suite at the Sir Francis Drake Hotel. As soon as I arrived and set my gear on the piano bench a large man in a blue suit approached. His name tag read "Art Kilkenny, Little Rock."

"What's required here," he said emphatically, "is ice-cream music." He indicated a tiered oval bar—a voluptuous, unintelligible ice sculpture at its center—holding frosty cylinders of ice cream in a full spectrum from mocha brown to snow white; stacks of telescoping sugar cones; ladle-equipped tureens of whipped cream, hot fudge, ruby toppings, and gooey syrups; brimming bowls of nuts, cherries, and sprinkles; and green-yellow jungles of bananas.

The idea was innovative. Instead of the traditional booze and hors d'oeuvres, Arkansas Diesel had chosen to dispense postprandial sweets, but with a flair. The corporation's employees and guests would concoct their own desserts—sundaes, splits, double- and triple-decker cones—from the confections at hand. I was to supply thematic piano accompaniment.

"What's ice-cream music?" I asked.

"That's why we hired you. My contact said you had expertise in the field of mood establishment."

My mind spun out. Something summery, good-humored, flavorful—but not vanilla, which is musicians' vernacular for bland. There are a couple of antique musicals, *The Chocolate Soldier* and Eubie Blake's *The Chocolate Dandies*, but I'd be hard put to dredge up a tune from either. Besides, who under the age of seventy would recognize the score? Surely Kilkenny didn't expect me to play "I Scream, You Scream, We All Scream for Ice Cream" all night. (Was there even a melodic line attached to that inane chant?) I scanned the bar for inspiration. "Casey Would Waltz with the Strawberry Blonde." "Yes! We Have No Bananas." "Goody-Goody." "When My Sugar Walks Down the Street." "Big Butter and Egg Man." (Ah!) This was going to be fun. "If I Knew You Were Coming I'd've Baked—"

"Here, shuck the soup and fish and try this on."

While my mind was wheeling, Kilkenny had opened an attaché case on the piano and removed a red-and-white striped vest and straw boater.

My heart sank; I thought I'd left those sideshow days behind. No way out. I got out of my tux coat and slipped into the new livery. The vest dropped below my waist and the straw boater covered my ears. Kilkenny looked at me. "I was expecting a larger man."

"I'm used to costume gigs, but I don't want to come on like Chester the clown," I said.

"Skip the boater. Leave it on the piano as a prop." He buttoned the vest and pulled it taut around my shoulders. "It's not Brooks Brothers, but then you ain't Rubinstein."

The first guests had begun straggling in.

"Nine bells, let's get this show on the road," Kilkenny said. "Keep 'em smiling."

I kept the tempo bright and upbeat, letting my imagination run free—"You're the Cream in My Coffee," "Cherry," "On the Good Ship Lollipop" (a tip of the hat to you, Shirley), "June Is Bustin' Out All Over," "Neapolitan Nights" (ha!), "Take Me Out to the Ball Game"—but no one was smiling. These were serious scarfers, the men hunched, stiffly inclined, holding their brimming, tulip-shaped glasses and sundae boats at a discreet remove as they made their deliberate rounds of the bar, eyeing unsampled sauces and untapped tureens, the smart ones tucking neckties into buttoned vests and coats.

The women, many in pantsuits, promenaded in similar fashion, bent like septuagenarians on a neighborhood stroll, mouths agape, craning for the succulent spoonful.

As I watched the busy, contorted mouths, it became apparent why smiles were in short supply. Eating ice cream while ambulant is an exacting business. Mouths, eyes, and hands must coordinate with precision, and pleasure is often punctuated by pain: sinuses are jolted, teeth hurt.

"Running low on Amaretto fudge and peach!" I heard Kilkenny holler to an orange-jacketed waiter.

Someone was hovering at the treble end of the keyboard. A fortyish blonde in a lilac blouse, gobbling pistachio and sporting a trim whipped-cream mustache. She inquired with oozing inflection, "Can you pay 'Apsody in Boo'?"

I have a stock response to requests for this venerable war-horse—which should be played only in concert format—and delivered it now: "Certainly, madame, as soon as the French horns and cellos arrive."

The hobbyhorse tempo of ice-cream music, with its headlong pace and galloping left-hand stride, was taking its toll. I longed to slide into an easy, loping "Days of Wine and Roses" or "Girl From Ipanema." Would Kilkenny or anyone else even notice if I throttled down? I decided to chance it, but I'd hedge my bet. Gershwin's "Summertime" is no rollicking flagwaver, but at least the integrity of the motif would be sustained.

On the sixth bar Kilkenny rose at my side like Banquo's ghost, a crimson smear on his loosened tie, carrying a three-humped concoction drenched in raspberry.

"What in the name of God are you playing?"

" 'Summertime,' in keeping with—"

"Gloooo-my. We're dying on the vine, dad, if I'd wanted to visit a morgue I'd've worn my armband. You wanna do summertime, do 'In the *Good Old* Summertime,' 'In My Merry Oldsmobile,' 'Smile, Darn You, Smile,' any goddam thing, but let's get the blocks out from in front of the wheels and light a fire under this crowd, we're going down for the count. I haven't seen a smile since hour one."

"Everyone's busy stuffing his face. Try smiling with that spoon stuck in your mouth."

Kilkenny shot me a frosty look. A man unaccustomed to insubordination from the lower echelons: gofers, busboys, piano players. He sucked lingeringly on the receding spoon. "I blame myself. I seem to have tapped the wrong power source for the job."

He sauntered off, spooning raspberry, leaving egg on my face. Well, what can you expect from Little Rock, a town whose medical center sends its yuletide babies home in outsize Christmas stockings, whose former governor operated an amusement park called Dogpatch USA?

To allay boredom I tried to make a game of it, seeking melodic inspiration in character and attire. At Bay Area fashion shows I'd been challenged to come up with extempore fragments of music to match a summery sheen of silk, leather minis, a swirling cape. But these industrial folks were in a much narrower sartorial mode. How do you get turned on by a seersucker jacket, a pink pantsuit? Arm-weary, I cranked out long chains of golden oldies: "Daisy, Daisy," "Bicycle Built for Two," "You're a Grand Old Flag." So where were the smiles? I was supposed to be the life of the party. That's what my Uncle Irwin told me twenty years ago when I was floundering through Czerny exercises, Bach inventions: "Keep at it, kiddo, one day you'll be spreading sunshine, breaking hearts with this stuff."

At 10:30 I took my break. Whatever stomach I'd had for a cone or sundae had long since soured. I headed for the coffee urn across the room and was adding a dollop of half-and-half when a ghastly sound assaulted my ears. It's what all pianists dread on their intermissions. Some poor deluded fool, an eat-your-heart-out Horowitz type, had taken over the Chickering. It's not that we mind being spelled. But if the usurper is totally devoid of talent (and the chances are twenty out of twenty-one), party guests who aren't aware you're on a break or can't be bothered to check it out assume the boiler-room dissonances are coming from you. What if Peter Duchin happened to be in the crowd or, worse, Peter Serkin? "Jesus, who hired the meatball on piano?"

The man sounded like he was playing with both elbows, neither one possessing a shard of artistry. If you've been on the Bayshore Freeway during a late-Friday-afternoon traffic jam, you know the character of the sound. I caught a glimpse of the elbow-banger across the room: sparse hair, bull-like shoulders moving beneath the kind of sports jacket that in my childhood we called a horse blanket.

My first thought was to forgo my break and reclaim the instrument, but in my experience these jokers are nearly impossible to dislodge. My second: circulate around, make my presence known, thereby disavowing responsibility (Here I am, folks, the size forty-four circus vest, the ten magic fingers—no connection with *that* . . .). My final thought, which I acted on, was to take my coffee into the corridor, divorcing myself from the festivities. On the way out I passed in the suite's open doorway the mustached woman who had requested "Rhapsody in Blue," attacking a dripping double-decker while glancing up and down the corridor. Surely she couldn't be on the lookout for the horns and cellos?

On my return the piano bench was mercifully deserted—Elbows taking his own break at the hot-fudge tureen—but someone else lay in wait. An imposing-looking man in a monogrammed green blazer wanted "Aba Daba Honeymoon" and greased the request, slipping a fiver into my vest pocket. To my everlasting shame I once committed this abomination to memory, and over the years the damn thing has stuck in my mind like boysenberry to white flannel. I don't play it well—it's not possible to play it well—and you hesitate to perform in public a piece notorious for its unparalleled unmusicality. As Yeats said, "How can we know the dancer from the dance?"

I whipped through a nervous chorus and exited fast, segueing into "Put On a Happy Face." But I was bucking an irreversible trend. A listless mood hung over the suite. A number of people were sunk deeply into chairs. Those still ambulant carried themselves differently, the rigid, inclined stance grown slack, careless. Coats hung open, pants drooped, ties had been yanked from necks. Few lapels, shirts, or blouses had escaped untinged, and the carpet surrounding the oval bar was dappled in pastel, as if a clutch of patient dogs with painted paws had been led around and around on their evening stroll. Those still working the bar appeared to be weaving, as if the sugar intake had infiltrated the delicate chambers of the inner ear. Women's cheeks puffed out periodically like those of little girls who have just completed a daring sequence of hopscotch leaps. The faces of some promenaders had a peculiar yaw; they looked to be on the verge of agony or revelation.

The ubiquitous Kilkenny surfaced off my right shoulder, announcing his presence with a volcanic belch.

"How's the Good Humor man?"

"Not grinning, bearing it."

"We're sinking under the waves, dad, we need fresh blood. How about if Billy took over again?"

"You can't mean the meatba—the chap who sat in during my—" A smiling Billy hove into view.

"If I have no choice." I stood up.

"Naturally this won't affect your wages. Why don't you give him the vest."

"He scarcely needs it." I slipped out of the sideshow garment and Billy handed me his horse blanket.

"Sure you don't mind?" Billy said.

I gave him a smile that hurt my face. "You guys are giving the party."

The vest fit Billy like a rubber glove. He eased onto the bench, nudging my cushion over the side, and Kilkenny popped the straw boater on his head. It caught at the ears and stayed put. A half dozen of Billy's colleagues gathered round, calling phrases of encouragement as he applied the elbows. Monogrammed Green Blazer began singing—somehow divining what Billy was playing—"If you knew Susie . . ." Others joined in; arms rose as if on signal, linking to shoulders. An impromptu barbershop sextet had materialized in the midst of the Bayshore traffic jam.

I backed off, feeling naked in my suspenders; Kilkenny had hung my tux coat somewhere. I draped Billy's blanket over a chair behind the ice-cream bar and fixed myself a modest butterscotch sundae: two scoops, coffee and vanilla, easy on the butterscotch; dollop of whipped cream, light sprinkle of walnuts, top it with (why not?) a cherry.

The voices lifted, unexpectedly robust, strident, several keys away from the one Billy was driving in. Didn't matter in the least. Carefree grins wide as banana splits were beginning to splatter across faces. Strange how potent, as Noël Coward said, cheap music is.

Kilkenny heartily pounded the brawny striped back. "Attaboy, Billy, great ice-cream music!"

Someone was tugging on my sleeve. With a mouth full of vanilla I turned and encountered a vision in lilac, a bloated, surfeited face, a faintly bewildered cast to the eyes. Sugary breath swarmed over me.

"When are the French horns arriving?"

(I scream.)

THE SIR FRANCIS DRAKE is one of four major San Francisco hotels located on the fringes of the Tenderloin, and emerging from opulent chandeliered rooms after midnight onto those looming, shadowed alleyways can be as jarring an experience as encountering a vulture in a sunlit parlor. In such nether regions a slight build in conjunction with a tuxedo, a telephone book, and a pair of frilly, silly-ass cushions can make a tempting target. I found myself adopting the same survival techniques (though older now and more fearful) I had employed when entering the Boston ghetto following a Rudy Yellin gig: remove the bow tie before leaving the hotel, wear a coat over the soup and fish, and walk fast, with purpose, to your car.

It was after one in the morning when I left the ice-cream gig, drained (blood sugar out of sight), and saw a man of about fifty walking back and forth across Powell Street singing snatches of old standards loudly, in a resonant, near-professional voice; a tattered, strutting, slovenly figure in stained clothes. His feet did a little dance as he sang, and his arms flailed. Knots of people had gathered on the curbs to watch, others veered away in fright or distaste. He may have been drunk, though he didn't move as if he were drunk. More likely he had a lot of marbles loose—who can explain the ranters and shouters? Careening across the cable-car tracks, oblivious to traffic, he would sing a few bars of a song before jumping abruptly to another. The lyrics were all highly sophisticated, as popular lyrics go; they were songs I knew and loved from the golden decades of the thirties and forties. I moved along the curb, staying with him, wondering what he would go into next. The voice boomed down the street, the lyrics sharply articulated. He sang of castles in Spain, of oysters and champagne and another fragment about a clandestine lover that caught me up, a line from an out-of-print tune I'd been trying to track down for years, "I'm in Love with the Honorable Mr. So and So." I felt lightheaded enough to confront the singer. I waited until his next swing back across the street. When he was within a few feet I said, "The lyrics from 'The Honorable Mr. So and So'—do you know the rest of them?" He broke off and stopped; a powerful reek emanated from him. His pale eyes burned at me for a moment, then darted away. He began to move quickly down the center of the street, south, toward the Tenderloin. I followed at a discreet distance, my arms bulging with cushions and phone book. After about a block he began to sing again. But I wasn't about to pursue him into those dim alleys. As I turned back to the humdrum night I noticed a peculiar thing. The passersby, the knots of watching people, were now regarding me with the slightest edge of distrust, of fear. The crazed sophisticate had tarnished me with his lovely passion.

17

"If someone is missing he'll eventually show up in San Francisco." Oscar Wilde was supposed to have said that, but it always sounded to me more like Mark Twain.

Amy Avallone wasn't really missing, but she had certainly been outside my sphere of activity. She was sitting at a sidewalk table at Enrico's Coffeehouse drinking something bright green on one of those sparkling blue California days that are like New England October without the autumn foliage and the threat of winter. She didn't look much different from the nights at Vincent's in Worcester all those years ago, except for differences of tint, accents of color in the eyes and skin that I didn't remember; then I realized I had never before seen her in daylight.

"We know each other," she said.

"You're Amy Avallone. Vincent's on Shrewsbury Street—nine, ten years ago."

"It's Avalon now." She spelled it.

"Closing night I asked if I could buy you a coffee. You asked if I was tired of living."

"Glad you survived. Pull up a chair."

"Are you still sitting on pianos?"

"Not since I left the bush leagues."

"Then you're still singing."

She gave me a flat stare. "How d'you mean, *still?*"

"Nothing beyond the word. Where can I hear you?"

"The hungry i."

"That's a big gig."

"I'm not in the show room. There's a supper-club annex called The Other Room. But the piano player they gave me can't read shit." She eyed me speculatively. "I suppose you still have that problem . . ."

"I'm not only reading these days, I'm writing," I said, sounding like I'd just been promoted to the third grade.

"What are you doing tonight?"

My hasty heart took a flying leap. "You aren't working?"

"I *am.* I need someone backing me who can read."

"Well, it's Monday, I'm off . . . But how can you bring in another pianist on such short notice?"

"I just *can.*" The big dark eyes flashed, precluding argument.

"Do we get to rehearse?"

"Let's go," she said, standing, and yes, I could see she was still stacked good enough to bruise walls with that marauding take-charge stride.

"Your place or mine?"

"My music's at home. But I better warn you, my piano sucks."

And so, a wise voice in my head stopped me from saying, do I.

Crossing Van Ness Avenue on our way to her pad I heard a guitar playing "When Sunny Gets Blue" and thought it came from a passing car radio. No sir. There was my old Beantown colleague Oscar working a street corner, guitar case open at his bare feet for gratuities. He was wearing a tattered straw hat, unbuttoned brocade vest, and stained sweat pants; the Ho Chi Minh chin whiskers were still tied with a yellow elastic band. It is not with pride that I relate driving past that corner with averted eyes, denying our common heritage—at the same time wondering if this carefree let-it-all-hang-out town so lacking in standard restraints had hastened the collapse of a fragile psyche.

Amy's charts—recent cabaret and show tunes ("You Make Me Feel So Young," "Guess Who I Saw Today") that I'd just begun to hear when I left Boston—still looked like flyshit on a screen door, but now I could decipher most of it. I was pleased to see she'd discarded the "Once in Love with Amy" opener. We rehearsed a complete show with encores in two hours. Then she told me she had to take a beauty nap, and to pick her up at seven bells; the first show was at eight.

I had been in the show room before, but not the supper room; its elegance, belying the dusty cellar-stairs entrance, surprised me. Recessed brick walls and green-glass candlesticks, the subdued light playing over snowy tablecloths and gleaming silver; on one side a short ornately banistered stairway that must have once led somewhere ran flush into weathered brick. We worked to an affluent crowd whose dinner tabs entitled them to preferential seating in the show room, and between sets I stood in the back of the packed theater listening to Mort Sahl dissect the Kennedys, and to the beauteous African folksinger Miriam Makeba (who in a few years would marry Stokely Carmichael) singing of Congo bazaars and the back of the moon in a voice as sumptuous and spangled as her silken gown.

After Amy's last set, proprietor Enrico Banducci took me aside in the L-shaped bar-lounge behind the show room; he also owned the

Broadway coffeehouse where I'd met Amy that afternoon. A barrel-chested mustachioed man in a red sweater and black beret, he moved with a natural roll and swagger that was part swashbuckler, part boulevardier.

"When can you start steady?"

"I already have a job."

"Not like this one you don't. And not behind Amy, that's small potatoes. In the theater room backing the acts. I'm losing my pianist to the cruise ships."

My head started reeling, a dazzling parade of international stars floating on the rim of my mind's eye.

"I'd have to think about it."

"Think fast. I know players who would trample your Aunt Sophie for this gig. I don't want to be bothered with competitions, auditions. I've heard you, you're here. The timing's right."

"How much time do I have?"

"Call me tomorrow noon at the coffeehouse."

I drove Amy home and told her of the offer.

"Take it," she said, "it's where everything's happening. And I'm being generous—I'll have to find another piano player."

"I've got such a good gig, security and—"

"It's the big time. Even The Other Room's going on a name policy. You know who's following me next month? Mabel Mercer, then Bobby Short. And that's just for supper, while you're waiting to see the show. Banducci's a step ahead of the New York cabarets, he's taking more risks. He's pulling unknown kids off the streets and making them stars."

"I don't know if I'm ready for this . . ."

"What's worrying you? You're not Erroll Garner but you can play. Anyway, there's not that much pressure. The really heavy acts usually bring their own backup people."

In front of her apartment house I cut the motor and she said, "Ten years ago you were after me. Are you now?"

"Now and ten years from now. You're beautiful." I was so horny I would have said the same to Kate Smith or Olive Oyl.

"Your timing'll never be better. The coffeehouse this afternoon, Banducci's piano player leaving on the boats, and now me. Let's go have our cup of coffee."

I implored the gods in charge of these matters that she was speaking figuratively and erotically.

My plea was answered.

In the close gloom of her Franklin Street pad with the postmidnight traffic rumbling past the window, a cat, dog, or something more sinister scratching on a bedpost, and thoughts of my impending decision (due in less than twelve hours) rattling around my brain like dice in a cup, I surprised myself by performing not like a champion, but adequately, a rung or two above adequately, if I may be permitted a modest boast. I guess if you're ready you're ready. Amazing the things that can sustain you. Detachment, I was beginning to suspect, is the key, detachment fuzzing into oblivion.

With Amy writhing underneath me like a fakir's cobra, I thought, Christ, I'm over thirty, am I going to spend the rest of my days playing "As Time Goes By"? . . . Bruce, Cosby, Makeba, the Limeliters, Mike and Elaine, the illustrious names flashed by like signposts on a highway to Valhalla. Was I ready for that company? If you don't have the right fare stay off the bus, Junie, the Carousel tenor man, used to say when I asked him how he did this or that.

"You always talk to yourself when you screw?" Amy grunted below me.

Another of the saxophonist's cryptograms recurred, equally applicable: Always take your best shot and go to the wall with it.

But there was a more pressing matter at hand. Last eight out . . . *Goin' home!*

And even before I'd clambered off, the decision was made. Seize the day.

"This'll have to be a one-shot," Amy said as a ball of fur catapulted from the floor and grappled my ankles.

"You're joking. Didn't you—"

"Like the guy who bombed at Carnegie Hall, the premiere performance became the farewell. I don't want you after me."

Bombed? "I thought it went okay. You didn't . . . get off?"

"Do you know how old I am? I could be your Aunt Sophie."

"What's a couple years when it's good? And how come you and Banducci both think I have an Aunt Sophie?"

"There's a guy I'm seeing who helped me get this gig." Beside me her body trembled and a low chuckle spilled into the darkness. "It's Vincent's brother-in-law."

I came up on one elbow. "*Our* Vincent? Shrewsbury Street?"

"The very same."

"You never laid eyes on me before in your life," I said.

SOME TIME TOWARD dawn I dreamed I was accompanying Sinatra on the fabled brick-backed stage. Entering the bridge of "Nancy with the Laughing Face," he broke off in disgust, the cold blue eyes raking me like glass chips. "Banducci," he called to the back of the room, "who hired this meathead on piano?"

18

Bad dreams aside, it was time to move on. I bid Charles adieu, thanked him for the class chow, the Johnny Walker doubles, the artistic breathing space. We had a last supper together under the revolving blades, toasting Rick and Ilsa in memoriam.

So I was back in a cellar—but a cellar with a difference, a cellar of contrasts where sandals mingled with sables and the luxurious collided with the makeshift: stately old brick walls that would make a decorator swoon, rising to a ceiling festooned with steam pipes; fastidious crimson-jacketed Chinese waiters soundlessly cruising the aisles while the light-sound man, Alvah, shuffled onstage in rumpled slacks and baggy wool sweater to arrange microphones and props—a screenwriter and charter member of the Hollywood Ten, it turned out, arriving in San Francisco via a federal correctional institution in Texarkana, Texas; The Other Room's gleaming banquettes beckoning from the show room's worn theater chairs, each with a tacky wooden drink ledge nailed to the back. A dank and vibrant subterranean chamber in the Manilatown corner of North Beach, which was not a beach at all but (at that time) an amicable grid of Filipino hotels, Chinese sweatshops, avant-garde bookstores, leisurely coffeehouses, folk clubs, jazz joints, Italian groceries, and Italian-Basque-French family restaurants. Pre-nude, pre-gimcrack North Beach, the heart of the scene a half-dozen congested square blocks with Broadway running through like a hot white arrow.

There were nights the bar-lounge was so packed with international performers and celebrities you might have thought yourself, with only the slightest prod of the imagination, transported to some glittering entertainers' halfway house between Beverly Hills and Manhattan, Piccadilly Circus and the Via Veneto. Sinatra flipping Porfirio Rubirosa and Leo Durocher for drinks, Gregory Peck sitting for a charcoal portrait by our flustered artist, Mandy, alongside the album-jacketed walls (*Lenny Live!, Limeliters at hungry i, The Kingston Trio from the hungry i, Jonathan Winters Whistle Stopping* . . .) while at the bar's lower end the leaky plumbing from the upstairs Hotsy Totsy Club rained relentlessly into the grasshoppers and Rob Roys. And I sat there drinking it all in (quieting my pre-show butterfly stomach with a double Peter Dawson) like a star-struck kid on the MGM back lot. Except now I was part of the show.

ON THE COCOA BROWN wall over the bar mirror, pastel-chalk lettering announced:

PHYLLIS DILLER
MICHAEL DUNN
ANGELINA CAMPAGNA

Miss Diller had dropped in briefly during the Monday afternoon rehearsal, quizzically regarded the network of playground bars filling the stage—Michael Dunn, the amiable midget actor who had hit it big in *Ship of Fools*, would be frolicking on them with a five-foot-nine blonde that night—and departed, instructing me and Alberto, the house bass player, "No sweat, dear hearts, just play me on with something fast, frenetic, and preferably unrecognizable."

Now, six hours later, lights down on a packed house, Alvah's introduction came over the PA system in sepulchral tones strangely at odds with the frivolous content: "The hungry i is pleased, proud, and *absolutely terrified* to present the one, and God help us the only, ding-a-ling dilly delirious doll from Donner Pass, Phyllis Diller."

A bizarre harlequin in barrel-stave silver lamé with ropes of pearls drooping to ball-bearing knees, tramping down the center aisle, waving a two-foot ebony cigarette holder like a conductor's baton (while Alvah fumed with self-vilification in his side-wall booth for agreeing to mouth the imbecilic introduction suggested by the mad Miss D. herself) . . . now hoisting the dress to reveal legs that should never see the light of night or day—"You sweetheart, I love you!" Alberto whispered fervidly—as she climbed onstage to my crashing play-on (taking her at her word) of ascending-descending dissonant clusters and waited behind a grinning imp's countenance for cheers and applause to subside.

"It's wonderful being back in San Francisco and opening at the world-famous hungry i"—a bleak sweep of barnyard eyes around weathered brick up to ceiling pipes—"Anyway, after all those posh East Coast rooms it's a refreshing change playing a sewer. Ha ha ha. Being the nervous type I must've swallowed a half-dozen heavy-duty tranquilizers in the past hour, and on the basis of the play-on I just received I think I better pass some on to my high-wire accompanist sitting over there on a tablecloth, two cushions and, I believe, his overcoat. Sorry I'm late, I was rushing here in my Jag and cracked up midtown. Staggered to a phone booth to call my ever-loving husband and give him the gory details. Fang, I said, you better get here fast 'cause I got a show to do. He said, Where are you? I said, Corner of Jones and Taylor. He said, Look again, they don't cross. I said, They do now. Ha ha ha ha."

ALBERTO AND I had a nightcap in the bar after the last show. I was just coming down from the excitement, my shirt damp with sweat. Forty-five minutes ago Alvah had come onstage during our entr'acte music to tell us, "It might interest you gentlemen to know that Ed Sullivan, Mitch Miller, and Ethel Merman are in the audience"; his dry tone indicating that he, at least, wasn't impressed. I had survived the baptism intact. The only actual accompanying I'd done—other than playing on Diller and Dunn—had been backing Angelina, the black-eyed, broad-beamed folksinger, some of whose tunes I'd played twelve years earlier at the Italian-American Social Club in Worcester. Heavy acts were on the way, however—next month Eartha Kitt, reputed to chew unsatisfactory piano players alive and spit them out, and further down the line Carmen McRae and Miriam Makeba for a return engagement. They might not be traveling with their own backup groups. I confided to Alberto my inexperience with singers of that stature and some apprehension over my ability to fill the bill. The compact, antic Latino, in his fourth year at the club, lifted one of my dollar bills from the bar, tore off a sizable corner, folded it into a tight shaft and began contemplatively picking his teeth. When he'd finished the upper row he put his hand on my arm and said, "Charlie Parker, whatever shape he was in, faced each night the same way."

I waited.

"He gathered his coal, he stoked his fire, and he burned."

Some advice. The last-show crowd was filing up the stairs, chuckling at Diller's self-denigrating bons mots. I was watching the Chinese waiters—some quite elderly with speckled skin and halting gaits—silently hanging up their red jackets and donning long, shapeless overcoats for the trek back to Chinatown through the fog-bound night, when my eyes got knocked out by two near-glamazons in silver spiked heels and black mesh stockings that went on and up forever, open cloth coats draped over the shoulders revealing rhinestone-studded satin corselets. They took stools a little down the bar from us, each with a wad of bills wound tightly around her fingers.

"From the Hotsy Totsy," Alberto whispered to me. "They drop in about this time for a fast blast." He thrust his face past me and called down the bar, "Como va la cosa, niñas?"

They paid him no heed, ordering bourbons and soda, dexterously peeling bills from their fingers.

"Quiereñ cojer?"

"Not tonight, doll, I got a bad back," one of the girls said, looking straight ahead.

"That's supposed to be a headache," Alberto responded.

"What did you ask them?" I whispered.

"If they wanted to screw, do the thing." Having finished his gin and tonic, Alberto started in on my scotch.

The girls polished off their highballs in no time and departed, heels clicking, their rear-end bustles switching violently under the loose cloth coats. I swiveled around for a lingering look, my elbow striking something solid and yielding; I thought it had connected with Alberto. "Sorry," I said, but Alberto was staring down at his feet. "*Carajo.*"

Michael Dunn, all three feet of him, was sprawled on the barroom floor, squinting up at the pale yellow ceiling globe as if sighting stars.

Alberto and I slid off our stools, bending low.

"God, excuse me . . . ," I said, mortified.

"I'm not the Holy Ghost and I didn't think my act was that bad."

Alberto was carefully lifting the little fellow to his feet, gingerly testing his bones the way my Aunt Lila used to prod chickens in Manny's Meats and Poultry.

"I never saw you. I was—"

"Not to worry, I think I'll survive."

"A shot of brandy, *amigo,*" Alberto said.

"No, *gracias.*" He brushed his suit coat and toddled off, calling gamely over his shoulder, "Next time pick on someone your own size."

"LADIES AND GENTLEMEN, the hungry i takes pleasure—," Alvah began and abruptly broke off. Something strange was going on in the control booth. The house was dark. Beside me, just offstage, the mantillaed Angelina Campagna (a Banducci favorite and holdover from the previous week) awaited her introduction. Through the lighted observation window I saw a small wild-eyed rumple-haired man seize the microphone from Alvah.

"LADIES AND GENTLEMEN," a different voice, resounding, doomful, boomed over the speakers. "It is with IMMENSE PRIDE, tempered by a distinct note of regret, that Enrico Dan-Ban-Dambucci, the hungry i, AND THE UNITED STATES GOVERNMENT—"

Hoots of laughter erupting from isolated sectors of the room as the main body of the audience stared in bewilderment at the observation window.

"—present our new thinging thong thrush, Miss . . ." *Wheeeep . . .* The maniacal little man, still grappling with Alvah, appeared to be turning knobs on the control board . . . "Miss—" *Wheeee-eek . . .* "—a young girl for many years . . ." Laughter simmering uneasily in far-flung corners.

"Jesus, Mary, and Joseph," Angelina breathed beside me.

"Is this planned?" I whispered to Alberto.

"Half and half," the chunky Mexican answered, softly plucking strings, seemingly disinterested.

"—Miss Cacciatore this past year has played the Palladium in London, command performances before various queen mothers and tutti frutti in that prestigious establishment—" *Eeee-op* . . . A full-blown wrestling match progressing in the booth . . . "You trying to screw up my act, Jim?" the madman's snarling aside picked up by the audio . . . "NOT TO MENTION, LADIES AND GENTLEMEN, the Tivoli in Melbourne, concert halls in Glasgow, Amsterdam, Paris, Vienna, and most recently the newly renovated Rhythm Inn in Bakersfield . . ." The laughter now streaming between tourists and club regulars, tumbling in waves across the room, a portly, tuxedoed man at the far end of the front row on his feet, teetering, convulsed, ricocheting off the wall. I saw Banducci poke his head through the rear swing doors, glance briefly toward the control booth and withdraw, chuckling to himself. I was beginning to understand why an East Coast columnist had written, "There are nights when the club's operation appears to be in the exclusive hands of the Marx Brothers."

"I'm tightening up," Angelina said in an agonized voice, clawing at her stretched throat with tensed fingers. "Do 'Non Dimenticar' first."

We shuffled our music around, my mind reverting a dozen years, registering, "Please Don't Dent My New Car".

"Who is that guy?" I whispered to Alberto.

"Irwin Corey. We play him next month."

"The Professor? World's Foremost Authority?"

"The same hombre."

"I've seen him on the tube, he's funny."

"Wait'll you work behind him," Alberto said dolefully.

"—WITHOUT FURTHER ADO—" somewhere in the far recesses a glass crashed to the floor . . . "I ask you, ladies and gentlemen, to excuse our waiters tonight. YOU'D BE NERVOUS TOO IF YOU WERE STEALING . . ." In the renewed flood of laughter Alvah alone remained sober, for the moment giving up the struggle, sulking, running a fretful hand through sparse hair; and beside me the earthy Angelina exhaling through her nose, snuffling like a rutting filly . . .

"But let us for the moment grow somber and respectful as befits the occasion, for the hungry i does indeed take enormous pleasure—nay, *pride*—in presenting for her eight hundredth appearance before a San Francisco audience, the inimitable, the insatiable, the in-*scru*table—"

Wheeeeek ping

Seeing his chance, Alvah seized the mike from Corey's grasp.

"LADIES AND GENTLEMEN, ANGELINA CAMPAGNA."

"I worship you!" Alberto whispered as she stepped onstage through the remnants of laughter—a scattering of applause—into a single dazzling cone of light. I counted off four beats and swung into the intro. Angelina clasped her hands reverently before her and drew a calming breath. "Non dimenticar . . ." She sang, smiling blindly into the bright, smoky glare.

IN THE BAR between shows—a new lineup of acts—Alberto and I settled down to some serious drinking.

Behind us, a voice from the sparse second-show line of ticket holders said, "Who's the illiterate misspelled the broad's name?"

Over the glistening bar mirror was lettered in peach chalk:

BARBRA STREISAND
WOODY ALLEN
ANGELINA CAMPAGNA

She was still in her teens; he was twenty-five, writing jokes for other comics. And for the first week of the engagement you could have shot off the proverbial cannon in the place because no one on this coast knew who either was.

"Que tal, muchachos?" Banducci greeted us.

"*Bien*. The *bambina* with the nose can sing," Alberto said. "You have an option?"

"Of course."

"Like always you are way ahead of me."

"Enrico, you should've put Angelina or the joke teller in the top slot," one of the ticket holders said. "You're gonna lose your shirt with this Barbara whoever she is."

"Bar-*bra*. Please. She insists. When word of mouth takes effect you'll see the room turn around, I guarantee you."

Angelina in a violet housecoat came down the bar scowling. " 'Rico, you've got to keep that maniac out of the control booth and the dressing room. What's he hanging around for? He's driving me bananas."

Banducci affably wrapped her in a huge *paisano* hug.

"Jesus, come on now"—vexed, struggling out of his grasp—"I get pushed around in this joint like a third-rate tank-town act." She strode away, mad.

"Come back here, you magnificent dumb broad!" Banducci roared (leading one to speculate that something beyond the traditional entrepreneur-chanteuse relationship had developed behind the scenes), stalking her the length of the bar, the line of patrons' heads turning as if in the wake of a fire truck.

"I'll just take a wee sip if I may," Alberto said, intercepting my second scotch and water. He sipped tentatively, mused, heavy eyes roaming, then in a twinkling downed it whole, banging the empty glass authoritatively on the bar. *"Bonito!"*

We played the joke teller on, then Alberto departed, leaving me to supply fragments of cued music throughout the act. Allen's delivery was awkward—it was his second or third time on a cabaret stage—but his writing credits were gold, and on the tapes Banducci had heard in the agent's office, the kid was saying some funny things.

This night he never had a prayer. Two hecklers on opposite sides of the room zeroed in on an irresistible target—a scrawny bespectacled 120-pounder clumsily jabbing his arms in the air like a comic-strip Mort Sahl to punctuate his lugubrious chronicle of growing up Jewish, homely, and middle-class in Brooklyn. Within ten minutes of his twenty-five-minute turn he was reduced to something pale and quivering, his back to the audience, elbows on piano, mumbling material to the brick wall. A barrage of whistles and catcalls brought Banducci barging through the swing doors. I called across the piano to this shell of a boy that the old man was coming down the aisle and he better get his act together (when that phrase was used only in its literal sense).

"What's with the comic?" Banducci said behind me.

"Couple drunks got to him. He's froze."

"Any chance of him coming out of it?"

"Not from where I'm sitting."

"Take him off." Banducci signalled to Alvah in the control booth. Alvah either didn't get it or was raising objections, mouthing something unintelligible and waving his arms. Banducci strode across the front row and into the booth. His deep-down voice came hurtling over the PA like a fifty-pound shot put. "THANK YOU FOR THE HUNGRY I AND COMEDIAN WOODY ALLEN." The room went to black.

La Streisand, as she was already being called by perceptive observers, arrived on a different wavelength. A smallish, nineteen-year-old semi-zaftig Jewish girl with the profile of a Sumerian queen and the presence of a twenty-five-year veteran on the Keith–Albee–Orpheum circuit, belting Fats Waller and Harold Arlen tunes with a Sophie Tucker-like moxie and pizzazz, inserting a turnaround rendition of "Happy Days Are Here Again" in Depression-era dirge tempo, unfailingly bringing the salt and sting of remembrance to middle-aged eyes. Spooning honey from a jar between songs to soothe her tortured fledgling throat (for which Banducci had voiced concern—"Careful, dear, you ought to be using more diaphragm"), simultaneously transfixing the audience with an impromptu, artful Mae West-inflected monologue about anything that happened to spring into her silly-wise head. And closed her act by introducing the boys in the band in the same brassy corner-of-the-mouth tones. "To my left, on the drums [added for the engagement]—or rather, *behind* the drums, in silver trunks with embossed Star of David, weighing in at one-seventy-four"—trotting over with tiny steps in the skin-tight robin's-egg blue shift to raise the flushed drummer's hand—"Bobby . . . Talman! In the opposite corner, in green bathrobe and lavender trunks, defending titlist and Cisco Kid of the bull fiddle"—trot, trot, trot—"Alberto . . . Rodriguez!"

The story of how Banducci discovered her became a San Francisco legend, subject to variations. He was in his New York booker's office lining up acts for the fall season when she burst in the door. A frizzy-haired teenager in muumuu and tennis shoes. "You the guy with the cellar club on the coast? Why don't you hire me—I'm gonna be a big star." "Will you get out of here, *meshuggena*," the agent said, "we're busy." "I'll be so big, making so much dough, you won't be able to talk to me. You'll go down on your lovin' knees and beg me to play your crummy joint." The agent apologized, got up, and hustled her out the door. "If she's free in November," Banducci said, "I'll pay two hundred a week and transportation." "Are you crazy? You haven't even heard her sing," the agent said. "She sings, too? Make it two-fifty." It was one of those quasi-accidents of booking for which Banducci had earned his notoriety and sometime sobriquets, The Billy Rose of North Beach and The Man with the Magic Touch.

By the second week, talk-show interviews and word of mouth had brought moderate lines to the club. By the third and final week the house was jam-packed nightly and reverberating with stomping glass-banging ovations. Woody had got his act together (it was a good one), and La Streisand was singing gloriously. On closing night Banducci joined her for the last show, the two hamming it up grandly, unashamedly, improvising operatic arias in commingled Italian and Yiddish into the wee hours as red-jacketed waiters brought bouquets of roses and buckets of champagne to the stage, passing out free bubbly to a joyous audience, on its feet and cheering as at Kezar Stadium in its glory days.

WHEN ACTS NOT requiring accompaniment were onstage, Alberto and I adjourned to the bar-lounge, where a nightly carnival was in progress. The two *muchachos*, from their observation-post bar stools, taking in the passing parade.

Or, as Alvah tartly addresses us: "Mr. Paderewski and Mr. Casals. When are you going to play some decent entr'acte music? All I hear is the same old crap." Meaning current show tunes, jazz standards, and my scintillating originals. "Why don't I ever hear anything from *Garrick Gaieties* or *Finian's Rainbow?*"

"We don't know anything from those moldy-fig shows," Alberto tells him. (Actually we know a tune or two from *Finian's* but aren't going to give him the satisfaction.)

One of the elderly Chinese waiters is tugging on Alvah's sweater. "Mr. Miller to see you in dining room."

"What Mr. Miller? I don't know any Mr. Miller."

The waiter peruses a scrap of paper at arm's length. "Mr. . . . Arthur Miller?"

"Why didn't you say so." Even Alvah is impressed, and moves rapidly, stiff-legged, toward The Other Room.

"He can't stand jazz," Alberto says. "He had a bit part in *Garrick Gaieties* around nineteen twenty-six, which is why he keeps asking for those mothball tunes."

"That's the year I was born."

"So you know how moldy those numbers gotta be," Alberto says.

I had recently seen film clips of Alvah's appearance before the HUAC, which is probably why Miller is here. Alvah had been stalwart, fearless; had not only refused to fink but had castigated his persecutors and gallantly done his year in Texas, where, toward the end of his tenure, he would enjoy the ironic pleasure of hearing on the grapevine that his prime accuser, Congressman J. Parnell Thomas, was cleaning out chicken houses at another federal institution in Danbury, Connecticut.

A few stools down from us a scent of jasmine wafts from the satin corselets of a trio of Hotsy Totsy waitresses, surrounded by attentive men wearing name tags on their business suits ("Hi. Hobart 'Hap' Wilkinson, Acme Machine Tool Corp., Sioux City"). Ignoring the leering prairieland overtures, the women drink their highballs and smoke their ciggies with bored, sullen expressions. (Earlier I overheard one, shaking a wandering hand from her shoulder, say: "I'll tell you, Charlie, my life's very simple. I feed my kids, I hustle drinks, I buy a few lids. That's it.")

Another (potential) jailbird saunters by in tooled cowboots, bleached-out jeans, and Nehru tunic.

"Hombre, como va la cosa?" Alberto says.

"Hey, amigo . . ."

The skin is drawn tight across Lenny Bruce's face, the pouched, bruised-looking eyes at once darting and reflective. He is currently on trial here for using a ten-letter obscenity (rack your brains) during a performance at the Jazz Workshop, and is nearing the end of his life. Later tonight he will take over the stage and empty the show room of several hundred conventioneers as effectively as if tear gas were dispensed through the air-conditioner ducts—and two hours later free-fall in such a carefree, boneless manner from the open second-story window of his Broadway hotel (next day the word would circulate that Lenny presumed he could fly) that he will engage the paramedic who attends him in lively, obscene chatter and come out of the fall with only a sore back.

A ripple of excitement down the line now, heads swiveling—not for Lenny, few know who he is on this tourist-laden night—as two identifiable figures descend the stairway and enter the bar, one moderately slim and dark-suited, the other broad-shouldered in a busy sport jacket, a slight swagger to his gait, which has more to do with physical proportion than deliberate manner. Both fairly large men, though not as heroic-sized as you'd expect from their films—Efrem Zimbalist, Jr., and Charlton Heston. Now it is the waitresses' turn: they all but melt from their bar stools, eyes gone soft and mouths slack.

"Boys, where's the powder room, please?" One of the name-tagged businessmen smiling loosely, a little drunkenly at us. Alberto politely points out the sign MEN at the far end of the lounge. As the man heads in that direction, Alberto lifts one of my dollar bills and says to the bartender, "Bet you this he does, Edmond." Edmond nods and the three of us follow the man's itinerary. The sign, painted high on a corner wall, refers to a door directly to the left on the adjoining wall, and like the kids in Jacques Tati's *Mon Oncle* who make book on which deliberately distracted pedestrian will collide with a lamppost, the employees wager nightly on which male patron, advancing on the sign, will walk virtually into the wall, feverishly searching for a nonexistent doorknob. The man arrives in the designated area. Edmond mutters something and Alberto begins chuckling as the man kicks gingerly at the base of the wall, one hand scrabbling waist-high, feeling for something rounded and of brass. A waiter advances expressionlessly, taps him on the shoulder, and directs him a short ninety-degree turn to the left. Edmond pays off and Alberto tucks the two bills in his coat pocket.

The sound of a distant drumroll from The Other Room signals Bobby Short's show. I have another twenty minutes before playing on the headliner and wander down the bar to listen to the elegant troubadour—not so much to his voice, which is an acquired taste, but to the surprising, unorthodox harmonies he finds in well-worn Cole Porter standards. He is waiting by a rear banquette, adjusting a lemon silk handkerchief in the breast pocket of his tux while the drummer's gathering roll builds suspense and a pin spot casts a blue moon's glow on the beckoning baby grand. A lavender-gowned matron stirs in the banquette alongside him, looking about her; now she reaches out, plucks Bobby's sleeve. I assume she is going to make an ill-timed request. She says briskly, "Waiter, more coffee here please."

Short pulls himself up to his full five-feet-eight or so, his baby face aquiver; he stares down at the woman with a frozen and incredulous smile. "Madame, I am not your waiter. I am your pianist and your singer."

IN THE SHOW room there is no verbal introduction of Professor Irwin Corey ("The World's Foremost Authority"). Alvah, a victim of long harassment at the hands of the prickly, annually booked comic, has refused to participate. Corey's entrance works better without it. In a darkened house we play him on with "Pomp and Circumstance" in heavy martial cadence. "Lights! . . . Lights, you uncircumcised philistine!" he howls at Alvah; and to me, "Slowly, dolorosa! Try sitting on the frigging keys, it might sound better—"

I was growing accustomed, though not yet inured, to the role of musician as straight man. There is a long tradition for it: the tail-end banjoist as butt of the minstrel lines; a winding trail of baggy-pants fiddlers from Red Bank to Fargo; Jack Benny's radio show in the thirties with Phil Harris and the boys playing willing pratfall-lushes. We are the comics' perennial fall guys, smiling bravely under our dunce caps—semi-mute and expendable, Laurels to their blustering Hardys, prepared to be flung into the breach when the first bombs start dropping. No other professional is subject to such public degradation. The options: (1) abandon dignity for the moment, forgo pride, and roll with the attack, knowing Oliver means you no real or permanent harm (you might even get to enjoy it); (2) squirm under the brutal lights and complain to management, who could be expected to react to such a cavil as they would to a waiter refusing to clean up after a customer's overturned highball.

A month earlier I had been an unsuspecting victim of Jack E. Leonard's curare-tipped barbs. After playing the massive, check-suited, progenitor of insult onstage with an up-tempo "The Preacher," I segued into "Clair de Lune" as instructed. Alberto, who had worked the act the previous year, set down his bass and departed with these words of advice in my ear: "Keep repeating 'Clair' no matter what."

"No matter what *what*?"

"If he sits too hard on you kick him in the balls and run like hell."

Sits too hard on me? He looked to be pushing three fifty.

"Hasta luego, Ricardo Montalban," Leonard called to Alberto's retreating back, "Arrivederci, Tijuana." Squinting into the blazing bank of lights, he began fanning himself with his straw boater. "I have forty-five minutes to do, these lights will be very good for my sinuses . . . Hey, Eichmann," he bellowed to Banducci in the back row, "open the doors, it's murder in here!" Then came my turn. "My colleague here, playing the sound-wired coffin, is one of the finest nonrecording artists in the Bay Area. He tries very hard, but what the hell, if ya ain't got it, ya ain't got it. The tune he's playing is 'Clair de Lune' and she certainly was . . . Smile, you little cocker, or you won't get any D-O-P-E after the show . . ."

I began to comprehend Alberto's meaning. It was going to be a long forty-five minutes under the arcs.

". . . You wouldn't guess it looking at him, but my fine-feathered friend with the spongy fingers here studied at the conservatory in Vienna for four years and another two at, uh, first-rate institutions in Antwerp and Hamburg, which explains why, if you listen carefully, he don't know a goddam thing about American music. What key are you in, sonny boy?"

"D-flat."

"And you certainly are . . ."

The sweat began trickling under my shirt as it became deadly clear that for three-quarters of an hour I was meant to function as a sounding board, subtly resonant and preferably inanimate. To twenty-five choruses of "Clair de Lune."

But the audience was sitting on their hands. Attuned to the scalpel satire of Winters, Sahl, Gregory, et al., they weren't taking to the cheap shots and burley-house patter; they weren't even warm.

". . . Seriously, folks, this boy is one of the best accompanists in the country, but when he's working the city something seems to go wrong."

My stride left hand for a double scotch over. This was worse than the most demeaning of the funny-hat-and-coat gigs back east; at least there I'd had anonymity. Gazing numbly out through the smoke-shot haze of lights—trying to escape the heavy hand and horn-rims—I focused on two familiar figures in the second row. Amy Avalon sitting beside a skinny guy with a hairline mustache (that would have to be Vincent's brother-in-law, filing or paring his nails with what looked like a stiletto). And Frank Sinatra, whom I'd seen earlier in the bar with his entourage; for a fleeting moment our glances met (my "Nancy with the Laughing Face" nightmare flashing on the retina), and I thought I detected a flicker of sympathy in those hard, show-wise eyes.

". . . had the misfortune of spending last Sunday in your sister city of Oakland across the bay. Oakland on Sunday. Peoria is Monte Carlo compared to Oakland on Sunday . . . Either you've got two baldheaded men concealed down there, madame"—to a strapless-gowned lady in the front row—"or the basketball season is early this year."

A pall had settled over the room. A silent rain of dud bombs had been falling for nearly thirty minutes, the yocks few and far between. Back I went into the breach.

"Try blowing your nose, junior, it might improve the refrain . . . Seriously, folks, my friend with the flat fingers here, José Iturbi, Junior, is one of the best accompanists of the day, but when night falls the bottom seems to drop out . . ."

Kick him in the balls and run like hell.

"You're in trouble, Jack," Sinatra, or one of his party, called out amiably, as amiably as one trouper can so advise another.

"I'm not in trouble—you're in trouble! Put your teeth back in and get the hell out of here! . . . 'Tea for Two,' two choruses, stop-time second," Jack rasped at me, and he looked troubled.

Now an amazing transformation took place. The bald, porky man suddenly feather-light on his feet, moving trimly in a classic soft-shoe, straw boater pinwheeling on one finger, soles softly swishing the planks. The audience, turned off by the cornball red-barn banter, willingly hitched onto this excursion down Memory Lane, lovely old strings plucked and sweet chords strumming, even the few youths in the house touched by the gossamer charm of something they'd heard about or seen in grainy old flicks—fat-man vaudevillian abruptly, astonishingly graceful, in two brief choruses evoking a half century's nostalgia, Eddie Foy and Bojangles, Pocatello to the Palace.

" 'We will raise a family,' " he sang, belting it with panache and tuneful pipes, " 'a boy for you and a girl for me'—Goin' home!" he roared and we took it out together, pulling out all stops, as they say, bagging redeeming boffs and applause on the bow-off.

I left by the side exit, sweat-soaked, and ran into him in the bar, where Alberto and Edmond were making book on the outcome of end-of-show traffic headed for MEN.

"Couple more nights like this," he said, mopping his face, "I'm buying into the marble-and-granite cartel. You don't mind those bits I use, do you?" He offered his hand.

"Sort of," I said, trying to smile away the animus as I reached for his hand. He recoiled as if I were proferring a live tarantula. "Don't touch me, I'm big-time"—and the next instant half my cheek was between a pudgy thumb and forefinger and he was tweaking hard, like a Jewish mother *kitzeling* a five-year-old. "Can't you smile a little more up there, *meshuggener?* Let's have a drink." His chins sank into his neck; he was chuckling at something over my shoulder, the broad wreathed face beaming like a lighthouse up close.

I turned. The Hoboken Kid and his gang were gathered behind us; recognizable were Pat Kennedy, Peter Lawford, Leo Durocher, Porfirio Rubirosa, and Mike Romanoff. What had caught Jack's eye was a little butterball of a guy in a black silk suit and silver tie flitting around the group, agitatedly tugging at various sleeves. "C'mon, let's take off," he was saying. "No action here, gang, let's blow this joint . . ." Now Sinatra half turned; his leisurely, controlled voice was edged with menace. "I'm telling you one last time, Louie, go wait in the car . . ."

"Now *that's* big-time," Jack chuckled.

Our drinks came. I reached for my wallet.

"Put your goddam money away," he said, affronted, "I make a quarter of a million dollars a year."

GRUDGINGLY, ALVAH BRINGS the lights up—"Pomp and Circumstance" continuing under—revealing a mock-crippled Professor bent almost double, face ravaged by grief and suffering as he is assisted up the stage stairs by Banducci (hard pressed to keep a straight man's straight face, for he enjoys Corey hugely). The diminutive Professor is moving excruciatingly slowly, attired for his impending seminar in moth-eaten frock coat, ankle-high sneakers, and frayed string tie dangling to the knees of wino pants. At the top stair he shakes Banducci off, makes his painful way alone, weakly scuffling and scrabbling like a marionette on loose strings to center stage, where, with creaking of bones and sighing expulsions of breath, he straightens slowly up—our cue to fade out.

Battle-hardened by past encounters with ruthless practitioners of the craft, I still am not prepared for the Professor's thrust, ten minutes into a tortuous opening discourse on Moses leading the Jews out of Egypt (but a Moses and a cast of Jews you would be unlikely to witness in your most windblown dreams). Suddenly wheeling on me (Alberto's urgent "On your toes, *amigo!*" brushing my ears), he inquires with Shakespearean gravity, "What key art'st thou in?" Tintinnabulations of Jack E. Leonard: these troupers come out of the same alley and have lines and attacks in common; only the delivery differs. But here the question is as illogical as it is unexpected: I haven't touched the keyboard. Of course, logic isn't the Professor's strong suit. For what seems minutes he fixes me with a stark and baleful gaze. Careful; I know I have to say something, and at the same time I realize it does not much matter what. "Shall I repeat the question," he intones, stony expression implying I am lousing up his act. "Please, Professor." We are worrying each other like cat and squirrel. "What key art'st thou in?" Well, pick a letter from A to G. "C-sharp," I say. His eyes blaze like a rabid evangelist's. "NEXT TIME I ASK YOU

SOMETHING SHUT THE FLUG UP!" Tatters of nervous laughter spill over the room. The conventioneers are not used to the F word, mutated or not, in public places. The voice turns prissy, schoolmarmish. "You may leave the seminar. All two of you. Dismissed." He waves a hand airily at Alberto and me. We troop single file down the aisle past the rows, and it's a long, long walk through that vale of fatuous cracker grins.

We watch the rest of the show from the back row. Despite our ordeal—and there is more to come—Corey is a spellbinder. The scruffy, manic pedant is a classically realized character, and he delivers his inspired gibberish with a jazzman's timing.

"*Time to get off, Corey . . .*" Banducci's voice blasting over the speakers. He has run well over his allotted forty-five minutes.

"Get off who?" Corey cocks his head in befuddlement; gazes around, up, searching the bank of lights and beyond for a source. "Gabriel? . . ."

"Get off, or I'm going to come up there and pull you off."

"In front of all these people?" The volatile face composes itself, the hands fold before the string tie in ecclesiastic earnestness. "Ladies and gentlemen, that concludes your show . . ." The eyes sparkle, a beatific grin flares. "Now I do mine." Banducci has left the booth and is marching up the aisle; if necessary he will sling the little man over his shoulder like a sack of nuts and carry him out.

"I would like to thank Tex Maynard, Clara Bow, S. Z. Zakall, Tom Mix, Vilma Banky, Phineas T. Barnum, and the entire orchestra . . ." This is my and Alberto's cue to return to the stage, back into the breach, the pits—not to play him off, would that it were that simple, but to stand abreast with our backs against the brick wall. "Two instrumentalists, separate individuals in their own right, who have banded together to form an ensemb' . . ." The Professor's voice is reasonable, complimentary, elegiac, as we squirm and blink in a hot glare of twin spots, aligned and pinned like specimens to a board. "Don, the leader of the entire orchestra"—an inclusive sweep of the arm—"came to us a poor boy. Today he is a poor man . . ."

The demeanor abruptly changes; the eyes turn manic, the body rigid as a bird dog's. He leaps offstage into the front row, tattered coat billowing behind, and seizes a graying, fur-stoled matron by the shoulder. "Tell me, madame, do you recognize any of them? Is *he*"—eyes burning demoniacally, a stubby, accusatory finger stabbing at me—"the sex maniac?"

The house fades to dark.

ONE FORTY-FIVE A.M. The lights are up, patrons turning back their seats, waiters shedding their red jackets, when the slight sallow-skinned figure in cowboots and Nehru tunic wanders onstage. Alvah says laconically over the PA, "You might want to stay for this, ladies and gentlemen," and I have never heard such deference and respect in his tone. Most of the patrons ease back down, looking about, whispering to one another, "What's going on . . . Who is he? . . . Do we have to pay extra? . . ." He paces back and forth for most of a minute, head bent in thought, knuckles to mouth; he might be alone, steeped in self-rehearsal, familiarizing himself with the layout (though this stage is hardly alien to him). Banducci is leaning against the rear wall, arms folded, alert with anticipation despite the long night. A few waiters have slipped back in, along with Edmond and David, the club manager—a roly-poly man with a bum right knee that causes him to roll and pitch like a tipsy buccaneer. "People back east would pay good bread for this," Alberto whispers to me in the back row. "I don't know why he's giving it away like a class whore."

"Now I happen to be Jewish"—Lenny is half-facing the audience, cocking his head at them, the slightly bulging eyes grave and speculative; his gratuitous self-identification has brought a stir, then a hushed pall to the heartland ranks of blue serge, plaid jackets and pantsuits—"and I know we're supposed to have killed Christ, though I think the Romans had a lot to do with it. But I'll tell you this much, the next time that *tzaddik* shows his face we're gonna stick it to him good."

A distinct ripple along the rows, you can feel it like a comber rolling onto a beach, the heads aligned and uniform as whitecaps, perched high in the seats, blanched, stern-visaged.

The strange one is pacing again, short, charged strides like a whippet in a cage—and stops. "You ever wonder why a lion, *macher* of the jungle, backs off from the animal trainer's chair?" No one deigns an answer. (*What's that got to do with Christ killers, for God's sake?*) "Alvah, you got a cane-bottom chair in there?" Alvah does, and schleps it out. Lenny raises it to the audience, sweeps it back and forth over the front rows like a carnival hawker. "Let's say in the life of this chair maybe five thousand asses have sat on it, and that's a conservative figure. Put yourself behind the eyes of the lion. You don't see a simple cane-bottom chair, you're looking five thousand hairy asses in the face—naturally you cut out."

A renewed bristling across the rows, unallayed by pockets of employee laughter; Banducci is chuckling quietly to himself, the avuncular swashbuckler's face fractured. A few patrons have slipped into the aisles, murmuring, faces stiff with affront. One is arguing with the club manager standing behind us—demanding his money back, though he has seen a complete show. (David, a soft-spoken and infinitely logical fellow, tells him, "Sir, that's like finishing a meal in a restaurant and refusing to pay because the complimentary liqueur sent to your table by the proprietor is not quite to your liking.")

". . . Rapped for a minute in the bar with a civil engineer from Cedar Rapids—he still here?" Lenny shades his eyes and gazes out over the lighted house; the Cedar Rapids native on pain of death will not admit to this acquaintanceship, no matter how brief. "Okay. Anybody from the Okefenokee Swamp? No. I'll tell you something about Cedar Rapids, Sandusky, Kokomo . . . Lesbians get away with murder in those small towns. Faggots're no problem, they're easy to pin, even the private *fresser*s. You all know what a faggot is, don't you?" He comes to the lip of the stage and peers out; the front-row patrons recoil slightly, bending beneath him like river reeds in a foul breeze. "He takes it up the *tuchis*."

An electric charge sweeps the house, a distant prairie-fire crackling, wool and rayon rustling like insects' antennae as more departees peel off the main body, spill into the aisles . . . Who *is* this guy? . . . And what's a *tuchis?* (Plain enough what he means but why call it something even more disgusting sounding than what it is?) . . . An unsavory look about him in the foreigner's coat with his putty-colored skin and nervous, hunted eyes. Something . . . unhealthy, not quite clean beyond the filth spewing out of his mouth . . . something, well, yes, *unkosher* . . .

". . . But the dykes, they haven't had the exposure even though we're sometimes married to 'em. I go into one of those little communities, see an obvious diesel dyke with a Bruce Cabot face"—a strange constricted chuffing sound emanating from the speakers, as if someone were quietly strangling; it's coming from Alvah, head bowed and hand covering eyes, chortling into his chest; of course, an ex-screenwriter, he must *know* Bruce Cabot)—"leather zipper jacket, short hair, army shoes . . . And the people are never hip. 'That's Mrs. Lovell' [fluting childlike tones], 'she's a real tomboy.' *Tomboy, I'm hip.* 'Boy, she can hit a baseball farther than a guy!' *Uh-huh, what's she do for a living?* 'Oh, she heads the Girl Scout troop.' *A troop fresser, I dig* . . . By the way, you all know what a dyke is, don't you? . . ."

They are waiting for this, they're standing as one, as if by cue, chairs slamming back, Alberto's bellow of laughter riding over the irate swarm and crush as they jostle their way out of the rows.

"I'll put it this way—an old shtick—if you can stand the smell you got it licked . . ."

They're streaming en masse for the exits, a middle-American tide, frozen-faced, demeaned, outraged, some turning to shake a fist, shouting abuse, epithets (*We don't have to sit here and take this shit*), giving back as good as they got.

"Could be worse, man"—he is hollering over the din to Banducci—"when they walked out on me in Milwaukee they walked *toward* me!"

It has not been one of Lenny's better nights, he has scarcely cranked up, and on Banducci's face proprietary enjoyment has faded to something rueful and elegiac—a look of resignation, disheartenment. But not for the animosity generated or future patronage lost: more an expression of sorrow that an audience, no matter what its origins, should see fit to walk out in concert on this abrasive, tormented man who contained within his slight tummler's frame the voltaic energy to goad, convulse, alienate, and enrage, to empty show rooms and transform minds—who would lift off and burn like a Roman candle for a brief time, and when he came down would leave an electric, bluish afterglow that would remind us of the sparks and scorch and illumination that had been.

19

I was gaining confidence—like Val on top of his talent, rising to the occasion and some nights going right over it. Weaned from entr'acte Valium and Kaopectate, shrugging off unpredictable comic dusters and beanballs. It was an inside curve Mort Sahl threw me on a Friday night following my strident impromptu play-on of "It's a Grand Old Flag." (He left the choice of introduction to me, and I had conceived the George M. Cohan oldie as ironic counterpoint to his material.) Sahl, whom Banducci likened to "a very acid Mark Twain," had been his first comic discovery in the early fifties, hired at seventy-five dollars a week. There was no liquor license; kids from Cal and State and Stanford sat on rickety chairs drinking Filipino beer out of wax cups listening to the first stand-up political satire ever, thrilled to hear subjects aired in public that had only been spoken of in the privacy of living rooms and fraternity houses (even then you were wise to choose your friends). The political climate was considerably chillier at the time and an FBI agent or two could usually be found in the audience, reacting to the intelligence that a snotty kid who hung around UC Berkeley was denouncing the government to a basement full of radicals. On that Friday night, a decade later, as I concluded the Cohan play-on and slid off the bench, I heard him complain, "Did you ever in your life hear such unmitigated noise?" Strange line to open with, I thought (nothing personal, let's hope), and made my customary exit down the right-side aisle. His voice, knifing over the speakers, stopped me cold. "MR. ASHER." I turned very slowly; for some reason my rendition or the choice of tune—a parody was currently making the rounds, "He's a Grand Ol' Fag," which hardly applied to the incumbent—had touched a nerve. Three hundred pairs of eyes converged on me. Three hundred and one: Sahl transfixing me with the gaze of God Himself and grinning like a sated jackal. "Have you ever contemplated an alternate means of livelihood?" "No," I replied truthfully and added, surprising myself, "have you?" (I'm not sure how far my unamplified voice carried. It could have cost me the piano bench; Sahl was as big as they come. But his moods were mercurial, and by the next show all was forgotten.)

I had never been surer of my talent nor more caught up in every facet of the trade. Assorted benefits accrued from my position as resident pianist of the West Coast's most renowned cabaret. Performers commissioned me to revise their charts; vocalists sought me out for rehearsal and coaching. Departing performers laid gifts on Alberto and me as tokens of gratitude—a cabaret tradition I had not been aware of: from Dick Gregory, pairs of silver cuff links featuring embossed grand pianos and bass fiddles; a half dozen pairs each of ribbed solid-color socks delivered in brown paper bags by Jack E. Leonard

(*Put your goddam money away, I make a quarter of a million dollars a year*); from the glorious songstress Miriam Makeba, pear-shaped bottles of imported cognac. (When I was taken to the dressing room by her manager to meet her for the first time, unsure of the extent of her English—though I had previously heard her sing one or two tunes in the language, the lyrics seemed to have a precise, rote quality—I nodded and bowed silently as befitting an African queen and illustrious foreign artist in flowing bands of spangled silk. She was standing with her back to the mirror, sipping tea from a thin, intricately figured cup. She looked upon my genuflection with amazement, then turned on a grin that was like the sun bursting over Cape Town; held out five, flicked a wanton hip at me, and spoke: "What's happenin', baby?")

The Hotsy Totsy girls now greeted me by name, pecked my cheek, and allowed me to buy them occasional drinks, a custom I discontinued when I learned they were all divorced mothers of two to four kids and sleeping or living with studs. Strolling the bar-lounge, I could admire my charcoal profile (designated House 88 Man) hung between Godfrey Cambridge and Peter, Paul, and Mary. "I appreciate the company," I told Mandy. She was amassing an impressive exhibition of luminaries—chalk and charcoal portraits of the great, near great, and promising in dramatic and/or humorous juxtaposition (Dick Gregory bleakly eyeing a prissy Shelley Berman, Zero Mostel ogling La Streisand), belters, comics, chirps and terps, a gallery as venerable and glittering in its inspired, heartfelt way as any that ever lined the halls of Versailles.

JACKSON STREET AFTER midnight on a starry September morning. The last-show line winding past the white-and-black brick facade (*Club des Artistes: Kingston Trio Bill Dana Maya Angelou*), snaking around the Columbus Avenue corner (much like the papier-mâché dragon that would soon wind a similar route commemorating the Chinese Year of the Rabbit), skirting a trio of youthful Beach denizens—the last of the beats or the first of the flower children?—huddled peon fashion in the Hotsy Totsy entranceway, naked gray feet splayed out on the mottled sidewalk. The bill had been pulling capacity crowds all week. The previous night, manager David Allen informed 125 people without tickets they might as well go home, all three shows were sold out. "Not a soul moved, it was like mass hypnotism," he told us in the bar. "A hundred twenty-five people stared at me like I'd just escaped Vacaville; I don't know what goes through their minds. I think they feel there's a conspiracy, for some dark reason I'm trying to get rid of them . . ."

"When it comes to crowds it's every tub on its own bottom," a black newsman remarked cryptically.

"I went up and down that line three times, repeating myself. You begin to feel silly after awhile. There was a fellow about a hundredth in the no-ticket line, well-dressed, patient, as sane looking as you or me"—David made a deferential wave of his hand toward Alberto—"as you. I said to him, 'Sir, just to satisfy a humble man's curiosity, I've told everyone without tickets three times that we're completely sold out for the night, yet you're still standing here. Do you think I'm some kind of imposter impersonating the manager or that I've escaped from the nuthouse or what?' He said, 'Well, you can never tell, someone with a reservation might die or something and I'd get his ticket.' But ninety-nine people would have to drop dead on the sidewalk for him to get in!"

Now, looking toward Enrico's Coffeehouse and the narrow moonlit dwellings hugging Telegraph Hill, their windows reflecting trinkets of light from the East Bay, I think what a long road it's been from the New England turnpike saloons, Rudy's chop-suey gigs, and the bug-infested pavilions of upstate New York to this congenial stamping ground. I'd slogged through the mud and reached the pearls; nothing but green leas ahead, as Val would have said. A week ago when David asked me when I wanted to schedule my vacation, I said, "What vacation? I'm already on it!"

I cross in front of the waiting line and descend to the reverberant cellar, feeling euphoric, stars in my eyes. "Who's that guy? . . . How does he rate? . . ." Envious voices trail in my wake. Muffled laughter erupts behind the swing doors, and Sylvia Syms's knowing, candy voice drifts from the candlelit Other Room, singing of a mythical skylark. A man in his seventies in an expensive loose-fitting dark suit, a gold watch chain straddling the vest, is being sketched by Mandy, his profile paralleling the gallery of immortals and seeming to incontestably belong in a patriarchal, guardian-angel sort of way. There is a hauntingly familiar cast to the ancient jutting face and merry eyes—he belongs in a Santa Claus suit with a lot of pillows—the tart, slightly lopsided great-auntie smile . . . I turn away, close my eyes and look again. Yes, the jaunty smile does it for me, at once melancholy and playful, reflecting distant plank stages in venerable red-barn summer theaters (think of the boards he has trod!). From Mandy's polite, detached smile I can see she is too young to remember Edward Everett Horton.

Fifteen feet down the bar a workman stands with a long wrench atop a rickety-looking ladder trying to fortify the ceiling against the relentless Hotsy Totsy plumbing, and I think of all the bar patrons I've seen holding cocktail napkins to cheek and bald head, gazing upward as if seeking a pigeon in a cornice. I get a scotch from Edmond—I have five minutes before Bill Dana (José Jiménez) finishes—and settle on a stool to watch the workman.

He's having a hard time of it, muttering to himself amid the exposed network of rusted, glistening pipes; he takes a red kerchief from his back pocket and wipes his face.

"That pipe's been leaking ever since I started here," I say by way of sympathy and solidarity.

He pauses, gazes down on me with a sour expression. "You work here?"

"I'm the house pianist."

"Well hand me that other wrench and hold the ladder."

Leave it to those union guys to let the air out of your balloon.

20

Christmas 1963.

Banducci has a theory about what constitutes a successful comic: he is invariably Jewish (five thousand years of strife and persecution an indispensable ingredient), unhappy, gutsy, screwed-up or out-and-out crazy, and has endured a painful childhood that still haunts him. Jackie Mason, a low-keyed melancholic cherub in a black suit, a thirty-two-year-old former rabbinical student out of Sheboygan (a promising genesis right there), fit the formula like chicken fat fits chopped liver, and Banducci backed his prediction of stardom with an escalating option and bonus arrangement.

Mason was booked Christmas week, and the old saw about the worst three weeks of the year in show biz reared its wizened head. Opening night was silent night, lonely night, and the rest of the week barely improved. We could have hauled in a water hose à la Morty Gelb, sprayed the show room, and bet on who got wet. In The Other Room a neophyte folksinger from Daly City, brought in to bridge name bookings, died a miserable, unattended death.

A visiting Chicago club owner and Banducci compadre emerged from the show room midway through the juggler-raconteur and said, "That's a rough opening act, Rico. I thought we left the Indian-war-club guys back on the Sullivan-Considine circuit."

"I had to take him to get Mason. It's Christmas week, Arnold, what am I supposed to do, bring in Kate Smith and the Mormon Tabernacle choir?"

"So what're you doing with a Jewish comic Christmas week?"

"That's the only time he was available. It happens to be Hannukah too, my friend. You're a single-act room, you're not confronted with this. To get a Cosby or Newhart I'm often forced to take dross in the opening slots. And the worse business is the more I get dumped on." (The previous week an L.A. agent had sent him an ex-territory band thrush, arriving from a Sparks, Nevada, engagement with hair in a silvery beehive and a single floor-length ballroom gown cum plastic orchid, triggering an uncustomary Banducci explosion at Monday afternoon's rehearsal: "David, I won't have her going on my stage looking like a Penney's store-window mannequin, we've got a prestige room, people have supper and see a show, they go back to St. Paul and boast about it. Get rid of the Elks club gown, do something about the hair. Take her to I. Magnin and get her a cocktail dress, hot pants and boots, anything—I know there's a forties trend, but we're gonna stomp it into the ground and bury it by Easter.")

"I'm surprised you still haven't hooked up with the bus tours," the Chicago man pressed.

Banducci made a rude noise. "I don't want those people jamming in here like families pushing through an amusement-park turnstile to gawk at the performers. They're the same folks who're chasing the beats around Grant Avenue and think satire is Don Knotts popping his eyes and doing a double take. They're wrong for the room. They've been preconditioned by the tube and the concepts of the promoters who set up the tours. They'll accept protest songs as long as they don't mean anything or actually *encourage* protest. They don't want funky street singers, they want inoffensive street singers who *look* like they're being funky. They'll listen to Peter Nero play what they think is jazz piano, but they'll walk out on Ahmad Jamal. The club's my second home, I don't want people in one that I wouldn't invite to the other. You get seduced by the steady numbers of them and pretty soon they're dictating policy."

"All I'm trying to say is there's trouble ahead. The kids're starting to take over. Have you been inside one of those converted halls? You'll see a thousand teenagers who look like they bathed last February in clothes I wouldn't dress my Airedale in—but they've got tens and twenties in their hands, buying weed and pills and God knows what else, screaming and hopping around to a band that comes at you like a Pan Am jumbo crash-landing in your backyard."

"I've detected a few vibrations. The musicians sound like they picked up their instruments for the first time two weeks ago and forgot to practice."

"It's more than vibrations, Rico. It's like 1906 all over again, the earth's moving and that isn't Caruso singing out the hotel window."

The week's dismal mood affected everyone. Alvah raised nervous titters from the sparse house, shlumping onstage in his tired pants and sweater to rearrange mikes for the next act, an inch of ash protruding from the burning ciggie in the corner of his mouth. He turned and glowered at the crowd like a peevish grade-school custodian, shuffled back to the booth mike, and scolded in a rasping voice, "What the hell's so goddam funny?" The chastised house lapsed into silence, broken by a high-pitched cackle of laughter from *San Francisco Chronicle* columnist Ralph Gleason sitting close by in the first row behind the piano.

Heads craned in bewilderment, glancing from control booth to the hysterical, possibly deranged man in the aisle seat. *This is the world-famous nightclub we were told we shouldn't miss?*

I thought of the bar-lounge nightly circus, patrons walking into walls scrabbling for invisible doors; Lenny emptying the house at two in the morning with his anti-Christ-faggot-lesbian turns; of Michael Dunn climbing monkey bars onstage and a future superstar comic turning to jelly his first time out, delivering his act to a brick wall. I leaned toward Ralph. "You've been around. Could Alvah and the rest of it happen at any other class club in the country?"

Gleason was half off his chair, still emitting soprano yelps of delight. "No way, not a chance . . ."

Alvah announced dourly from the booth, "If the laughing hyena at stage left will attempt to control himself, we'll continue with our show . . ."

DECEMBER 30. I have been drinking too much—chasing the blues of a lugubrious week—and it is only the second show. I swivel abruptly on the stool to catch the silver heels and fishnet stockings of one of the exiting Hotsy Totsies. The last time I did that I knocked Michael Dunn sprawling; this time I dump a tall Coke into the lap of a short button-nosed girl in a yellow button-down shirt, striped tie, and Dutch Boy cap.

"God, why don't you watch what you're doing?"

Mortified, I start clumsily dabbing at her suede skirt with a cocktail napkin.

"Forget it." She pushes my arm away. "Just buy me another drink."

Within six months—after a decade and a half of lusting after glamazons, mobsters' molls, strippers, and assorted ladies of the night—this fresh-faced kind-of-cute girl who dresses like a boy from the waist up will move in with me and eventually become my wife.

On the lee side of me Alvah says with unrestrained satisfaction to Alberto, "At last we get rid of the aberration from Daly City." Samantha, the nice, sweet, no-talent folksinger in The Other Room, has been given her notice by David. I'd been in the dressing room a short while ago, watching the stars in her eyes turn to tears.

"*Oye, hombre,* how come you hate everyone so much?" Alberto says.

Alvah is affronted. "I don't hate *everyone.* I like you and him [me] and him [Edmond]. That's three people within a square yard."

In the next hour it becomes apparent there will be no third show tonight. An unprecedented premidnight closing. The second-show audience, some twenty-five die-hard souls, files disconsolately up the stairs. For the past forty-five minutes the silence in the show room has been so total you could have heard a mantis praying in the carpeted aisle. Mandy has closed up her easel and gone home early, as have the manager, chef, kitchen help, and most of the waiters. No point loitering in a disaster area, not if you have any choice in the matter. I decide to have one last belt—not so much for the road as in eve-of-New Year's Eve celebration of my third year in this basement citadel of satirists and songbirds, whose hallowed walls are beginning to shudder (the first minuscule cracks appearing) with the reverberations from an inchoate revolution under way in not-so-distant outposts. Alberto waves off, "*Hasta luego,*" and Edmond follows, leaving his second-in-charge, Duane, to kill the lounge lights and close up shop. Only quarter to twelve, it feels like three in the morning. I watch the ex-rabbinical student in the black suit round the bar's lower end, glumly inspecting the remnants of the departing house. He has laid an oversized (undeserved) egg this week and cannot be feeling too chipper. He raises himself onto the end stool like a mournful elf mounting a toadstool, rubbing his hands together as if to warm them, staring at his melancholy image above the dark gleaming bottles, perhaps seeing nothing. I turn away. The last show-room waiter, a tiny ancient Chinese man, discards his baggy red jacket and struggles arthritically into an ankle-length overcoat; clutching the banister, he climbs, aligning both feet on each successive step, into the misting night.

I drain my scotch, feeling suddenly lonely and rueful, the memory of past euphoric nights fading like streamers of fog. Thirty-seven years old and looking back, always looking back. Is it peculiar to musicians to spend so many hours in retrospection? Were the tunes that much better back then, the strippers more sensational? But the strippers are no more; they've become go-go girls, about to become topless dancers, and then bottomless, and in that pristine state will be humped by long-lasting studs (*la grande illusion?*) athwart stages where road companies once performed *Brigadoon* and *Under the Yum Yum Tree* . . . All those New Year's Eves in all those roadhouses, saloons, ballrooms. Will Jackie Mason break off in midroutine tomorrow night, don a paper-hat yarmulke, and jovially lead the congregation in a medley of "Eyn Kelohenu" and "Auld Lang Syne"? . . . I consider asking Duane for one last taste, the good stuff, Chivas Regal or the twelve-year-old Ambassador, when I sense Mason's gaze on me and turn with a faint shudder to glance down the barren, polished wood to the forlorn figure nodding ever so slightly to me out of the gloom. Though I have played him onstage for six straight nights, he is a modest, reserved man, has kept to himself, and the exchanges between us have been spare and functional. I nod back uneasily and am about to signal Duane for the nightcap, to break off the discomforting alliance, when he leans toward me out of the shadows in an earnest, almost supplicating way, the rich rabbinical voice carrying plaintively up the bar, "Excuse me, but are you by any chance Jewish?" I nod again, affirmative, and think I see the faintest consoling smile cross the cherubic face.

A few minutes later he leaves by the rear exit for his hotel, and it is just Duane—closing up—and me with a sixth (seventh?) scotch, and the custodian making a muffled clatter in the room to the left of the wayward sign MEN . . . A sweet and mournful sound has insinuated itself, as if a radio has suddenly been turned on in the club's recesses: a single line, a fragment of violin concerto, but the melody and timbre, though full-bodied, is slightly faltering, not quite accomplished. I carry my drink to the entrance of The Other Room, dark and empty, then back past the show room, where the sound swells. I push through one of the swing doors, and in the dim light slanting from the side dressing room see the bulky, sweatered figure pacing the bare stage, a small fiddle cradled in his shoulder like a swaddled baby. I have heard that Banducci was a promising violinist as a child, and that he still plays occasionally, but no one has caught him at it in years . . . What he is playing is keening, elegiac, the sorrowful refrain singing off old brick (*Slowly, molto doloroso,* I can hear Professor Corey hiss from the wings), and the wavering, forlorn sound (an unsuspected corner of his nature, or does he have a premonition about his noble club and second home?) oddly conjures my own childhood, the sweet pensive fledgling tones of Eric, the wiggy prodigy next door, practicing from midafternoon into dusk; and on a snow-muffled night standing in his backyard at two in the morning in pajamas and overshoes, head cocked, listening to the sound of the world turning in five flats . . . Enrico is playing more confidently now, the burnished wood tucked lovingly into the curve of his neck, moving not with his customary swagger but a big man's sure-footed grace (akin to Jack E. Leonard's going-home soft-shoe), his looming, engorged shadow on red brick trailing a beat behind. The sound begins to soar, grows tender, piercing, like a beseeching voice. I feel I am eavesdropping on something much too private and let the door swing softly shut.

Mounting the stairs, I realize I am weaving and shouldn't drive. But the logistics of getting home, returning tomorrow by bus or cab, a ticket on the windshield . . . I'll be careful. Slowly, doloroso. I take a wrong turn in the Falcon and find myself on Montgomery Street, a darkened canyon of office buildings, a scaled-down touch of Gotham in the city of light and water. And on this deep-shadowed, near-deserted concourse—a horn blaring somewhere behind me, a premature reveler crying "Yippee!" from a glassed doorway—a curious happening is about to enliven if not salvage the desolate evening. For two blocks now, my whirling peripheral vision has been distracted by something extraneous in the gutters and on the sidewalks, a congealed, whitish, confetti-like substance—refuse, perhaps, except a lucid compartment of my mind recalls that these affluent streets, the financial heart of the new West, are assiduously maintained and never less than immaculate. Still, something is there, and there's a lot of it; if I were a little more loaded and/or hallucinating, neglectful of the area's temperate climate, I would say it was freshly fallen powder snow. Curiosity roused, I veer to the curb, where my headlights pick out and clarify the whiteness: small sections of paper, thousands of them, carpeting the street and sidewalks, clogging gutters, blown into doorways; decorating awnings, car hoods, flattened on windshields like traffic tickets—and, unlike confetti, evenly cut in squares and oblongs. It takes a few moments to relate this alien litter to the date, the wall of buildings on either side of me, and a quaint San Francisco custom I have read about: desk-calendar pages ritually flung from office windows on this last workday of the year. A snowfall of private memos! No telling what secrets they might reveal—confidences, inducements, celebrations, confessions, dreams old and new buried among the luncheon dates, dentist appointments, anniversary and birthday reminders—incitements for future compositions (another "Manhattan Serenade," "Jitterbug Waltz," "Boulevard of Broken Dreams")—a treasure-trove for the taking. Angled from the curb, I eagerly kill the motor, empty my music folder on the seat and clamber out. Call it unseemly, a failing of character, but I have never been able to resist exposed communications, no matter how private. I have found myself leaning at precarious angles in buses and restaurants to catch fragments of conversation; poring over cryptic scribblings in the margins of library books with the attention archaeologists might accord hieroglyphs; in apartment-house corridors I stop compulsively at strange doors whenever voices emerge and have been known to scan postcards on foyer tables; and I have lost track of the number of sodden letter pages I have retrieved from gutters to take home, dry in the oven, and avidly peruse. The ring of epithet, the unexpected turn of phrase, the startling image: it's why poets, novelists, and lyricists loiter in bars and streets, ride city buses with tape recorders. Artists are inveterate snoopers, and it is out of such shameful, overweening curiosity that songs and books get written.

Giddy with scotch and fantasy, I reel along the misting boulevard, periodically stooping to gather and horde these pieces of private lives, plucking them from hoods and windshields to stuff into the gaping maw of the folder, manna for the imagination, an obsessed, half-tanked archivist caught up in a ludicrous game . . . Pausing now and then to peer in the dim lamplight at the scrawled memoranda, gleanings of mortality . . . "July 12: Get haircut. E says you look like something out of jungle, 'Wild Man of Borneo' . . . December 4: Ginny off for Big Sur Sunday. Ask once more if I get to go and if not why not and why go on . . . September 23: Walter's operation for you know what. Visit tomorrow w. fruit/flowers/lotion/pajamas? . . . May 5: Call Sue tell her je t'adore . . ." Would a stranger watching from a doorway or passing car consider the slight man in the rumpled raincoat a drunk or derelict scrabbling for refuse to take back to his pitiable hovel for some degrading purpose?

In my apartment—with no recollection of the route taken or time elapsed—I concentrate my spinning vision and sift eagerly through the pages; then, kneeling, begin to lay them out like tarots across the floor, arranged according to month, keeping a red eye peeled (as would any of us) for the special date, my own momentous birthday—a chance kinship with some unseen occupant of cubbyhole or executive suite, lowly clerk or board chairman, whose workaday path I would never cross—my inflamed mind envisioning some secret disclosure encoded on the ledger of our shared destiny, a form of benediction, perhaps, or chilling memento mori; a startling insight or sublime revelation, intimations of a grand design . . . and suddenly there it is, turning up like a trump card unexpectedly soon: *March 7*. My pulse races, I rear back and let out a shout of surprise . . . "Appt. VD clinic 4:30. This time keep it!"

WITHIN A MONTH Alberto and I would present on the brick-backed stage—as entr'acte following Rod McKuen—the world premiere performance of yet another jazz original: the sprightly, loping, raffish "Venereal Material."

21

My mother wrote that Uncle Allie had died of a heart attack in Florida. That stalwart cigar chomper and surrogate father who had been so concerned about my equilibrium in a topsy-turvy world that turned day into night and night into a lake of fire and brimstone, and had recommended the early purchase of a sizable chunk of life insurance. I wondered if he'd be pleased, astonished, or what, that I'd retained both my health and balance, was addicted to nothing stronger than scotch and Mexican food, and spent my working hours not with *shikkers* and *nafkas* (drunks and disreputable women) but with internationally known performers and celebrities of stage and screen. Irwin (Duke) Goldman, the letter went on, was selling Chryslers and Plymouths "like pancakes," had married one of the Shapiro girls, and bought a house in Westwood Hills (Worcester's Grosse Point). My brother, Herbie, now in the sales end of chemistry, had just paid the government a quarterly installment of three thousand dollars—in *estimated* taxes alone. Did I need any money, and when was I coming home?

I wrote back in detail about my new job, having previously told her only that I was working in a famous nightclub, knowing that description would set up for her a contradiction in terms. I was now "musical director," I wrote—choosing the phrase for its cachet; the more accurate "house pianist" would sound in her ears like "building janitor"—of the renowned cabaret, and intimated that I had achieved not only respectability but a measure of vicarious stardom. I played names like Bob Newhart, Mort Sahl, Shelley Berman, Vaughan Meader, Oscar Brown, Jr., and Phyllis Diller onstage nightly; I consorted with Burns and Schreiber, Peter, Paul, and Mary; Zero Mostel had bought me an Irish coffee, Joe Louis shook my hand (his was astonishingly soft and gentle; of course he was no longer decking ofays); Lenny Bruce addressed me intimately ("Hey baby, what's shakin'?"); Jackie Mason had established sociopolitical ties; Jack E. Leonard insulted me gratuitously; and in The Other Room Bobby Short had flung his perspiration-damp yellow silk handkerchief at me in a postshow gesture of (I think) fraternity.

Having seen many of these stars on television, my mother was impressed. She phoned me for more details. Flattered by her interest and appreciation of my newfound stature, I acted impulsively. As there was scant possibility of my making a trip home in the near future, I suggested she come out and visit for a few days and see the stars in person. If the vibes felt right I would introduce her to my future wife, who unfortunately was not Jewish. (I was now seeing her a couple of times a week, having run into her again at a Haight Street fair. "How you doin', man, remember me?" I'd greeted her, unaccountably lapsing into my Coffee John's vernacular. "How'm I doin', *who?*" she said.) After several more back-and-forth calls and letters it was finally arranged. The visit would take place during the week Bill Cosby, one of her favorites, was headlining. She insisted on a multistop night flight to save money, though I was paying the fare, and would arrive before dawn. I told her the limousine would take her downtown, within a half block of the hotel where I'd reserved a room. She should sleep as late as she wanted, then take a taxi to my apartment. I'd be busy most of the morning working on charts, but when she arrived I'd make us lunch and we'd spend the afternoon sightseeing. At night she'd have a front-row seat at the club. She said she didn't want to interrupt my work; I said that was no problem, I'd have the decks cleared by noon.

The big day dawned. My mother, as I've said, is a proper and conventional woman; the everyday amenities are important to her. She arrived for our luncheon and sightseeing in a black dress and fur stole, her gray-white hair newly coiffed. I opened the door at her ring. She looked smaller, frailer; a lifetime of *tsuris* and hardship, real and imagined, had furrowed her face. It had been a lot of years, and I felt a quick sting of tears as I moved to embrace her. "Mom," I said, my voice a heartfelt croak, arms wide in welcome. She drew back, recoiled almost, the thin, worn face falling as she took in the stubble on my cheeks, my rumpled hair, my frayed sweatshirt and dungarees. "This," she said, "you call *work?*"

2 2

It started like a dim cloud spreading across the skyline—like the pall you see on the horizon in old westerns (dust storm? prairie fire?) before you feel the trembling of the air, the far-off reverberations that presage the drumbeat of tens of thousands of hooves.

The first signs visual. Down the hill from me on Haight, Cole, Page, and Ashbury streets, masculine hair drooping to the shoulders lank and lifeless as a farm girl's or jutting in volute curls like an electrified Harpo Marx wig. The boys in army and Goodwill castoffs, the girls—slim, shapely chicks—dressed like their great-grandnannies, except their bare feet are bruised and raw, gray with crud. Strange appliances and bric-a-brac in the storefront windows on streets that in a few years will resemble bombed-out wastelands: hookahs, joss sticks, roach clips, candles in ice-cream colors, bubble blowers, fantastically curved pipes, god's eyes, exotically illustrated boxes of incense, indecipherable posters evoking—it helps to be high—Never-never Land and Nightmare Alley; the salesboys staring stonily at you from behind greasy Veronica Lake peekaboos. Weird scenes in the parks, thousands of kids squatting on trampled grass, in dirt and mud, incongruously waving joss sticks and blowing bubbles as if, while awaiting the Second Coming, they've drifted back in their minds to some sylvan childhood playground. The smells. Incense, liberated animals, crap-dappled walks, wretched feet, sweet reek of pot and sour wine and unwashed bodies masked by patchouli, unplaceable mossy exhalations as from a mongrel's ruined gums, a great acrid scruffy grimy pungency of self-willed poverty and dog shit. And shining through the putrescence an ineffable, selfless, idyllic, maddening, admirable charity and sweetness of demeanor.

The looming pall of dust first, then the gathering thunder of drumming hooves bestriding the plains, spilling into the continent's corners, filling the horizon. Stampede.

In *Variety* a prophetic headline: "How Troublesome Decibels Gonna Be?" Very. Out of behemoth speakers the size of small garages the otherworldly roar emerged like voltaic belches from the massed mouths of bottlenosed whales—an implacable vortex of sound that engulfed, lifted, and spun our world away as effortlessly and irreclaimably as Dorothy's Kansas farmhouse.

Banducci was listening to the new music with gritted teeth. "Since ee-yew been gone, bay-bee, I'm so forlorrrn . . . ," he piped in falsetto, pumping his arms, shuffling his big feet. "What kind of crap is that? You don't even have to practice to do that." Against the grain of his creditable taste, perhaps prodded by David (holding a wet, plump finger to the howling wind), he made dispirited attempts to accommodate youth. "Behind the vanguard, into the future!" he bellowed, appropriating Professor Corey's involuted line. He hired Lovin' Spoonful, Barry McGuire, Ike and Tina Turner, et al., and took a miserable ice-cold bath. As a fellow club owner ran it down, " 'Slaughter on Tenth Avenue' got transposed to Jackson Street." It was a month of bleached bones and dim stars, of klaxons of sound ricocheting off red brick. The regulars fled in droves, clutching their heads. The kids never materialized. Why should they when they could see the same fare unconstrained on their home grounds, leaping, hollering, pogo-ing, popping pills, sucking grass, and watching light shows of fan-rippled oil and water filtered through colored lenses and projected on thirty-foot walls, producing amorphous streaks and curlicues that conjured for the more frenzied and stoned the dawn of Creation, the giant amoebae of Sirius, the myriad faces of Jesus Christ?

On a midweek midnight I reported uneasily to Enrico, "Boss, the headliners don't want to do a third show."

"Why the hell not?"

"There're only about twenty people left."

The ragtag rockers straggled up the bar; Banducci met them halfway.

"I don't care if there are twenty people or two thousand—You're paid to entertain them!"

"We're not playing to brick walls, man."

"Your contract, if you're capable of reading it, reads three shows a night."

"We've never gone on to this small a crowd. We'll play longer shows tomorrow if you want . . ."

"No, I don't want. What I want is to terminate this abortion now. David, write a check for the whole amount."

"Hold it, you've got the weekend coming."

"The weekend isn't going to improve. We just buried the new sound in Tombstone, Arizona. Write a check."

"Enrico, it's not in the bank."

Banducci furiously emptied his pockets as in a Keystone two-reel hold-up, wheeling on Edmond—"Give me what's in the register"—

stuffing bills in David's hands as the cow-booted leather-vested group looked on with placid detachment.

"Will you just ease off a minute and—"

"No. I'm sick of this crap, pay them. Lenny, Mike and Elaine, Makeba performed for a half dozen people and worked out like they were playing the Court of Saint James. And these kids with the jackhammers drilling holes in our heads won't go on. But they'll take off and jam for free at some hole-in-the-wall till five in the morning. I say something's goddam out of whack."

AT A TWO A.M. postmortem David protested to Banducci, "You never gave it a chance. You brought in Hollywood Bowl shows on a Coney Island budget. The kids never felt welcome, not one night. They detected the vibes, they're not insensi—"

"Don't talk to me about vibes, I got vibes bouncing around my head like footballs. I have nothing against the kids in their gypsy clothes protesting the war, questioning the corporations—they're earnest and they're refreshing. It's the entertainers who represent them—I'll tell you something, I understood Tom Lehrer, the Limelighters, Dick Gregory. Even the blacks walked out on him when he first worked for me. He kept telling me, 'Enrico, you wuuuury too much, we got to luuuuv one another.' I understand Ray Charles and Bob Dylan. I don't understand the Lovin' Cupful or the Yellow Cobblestone Wrecking Company or whatever the hell it is they call themselves . . ."

"What can I say, today's kids aren't used to sitting in a formal environment, in theater chairs—you have to give them time to get weaned from the coffeehouses and halls. You can't operate a Basque family restaurant at the same locale for fifteen years, suddenly switch to Cantonese and expect to turn a profit the first week."

"The walls haven't stopped shaking, we're not extending this policy," Banducci said. "I got a bad headache."

The next night between shows I talked to a girl in the bar; she had come in with the band, a hanger-on, I assumed—a groupie, as the term was coming into vogue. She looked to be nineteen, twenty-two at the outside, lank-haired and sallow, sucking on a Pall Mall as if it were Columbian Gold.

"You guys play okay," she said, referring to Alberto and me, "but you lack energy." And a little later, when she'd established that she was in the business, too—a singer and guitarist: "I'm opening at the Palladium in the fall."

"The Palladium—where?" I said, thinking Petaluma, maybe, Passaic, New Jersey.

She looked at me blankly, askance. "It's in London."

"Oh." That one.

"They're only paying fifteen thou', which is down from my usual price, but I figure the exposure's worth it."

"Fifteen—?"

"Thou'." A slight frown. "Thousand."

"For the . . . season?"

A wide-eyed stare. Dummy. "A week."

I asked her her name; I'd never heard of her. The handwriting, along with the amoeba of Sirius, was on the wall.

MARIO SAVIO WAS the new Adlai Stevenson.

Suddenly Mort Sahl was as stale as last week's bread (he'd bounce back).

In the record industry a cataclysm was under way.

They weren't writing songs with thirty-two bars anymore.

The Kingston Trio drew more laughs than applause.

Professor Corey joined the Playboy Club circuit.

Jonathan Winters was wearing drag on network variety shows.

Mike and Elaine were directing flicks.

Shelley Berman was deader than smoking jackets and Lifebuoy soap.

Lenny was dead.

There was a short-lived, ill-starred move to luxurious quarters in Ghirardelli Square—a multitiered waterfront restaurant-and-boutique complex that had once been a chocolate factory. Cosby and a handful of surviving stars returned to help launch the new operation, performing gratis for the man who had given them their first breaks. The sturdy old tub in its new coat of paint stayed afloat for a while, but the troublesome decibels had set off a tidal wave. Within a few months the revamped club was foundering. Banducci studied the barometer, surveyed the towering combers, sighed deeply, and said, "Close it, David."

It was one of the city's premier ambassadors in an era when wit had bite and flavor, when style and sophistication ruled the boards, and tunes had titles like "Violets for Your Furs" and "Miss Otis Regrets." A warm, vibrant, rather funky place that was home for jazz musicians and an advance guard of satirists and folksingers during the dawn of political protest.

Light-filled antic nights in that dear dank cellar on Jackson Street. I miss them like a dead brother.

I thought of the bumper sticker I'd been seeing over and over during the past month: W. C. Fields Is Alive and Drunk in Oakland. Weird. At the same time that the teenage millionaires in Veronica Lake peekaboos were scrambling our brains with their power plants, Fields movies and Flash Gordon serials were jamming the theaters. Bogart and Mae West posters hung among the hookahs and joss sticks in Haight Street head shops, and in New York the Stork Club had been closed a year but they were reviving *No No Nanette*. It was crazy, everything had gotten turned around. The bell-bottoms I saw on the streets now, which made me think of Kelly, Sinatra, and Munshin in *On the Town*, were the pegged pants of the forties.

The hungry i name and logo were sold for $10,000 to an organization known as Chowder House, Inc., and now adorns the marquee (*Totally Nude College Coeds*) of a narrow bar on Broadway—just a few doors west of Enrico's Coffeehouse—where the barkers agitate and nude terps do their somber turns. The quintessential rube hangout, *Variety* might say.

The girl into whose lap I had knocked the Coke—Poe, a name that would generate endless confusion in the coming years (letters addressed to Ms. or Mr. Poe Asher, five hundred bank checks printed Joe Asher)—found a sunny five-room pad with garden for us on Buena Vista Heights. We pooled our resources and, projecting long good times together, took out a mortgage. She was a forthright, laconic, gutsy lady, a schoolteacher with unsuspected talents: she could construct picket fences, install dimmer switches, lay bathroom tiles or a flagstone path through a garden. "Where did you learn to do all that?" I asked. "Nowhere—I just know," she said. If we had a great meal at a Mandarin or Indonesian or Japanese restaurant, a few nights later she would effortlessly duplicate it. Flesh accrued to my thin bones, dimensions were added to my life.

I now had time to spare and Poe, fourteen years my junior, took my education in hand, dragging me to rock halls and park concerts, trying to instruct me in how to listen to the "big beat." In the Golden Gate Park Panhandle I listened for an hour to Jimi Hendrix playing from the back of a flatbed truck, cradled in a cobra's nest of black cables, the sound emerging from speakers the size of master-bedroom chests of drawers stacked against tree trunks. I thought, It's frantic, it's passionate, Christ knows it's loud enough—but here's a guy who's supposed to be a superstar, I told her between numbers, and there must be a dozen jazz guitarists in the Bay Area alone who can improvise rings around him. Poe, born in 1940, said, "You're listening to the stuff the wrong way," and suggested that I put my conventional harmonies and melodies out of mind and think instead of the soloist astride a Harley chopper roaring down the Bayshore Freeway at full throttle, exuberant, wailing, riding like a demon, like the wind, but in control all the way. "That makes sense for describing the *sound*," I yelled (the band had started in again) through cupped hands into her ear, "but—" and gave it up, the voltage having shaken my brains free and sent them rattling around my skull.

I reciprocated, taking her to jazz clubs. She listened politely and patiently to the old-time melodies and harmonies. And warily approaching each other from opposite sides of the chasm, we arrived at a halfway place, a precarious musical standoff.

A CULTURAL GENERATION had passed, and among the ranks of musicians who had been nurtured by the music of the thirties, forties, and fifties it was a time of artistic upheaval and personal havoc. Overnight, it seemed, those of us who had come up during those decades were no longer playing the comfortable Gershwin–Berlin–Porter–Kern–Rodgers and Hart tunes we'd played countless times and never tired of because of their fluent lines and enduring architecture. Our tight, ingrown world wobbled violently on its axis. Suddenly kids wearing soup-line motley and fright-wig hairdos, wielding skinny lethal guitars, were jet-whining and wrong-chording in our ears. The plump, sedate walk of the stand-up bass gave way to the raw reverberations of a scrawny instrument held like a guitar or submachine gun; the drummers turned stiff-wristed and brutal, no longer swishing their brushes in graceful arabesques; the singers—in requiem for the sweet warblers, canaries, and orioles from the big-band sanctuaries—were shrieking: "She loves you, yeh, yeh, yeh."

The professional pianists and bassists of my generation had trouble learning—or faking—those early rock tunes; we couldn't hear the changes, the harmonic movement was alien, hence wrong. Young musicians and singers with no formal training and the most primitive harmonic knowledge were writing their own material and hiring older studio musicians to set it down on paper for copyright purposes. The music gaped with structural wounds; chords failed to resolve, tunes came out in odd numbers of bars; the up-tempo pieces lacked fluidity and couldn't be jammed. When we tried to play the Beatles' "Yesterday," with one bar missing before the turnaround between phrases, we got thrown out of whack. Who ever heard of a seven-bar phrase, a twenty-nine-bar tune? In the tribal love-rock anthem "Aquarius," single notes were held for nine, eleven, and thirteen beats for no logical reason. Accomplished musicians were counting beats like preschool kids adding up their toes. Conversely, when contractors—hedging their bets, trying to cover all bases—provided us with rock rhythm players, these kids proceeded to butcher standards like "My Romance" and "Fly Me to the Moon," whose chordal structure seemed to us as basic, congruous, and inevitable as shoulder padding in sports jackets or cheering MacArthur and Eisenhower in the newsreels had been two decades earlier.

Music wasn't fun anymore. We felt that staying alive in our profession meant being forced back to a musical Stone Age; long years of training and apprenticeship went by the board. We yearned for the champagne sparkle of Porter ("You're the purple light of a summer night in Spain / You're the Nation'l Gall'ry, you're Garbo's salary, you're cellophane!"), the sophisticated heartbreak of Rodgers and Hart ("Now the young world has grown old / Gone are the tinsel and gold"). A ghostly, top-hatted Astaire no longer glided in from the terrace with his silken-gowned partner when we played "They Can't Take That Away From Me." We turned hostile and bitter. The black rhythm-and-blues and jazz players, whose gritty music had furnished the raw material for the new sound, were furious. "How can they steal our stuff," asked Hampton Hawes, "play it so bad, and make all that bread?" Kids who had bought their first guitars ten months ago and learned to twirl the volume knobs and run a few stereotyped licks were generating gold records, playing to twenty-five thousand people in stadiums and arenas where livestock shows were once held. We were drowned in decibels; when we shared the stage with rockers we packed our ears with cotton. Our tight little thirty-two-bar island had been overrun by Visigoths.

We didn't cope very well. Those who found it spiritually and artistically impossible to adjust retreated (like the work-starved alumni of the Classical High Gang twenty years earlier) to the non-performing corners of the profession—teaching, tuning pianos, arranging; others dropped out entirely and never looked back. Many hung on, stubbornly cavalier, making halfhearted accommodations and hating every minute on the stand. But they underestimated the difficulty of playing good rock (a contradiction in terms for them); they failed to learn the new musical language and saw their work calls dwindle. (*If you don't have the right token don't come through the turnstile.*) Others, goaded by necessity and the lure of more money than had ever been available, studied the new technology, grew their hair long, and joined the enemy. Pianists, formerly the envy of encumbered bass players and drummers, were suddenly lugging hefty amplifiers and collapsible electric pianos into country clubs and along hotel corridors, cursing and sweating into their tuxes.

Wedded to the sweet sound of good wood, I took what society work was available for nonelectric keyboard players, steeling myself when the new tunes were called and wincing as I watched dancers my age and older pulling muscles and throwing out backs in the process of getting it on with the kids. Writing and rehearsal fees provided a living. I sought refuge from the revolution in six-hour practice sessions, renewing old, neglected acquaintanceships: Bach, Chopin, Debussy, Prokofiev. There were occasional solo gigs at house parties for die-hard melodists, and four months as accompanist for The Committee, a satirical revue, that was an invigorating change of pace and brought out the latent ham in me as I was incorporated into skits in a variety of walk-ons and against-type minor roles—disturbed pedestrian, head-shop customer, junkie. Bill Cosby sat in for the improvisational sets when he was in the area, and one night after hours I cut a demo record for the girlfriend of one of the troupe players, who had aspirations as an actress-singer and was on her way to New York; I donated my services and wished her luck, though I wasn't much impressed. I knew only her first name, Valerie, and within a year would learn the rest of it from a national magazine cover—Harper. And that spring I turned forty.

The emergence of more skillful performers and composers—the later Beatles, Jim Webb, Paul Simon, and Carole King, whose songs were vital, technically sound, and frequently poetic—provoked some of us to a grudging reevaluation: How good, really, were those romantic ballads that Gershwin wrote for "young girls sitting on fire escapes on hot summer nights in New York dreaming of love," as a journalist piquantly phrased it? Were the sentiments more saccharine than genuine? And if so, why did we feel such anguish when they were all but blown away by the cannonade of new sound shelling the country? Was it possible the kids' tastes were more catholic, even more refined, than ours when we were young? (Consider "Mairzy Doats," "Pistol Packin' Mama," and "Three Little Fishies [Itty Bitty Poo].") But the pre-sixties tunes reflected a blander, more innocent time. Lovers lived in sky-high penthouses and danced the night away on moonlit terraces; if poor, their pockets were filled with dreams. We were determinedly optimistic; the world was good enough and it was going to get better. We put heartache behind us and believed we'd grow up happy. "Look for the Silver Lining" . . . "Guess I'll Hang My Tears Out to Dry." With the new decade came assassination, pessimism, and protest. The sardonic gloom of the Vietnam-connected "Fixin' to Die Rag" contrasts vividly with the buoyancy and confidence of the World War II songs: "Praise the Lord and Pass the Ammunition" and "When the Lights Go On Again All Over the World." Many of the sixties love songs were elegies of loneliness. The music was written for a generation of rebels. Bob Dylan and the Beatles not only reflected but defined their times; their impetus helped forge new mores. There were no Woodstock celebrations of generational apartness in the earlier era. Perhaps the closest parallel from the past was the abandoned jitterbugging to Benny Goodman's band in the aisles of the Paramount Theater.

Over the past decade a merging of boundaries has taken place, a cross-fertilization of cultures. Jazz improvisation enriches the more progressive rock groups today, and the pulse of rhythm-and-blues and Latin powers many jazz rhythm sections. Those of us who survived the shattering of the thirty-two-bar icon are the better for it.

2 3

An old Worcester classmate sent me a *New York Times* notice of Jaki (formerly "Jackie") Byard's appearance at the Village Vanguard. I dropped him a card in care of the club letting him know my whereabouts and telling him I'd been following his career from afar with avid interest and hometown pride. Worcester forever!

It suddenly seemed a good time for a trip back—if for no other reason than that my days were more leisurely and I missed seeing the leaves change color and hearing the sound of night rain on the roof.

I arrived in Worcester on a Saturday

afternoon, rented a car and began a nostalgic prowl of downtown. Union Station, that white-marble monolith and major depot on the New York, New Haven & Hartford line, wore a shawl of grime on its burly shoulders and was boarded up except for a side entrance over which a sign announced, Barber Shop. At least the longhairs hadn't yet overrun the town.

The marquee of the Plymouth Theater, temple of big bands and flamboyant floor shows, was barren. I glanced through the dusty, barred glass doors; daylight was leaking in from somewhere, and I could see most of the way through to what used to be the stage. The structure looked gutted, sans curtain, seats, chandeliers, everything. I drove a few blocks east of the theater, trying to find the Saxtrum Club and Jackie Byard's house ("Jaki" seemed an incongruity here); I kept getting turned around, finding myself reentering the same unfamiliar curlicue of connecting roadways. The colored district had vanished in a tangle of traffic interchanges shadowed by a high-rise orange-brick housing project.

My mother was in Florida, visiting her sister Lila, Allie's widow. I stayed with Herbie, who was rolling in dough now and had bought an eight-room Cape Cod house with sunken living room and flagstone patio high on one of the west-side hills.

The Bancroft Hotel on Franklin Street was now the Sheraton, and the Pollywog Lounge had metamorphosed to the Flamingo Room. The lighting was much brighter; the murky green aquariums had been replaced by tubs of spearlike plants from which emerged the scarlet necks of ceramic flamingos. A silver-haired man in a white Palm Beach coat and black bow was playing "The World Is Waiting For the Sunrise" in three-quarter time on a console organ. I noticed he kept a cloth napkin at the end of the keyboard, as would a jazz musician to periodically mop his perspiring face. I watched for another minute or two: the man in the white coat was drooling.

Some of the lakeside clubs were still operating, though under different names. Others were either boarded up and crumbling or had been converted to fish-and-bait shops; a few had been demolished, leaving excavations like pulled teeth along the luxuriant banks. Inland, the Blue Marlin and Good Ship Madam Zucchini had gone the way of the Titanic. Carl Seder's Music Mart, where I'd picked out my first melodies standing at the player piano, was a dental laboratory.

The second day of my visit this headline appeared in the morning *Telegram*: "Harold Harganian, Noted Bandleader, Dies." I attended the funeral two days later with Warren, my old confederate from the Blue Marlin–Foxes and Hounds–Shanghai Bess days, now gray-haired and teaching music in the public schools. The strange morning started on a macabre note when a pale mortuary official in morning coat and striped trousers directed Warren to a space in the parking lot thusly: "Just pull into that hole over there . . ."

"Jesus." Warren pursed his lips, giving a helpless little smile.

It was a crisp, blue October morning, the leaves scarlet and gold on this tunneling street of wide-branched maples and oaks. We entered the O'Donnell Funeral Home. The O'Donnells were an old Worcester family, and as one of the patriarchs had been a violinist and lifetime member of Local 143, the union hierarchy threw most of the trade business their way. "What a day to keel," Warren said as we passed out of the brilliant morning light into candlelit gloom and a cloying reek of pale flowers. Tinny music was coming from somewhere. I thought fleetingly of Alvie Drake (whose obituary I had read in a spring issue of *International Musician*) and the convention of morticians we'd played for in upstate New York, the rowdy barbershop harmony and whoopee cushions. Adjusting to the dim light, I nodded to faces I half recognized milling around at the rear of the chapel and in the aisles. An icicle chill ran down my back. At the far end Hal was reclining on billowing white satin, tilted at about twenty-five degrees and enclosed by a picket fence of tall white candles. A parody of one of his Foxes and Hounds routines echoed in my inner ear, "Let's give this unique leader a great big hand . . ." The sound in the chapel had become intrusive, a bleak, mournful screak of violins playing "Beyond the Blue Horizon" slightly out of sync, as if a warped record were playing on an old Gramophone. I looked around for the speakers and then saw Warren, who had wandered down a side aisle, beckoning to me from an archway opposite the dais. I walked toward him—the fretful sound swelling as if I were passing directly under one of the invisible speakers—averting my eyes from Hal's rouged, chalky face and black suit. "Dig," Warren said. On the other side of the archway was a small, draperied alcove. Three live but very old musicians were seated in a circle on bentwood chairs, reading from metal music stands: two tuxedoed gentlemen, whose faces looked as white as Hal's, sawing on fiddles, and a tall, spare woman in a blue gown bowing a cello propped awkwardly, almost obscenely, between her legs. She looked up from the music and smiled thinly at us, her powdered face cracking into a thousand pieces.

The minister was mounting the dais, the chapel now about two-thirds full. Warren and I took rear seats. A frail, thin-lipped woman with pixie-cut white hair eased into the row ahead of us. It had been a long trail of years, but I was sure I recognized Valerie Bismel, who had led the band at the Hartville Academy for the Deaf and Dumb.

"Is Pepto Bismel still alive?" I whispered to Warren.

"Nursing home."

The string trio had segued waveringly into "Over the Rainbow." "Rainbow, three grapes," Hal used to signal us at the Foxes and Hounds.

"Hal looks awful," Warren said.

"No worse than the morning after a bad New Year's Eve," someone said behind us.

"Dear friends, we are gathered here this morning," the minister began, "to pay tribute to the memory of a man who made a joyful noise unto the Lord . . ." No one had notified the string trio, who were out of view of the dais. Hearing the service begin, they trailed off miserably, one by one; it sounded like a wind-up Victrola running down.

After the service, musicians and their wives swarmed on the sidewalk, chatting casually in the bright late morning; there was no feeling of bereavement; we might have all been on a union outing in Green Hill Park. I recognized Coe Wittig, the Good Ship Madam Zucchini's blind drummer, shockingly snow-haired (mine was still brown). He was holding the arm of a small, stout woman in a veiled round hat, and at that distance I could not have said whether she was his wife or mother. Other faces were less familiar, an identity snapping into place when a feature jogged my memory—a curve of mouth, a shock of hair though the color was gone, a shyness or arrogance of bearing. There, a few yards away on the curb, one foot (appropriately) in the gutter, the peculiar sour aspect and crooked smile of Arnie, the baritone saxophonist at the deaf-and-dumb academy dance.

"Hear you're living it up in Frisco now . . ." A few of the old crowd recognizing me (which features? I wondered), tentatively approaching, the voices as careless as if it were yesterday.

"Except out there you can get punched out for calling the town that," I said lamely, smiling.

Strange, I felt shy, awkward in their presence, though it was I who had managed the departure, fashioned a small identity for myself in the big floor show beyond the town line.

"Ever run across Joe Dimaggio?"

"I see him in restaurants now and then, but he's out of my league."

"I keep waiting for those calls, Freddie . . ." Threads of other conversations floating around me, none of them relating to Hal.

"Got the next two Saturdays open, Freddie, afternoon or night, if anything pops . . ."

Freddie, whom I didn't know, was holding court nearby, manifestly a big operator, filling the vacuum left by Harganian and Bismel. A well-fed, sleek, thick-chested man, wisps of long blond hair blowing across his blue-tinted shades, light-gray topcoat draped over the shoulders of a pinstripe suit.

". . . Charlie's a nice enough cat but he's got a tone like a frog in a sewer pipe . . ."

". . . I tried to warn her in front, man, I told her, baby, never eat in a club with acts or a piano bar . . ."

And a voice directly behind me: "That's the third cat keeled this month, watch the assessments go up next quarter . . ." Finally an allusion to the corpus inside.

More people gathering around, asking about Frisco. Was it true the fags had taken over the town? That people flipped off the Golden Gate Bridge like it was a diving board?

And as the blurred faces made their connections, rekindling memories, I turned the questions around, asking about Dinah, the voluptuous stag-show stripper from the Good Ship Madam Z. and Silverella (a.k.a. Ginger Rhale), who had grown up on a boulevard of broken lights. Eyes squinted and roamed in the glare of autumn noon . . . Dinah what? . . . *Cole, I think, Coles. Her hair was a reddish orange, she could prance like a pony* . . . Silverella—you don't mean Ella Reynolds, stacked little blonde? . . . *No, no, she was black too, tall as a tree, stripped to Fats Waller tunes and ended up in just a coat of silver paint* . . . Heads were scratched, memories ransacked. No one could say; no one really remembered.

"Do you know how long it's been, man? Those chicks could be in old ladies' homes."

The conversation dropped away, almost to a hush—people suddenly diverted and self-conscious, making way. The casket had emerged, tilted down the steps by white-gloved pallbearers, brass handles gleaming in the sun. "Timmmmmmm-ber . . . ," someone called wistfully—one of the better routines of the late great master of whimsy—as he was borne across the thronged sidewalk, a felled splendid oak, and eased into the polished hearse. *Give Us a Ring*, I remembered, *We Would Like the Engagement.*

"Keep on swinging, Hal," a voice piped as the hearse door soundlessly closed.

I decided I wouldn't go to the cemetery. I thought again how glorious the leaves looked, beginning to fill the gutters and drift across the lawns, how blue and clear the sky—a depth and clarity you don't often see in California. And as the hearse pulled quietly away, its simonized sheen throwing off sparks of sunlight, I had an idle recollection from a half-forgotten history class of one of Henry VIII's wives (or mistresses) moments before the blade fell; she had arched her youthful neck to the sky and said, "But it's such a beautiful day."

24

Back on Buena Vista Heights the phone was ringing as I let myself in.

"I've been trying to reach you, *amigo*, they're excavating," Alberto said.

"Excavating what?"

"On Jackson Street, the club. Don't go by, it's a big hole in the ground. I've saved you a brick."

"A brick . . . ?" It wasn't quite registering.

"From the stage. One of the excavators gave me a couple. He looked at me funny—maybe he thought I wanted to throw them through store windows. I said I wanted them for—I couldn't think of the word—old times . . ."

"Sentimental reasons."

"You got it!"

A hole in the ground. The music, the laughter. "How's work, Alberto?"

"Oh, it's around. But not for me. I'm back in the barbershop with my brother. You remember—Mission and Twenty-sixth. Come by, I'll make you a duck's ass."

"I will. Hold onto that brick for me."

"I guard it with my life. *Qué tal?*"

"Not bad. I'm thinking of getting married."

"You sex maniac! *Bonito!*"

WEDDING DAYS. AS Poe and I were contemplating ours Amy Avalon phoned about hers. She was taking on Vincent's brother-in-law, Mario, and wanted me to play for the reception. A Sunday night at Bimbo's 365 Club.

"I better tell you—outside of a couple of show tunes I know hardly anything written after nineteen seventy."

"Who needs it? These folks are all good-time Charlies."

Easy on the DiMaggios, I remembered. "Can I talk you into a bass player?"

"Uh-uh. Mario's popping and he's very tight in the bread department."

It turned out to be a rowdy, heavy-juicing affair. Lots of spilled booze and foot-long cigars and wrong-key vocalizing around the baby grand. Italian medleys into the morning hours, "Come Back to Sorrento," "O Sole Mio," "Volare," "Vieni Su," "That's Amore," "Ciao, Ciao, Bambina," the same tunes over and over, no end to them, like seventy-five choruses of "Never on Sunday" at a Greek restaurant; half-eaten plates of antipasta, linguini, fettuccine draping the piano, vino trickling onto the hammers and felts, smoke in my eyes, hands pounding my shoulders, slamming my back. Amy got tanked early, leaving a tracery of gooey lip prints on my face, fending off requests to sing. "What're ya talkin' about, sing? I can't even stand . . ." Some of the tunes went back to the *Niña*, the *Pinta*, and the *Santa María*. When I said I didn't know one, they said play it anyway. I half expected a beetle-browed patriarch to lift me by the scruff of the neck, briskly slap my face, and drive a right to the breadbasket, smiling all the while: "My wife has asked you three times for 'Neapolitan Nights.' Now be a good boy and play it, *capisc?*"

Turning the corner of midnight, following the tenth reprise of "Volare," Mario's best man, Alfredo, an amiable all-beef sausage stuffed into a chocolate-brown tux, put on an impromptu show of comedy and magic, incorporating your accommodating keyboard artist. An aspiring clown, Alfredo had been auditioning in northern California clubs for ten years, to no avail. "In case ya haven't noticed it, my *paisano* on the keys, Liberace, Junior," he said a little way into his act to the three-quarters-bombed crowd—his fat hand squeezing the back of my neck like a kitchen sponge—"possesses on each hand six magic fingers, count 'em, six, with which he'll now play the fastest 'Minute Waltz' ya ever heard. (Pause) Now he'll play it again . . ."

So some things never change, and in the end the turns all come full circle.

A FEW MONTHS later Jaki Byard came to San Francisco to play Kimball's, a prominent jazz room. Over the past decade he had acquired, along with his new moniker, critical accolades and an international reputation. He arrived a day early, phoned, and Poe and I had him to dinner. He had lost a lot of weight and hair, and sported a trim gray beard flecked with white. It had been a good twenty-five years since he turned me upside down, slapped me on the butt, and pushed me howling into the world. We reminisced endlessly about Worcester and the old haunts, sending Poe—whose eyelids drooped progressively lower as if she were watching the neighbors' vacation slides—to bed in a stupor an hour before her accustomed time.

After dinner he played some of his original compositions for me.

It isn't often you get to hear a virtuoso of the first rank in your living room. I was awed. The pieces were rich, orchestral, and the bravura technique he brought to the improvisational passages left me smiling weakly and shaking my head in astonishment and frustration. A hard act to follow, as they say, but fortified by predinner drinks and the superb wine Jaki had brought, I found the courage to sit down and play some of my things for him. Musicians are always striving to shine for one another, to attain esteem in the other's eyes; envy and admiration, competitiveness and support are complexly linked. An exceptional attachment prevails. We honor and look after one another, embrace when we have been out of touch for a spell—a fond and unselfconscious laying on of hands. Within the boundaries of artistic rivalry lies a common pride and sense of family: the shared genetic inheritance, or accident, that enables us to make music. In our mutual respect the divisions between former teacher and pupil, between wizardry and mere proficiency, vanish.

It was after two in the morning when Jaki finally split. Before he did he related a curious and indelible experience he'd had on his recent trip home (Worcester still "home" despite our having been away all those years). The story embodies that peculiar distortion I'd first noticed during my Happy Hour solo sessions at Lake Laramee—the layman's uncertainty or uneasiness with the idea of someone earning a living from what is usually conceived of as a hobby or party activity—and it comes to mind whenever I get to feeling too complacent, too pleased with my achievements.

On the streets of Worcester, in the space of a week, Jaki had encountered numerous old nonmusician friends and classmates. Now at the time of his visit he was, as I've said, an acclaimed pianist of international stature. He had recorded some thirty albums under his own name; he had been featured at major jazz festivals throughout the world; he was (and is) on the staffs of eminent music schools and had played solo concerts illustrating the history and evolution of jazz piano in prestigious halls; he had written countless arrangements and jazz suites for Charles Mingus, Maynard Ferguson, and other luminaries; during the last months of Duke Ellington's life, when he was too ill to perform, Jaki was asked to take over the piano bench; other musicians speak of him in awed tones; the late multi-instrumentalist Rahsaan Roland Kirk called him "The Living Emperor of Jazz Piano." But on the streets of Worcester his old friends and classmates greeted him—and the wording each time was virtually identical—"Hey, Jackie, still foolin' around with the piano?"

THAT BUTTERFLY, SECURITY, hovers and tantalizes, ventures within my grasp, then flutters away. Still I remain stubbornly selective, choosing carefully among the jobs that come my way. A middle-aged dog unable to learn new tricks. But it's a strange thing—every now and then, taking a late-afternoon nap on the day of an important gig, I'll waken abruptly in the gloom, heart pounding, a light sweat breaking out, experiencing that displacement Val spoke of—the confusion of dawn with dusk. In the moment before my senses realign and I shoot a look at the clock face, a number of possibilities dart in my mind. What time is the gig? What month is this? If we're on daylight saving then I'm already late, and the sweat begins running in earnest . . . Six-fifty, the hands read. But *what end of the day?* And while the disorientation lasts, old premonitions surface—half-formed anxieties, Sincere Hotel, a veiled longing for the order of a workaday life, regulated hours, schedules, almost wishing I'd followed in my father's and Herbie's footsteps (notice I said *almost*)—and the specter of Uncle Allie looms in a long line of rigid, unbending uncles like blackbirds on a wire, robed justices on a bench: their stern admonitions and fears for me. Then my heart quiets, it's November, a Friday night, the gig doesn't start till nine; the sweat dries. They're only apparitions, these anti-night people, day-trippers with their strange conventions and rituals. They inhabit an alien country on the far side of the horizon; they have nothing to do with me.

EPILOGUE

Not long ago I got a free trip to London to work on a screenplay about musicians and entertainers for an English film director. The hotel where I was put up was in Mayfair, less than half a mile from Berkeley Square. Early each morning I'd wander out into the silvery London light, down Hill Street, past Charrington's Coach and Horses, and sit on a bench, gazing into the trees, listening for the nightingale of my youth in a tiny park ringed by auto agencies, banks, and gambling casinos. The director and his aides must have thought I was a touch flaky, even for a Californian.

For many musicians and lovers who played or danced through the forties, there was a piquant, fanciful ballad that served, perhaps more than any other, as the decade's romantic anthem. "A Nightingale Sang in Berkeley Square" (*Bar-kley*, the sheet music parenthetically instructs at the close of each refrain) encompassed star-paved streets and angels dining at the Ritz: a lilting serenade infused with the stateliness of a pavane. The tune still fills me with yearning, a sweet languor, and the sentimental, dated lyrics ("This heart of mine beat loud and fast / Like a merry-go-round in a fair") only heighten the spell. I have been playing it on roadhouse, cabaret, hotel, and country-club pianos for as long as I can remember; whenever there are people over forty in the room, I'll always see a graying head or two turn in my direction, a misty look in the eyes.

SOMETHING HAS BEEN happening of late. The quality of work is improving; my phone rings more often: restaurants, clubs, party hosts wanting the old songs, the pretty ones: At the Café Majestic, where I now play dinner music nightly, kids in their twenties approach the piano, patronizingly, affectionately call me Sam (curse that tune!) and then—I hold my breath, expecting a request for the latest Stones track, something by Guns N' Roses, Run DMC—they ask for "Lush Life" and "What's New?" and "My Funny Valentine." It gives me pause, turns me around. A boy wearing an earring and a camouflage jacket came up one recent evening holding hands with his girl. They could have been seventeen or twenty-four, I no longer can tell. She smiled and said, "Hiya, Sam." He asked politely if I knew Willie Nelson's "Stardust." *Willie Nelson's!* "I know that tune like I know my mother's touch," I told him, "but what happened to Hoagy Carmichael?" The girl's smile wavered, the boy's face went blank. "I'd be pleased to play it," I reassured them, and did, lovingly, throwing in the verse as a bonus.

Something is decidedly in the air. I think those long-sequestered songbirds have taken wing again, their melodies as beguiling as ever.

It takes very little these days to stir my imagination, the most fragile of catalysts can send my mind winging back to that Mayfair park—

> That certain night, the night we met,
> There was magic abroad in the air
> There were angels dining at the Ritz . . .

—and I'm there again strolling like a dreamer, a lover, among the benches and trees, a veiled moon riding low through the mist. The surrounding streets, the casinos, banks, auto agencies recede in deep shadow, a quick breeze rustles the summer leaves, then . . . Later, to anyone who'll listen, I'll swear I heard it, that sweet, melodious refrain like an echo far away, *like the tap-dancing feet of Astaire*, the nightingale singing once again in Berkeley (*Bar-kley*) Square.